Off the
Beaten Path®

georgia

Help Us Keep This Guide Up to Date

Every effort has been made by the author and editors to make this guide as accurate and useful as possible. However, many changes can occur after a guide is published—establishments close, phone numbers change, hiking trails are rerouted, facilities come under new management, etc.

We would love to hear from you concerning your experiences with this guide and how you feel it could be improved and be kept up to date. While we may not be able to respond to all comments and suggestions, we'll take them to heart, and we'll make certain to share them with the author. Please send your comments and suggestions to the following address:

The Globe Pequot Press
Reader Response/Editorial Department
P.O. Box 480
Guilford, CT 06437

Or you may e-mail us at: editorial@GlobePequot.com

Thanks for your input, and happy travels!

INSIDERS' GUIDE®

OFF THE BEATEN PATH® SERIES

Off the EIGHTH EDITION
Beaten Path®

georgia

A GUIDE TO UNIQUE PLACES

WILLIAM SCHEMMEL

INSIDERS' GUIDE®

GUILFORD, CONNECTICUT
AN IMPRINT OF THE GLOBE PEQUOT PRESS

The prices, rates, and hours listed in this guidebook were confirmed at press time. We recommend, however, that you call establishments to obtain current information before traveling.

To buy books in quantity for corporate use or incentives, call **(800) 962–0973, ext. 4551,** or e-mail **premiums@GlobePequot.com.**

INSIDERS' GUIDE ®

Text design by Linda Loiewski
Maps by Equator Graphics © Morris Book Publishing, LLC
Illustrations by Carole Drong
Spot photography throughout © James Randklev Photography

ISSN: 1541-6615
ISBN-13: 978-0-7627-4199-1
ISBN-10: 0-7627-4199-6

Manufactured in the United States of America
Eighth Edition/First Printing

To Roscoe, my special friend

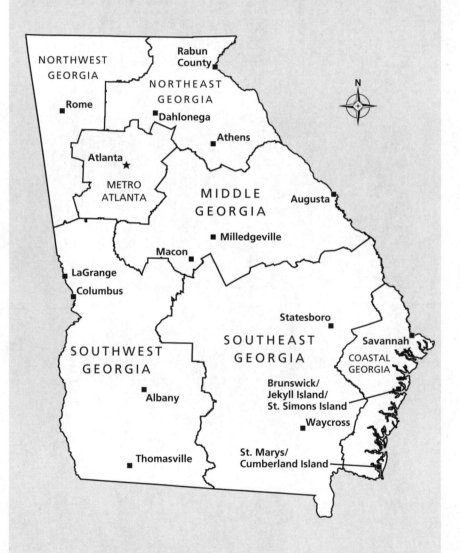

NORTHWEST
GEORGIA

Rome

Rabun
County

NORTHEAST
GEORGIA

Dahlonega

Athens

Atlanta

METRO
ATLANTA

MIDDLE
GEORGIA

Augusta

Milledgeville

Macon

LaGrange

Columbus

Statesboro

SOUTHEAST
GEORGIA

Savannah

COASTAL
GEORGIA

SOUTHWEST
GEORGIA

Brunswick/
Jekyll Island/
St. Simons Island

Albany

Waycross

Thomasville

St. Marys/
Cumberland Island

N

Contents

Introduction

After spending a good deal of my life wandering Georgia's byways, I'm happily convinced my home state will never run out of ways to surprise and delight me. From the Blue Ridge Mountains by the Tennessee and Carolina borders to the Okefenokee Swamp and piney woods bordering Florida, from Savannah and "The Golden Isles" on the Atlantic Coast to Columbus and La Grange and Lake Seminole on the westerly Chattahoochee River, I'm ever amazed at Georgia's depth and breadth. It's like an incredible attic stacked floor to ceiling with a never-ending cache of treasures.

I've attended Sunday morning services with Macon County's Mennonites and been transported by the Gregorian chants of the Benedictine monks at Rockdale County's Monastery of the Holy Ghost. I've awakened in the depths of the swamps to the eerie symphony of gators and owls and at sunrise by mountain lakes to the siren songs of loons and geese.

I've encountered ghosts, and tales of ghosts, in antebellum mansions where Sherman and Lafayette once slept, and I've half-believed the outrageous lies of anglers and small-town sages. I've attended festivals exalting rattlesnakes, chitterlings, sorghum syrup, pecans, autumn leaves, spring dogwoods, and Greek, Chinese, Middle Eastern, East Indian, and Native American heritage. Along the way I've eaten a fair share of barbecue, catfish, and fried chicken, as well as accomplished European cuisine, in mountain valleys and small-town cafes.

I've beheld a likeness of the Roman she-wolf nursing Romulus and Remus, donated to an embarrassed small town by Benito Mussolini, and best of all, I've met Georgia's proudest monument, its own people, in their natural habitat. A few grouches notwithstanding, they're warm, wise, and witty, and when you wander off the beaten path, they'll be pleased to point you in some fascinating directions.

I hope you'll enjoy using this book half as much as I've enjoyed researching it. When you discover some off-the-beaten-path adventures that I've yet to come across, please let me know by writing to me c/o The Globe Pequot Press, P.O. Box 480, Guilford, CT 06437.

Restaurant cost categories refer to the price of entrees without beverages, desserts, taxes, or tips. Those listed as inexpensive are $10 or less; moderate, between $10 and $15; and expensive, $20 and over. Places to stay listed as inexpensive are up to $100 per double per night; moderate, $101 to $200 per night; and expensive, $201 and up per night.

Before you launch your off-the-beaten-path adventures, gather information from these sources: Georgia Tourist Division, P.O. Box 1776, Atlanta 30301, (404) 656–3590; and Georgia Department of Natural Resources, Parks and Historic Sites Division, 1352 Floyd Tower East, 2 Martin Luther King Drive, Atlanta 30334. For general information call (800) 869–8420 from anywhere in the United States; in Metro Atlanta call (404) 656–3530.

The Parks Division's Reservation Resource lets you make one toll-free call for campsites, cottages, picnic shelters, and lodge rooms throughout the system. Rates vary at different parks. Campsites, with electrical and water hookups, range from $12 to $17 a night. Completely furnished cottages are $45 to $55 for one bedroom, $65 to $75 for two bedrooms, and $75 to $125 for three bedrooms. Rates are higher on weekends and in certain seasons. Double rooms at state park lodges are $50 to $125. Call individual parks for exact rates. In metro Atlanta call (770) 389–PARK; anywhere else in the United States call (800) 864–PARK or go to www.gastateparks.org.

In 2000 the Georgia Department of Transportation changed the numbering system for interstate highway exits. The old sequential system, in which numbers are in chronological order, has been replaced by a mile log system, in which exit numbers correspond to mileposts. For instance, exit 2, on I–75 in southeastern Georgia, is 2 miles from the Florida border. Exit 353, near the Tennessee border in northwestern Georgia, is 353 miles from the Florida border. For a brochure of the new numbers, contact Georgia Department of Transportation, 2 Capitol Square, Atlanta 30334, (888) 419–4368.

If you're interested in a particular area, contact the local convention and visitors bureau or chamber of commerce.

Facts about Georgia

State tourism toll-free phone number: (800) VISIT–GA

MAJOR NEWSPAPERS

Atlanta Journal-Constitution, Augusta Chronicle, Macon Telegraph, Savannah Morning News, Columbus Enquirer

POPULATION

Georgia has 9.2 million people, the tenth most in the country.

MAJOR METRO AREAS

Atlanta, 4.7 million	Augusta, 200,000
Savannah, 300,000	Macon, 225,000
Columbus, 300,000	

SIZE

With 58,910 square miles, it is the largest state east of the Mississippi, twenty-first in the nation.

FAMOUS PEOPLE

- 39th President Jimmy Carter
- Juliette Gordon Low, founder of the Girl Scouts
- Dr. Martin Luther King Jr.
- *Gone With the Wind* author Margaret Mitchell
- Milledgeville novelist Flannery O'Connor *(The Violent Bear It Away, Wise Blood)*
- Columbus novelist Carson McCullers *(The Member of the Wedding, The Heart Is a Lonely Hunter)*
- Eatonton Pulitzer Prize–winning novelist Alice Walker *(The Color Purple)*
- Eatonton folk story author and humorist Joel Chandler Harris *(Uncle Remus: Tales, Uncle Remus: His Songs & His Sayings)*
- Moreland novelist Erskine Caldwell *(God's Little Acre, Tobacco Road)*
- Popular performers Ray Charles, Lena Horne, Otis Redding, Little Richard Penniman, bandleader Harry James, opera superstar Jessye Norman, songwriter Johnny Mercer, comedian Oliver Hardy
- Danielsville's Dr. Crawford W. Long, who performed the world's first painless surgery with ether in 1842
- Baseball's "Georgia Peach" Ty Cobb, from Royston
- Actress Joanne Woodward, from Thomasville
- Actor Burt Reynolds, born in Waycross
- Folk artist Howard Finster, from Summerville
- Western legend John "Doc" Holliday, born in Griffin

PUBLIC TRANSPORTATION

Atlanta has a rapid rail and public bus system, Metropolitan Atlanta Rapid Transit Authority (MARTA). Other cities with public transportation systems are Macon, Savannah, Augusta, Athens, and Columbus.

READING FOR KIDS

Joel Chandler Harris's *Uncle Remus: Tales* and *Uncle Remus: His Songs & His Sayings*.

CLIMATE

Summers are hot and humid, especially in the southern half of the state and the coast; spring is beautiful and balmy; winters are usually mild, with some snow accumulation in the northern mountains; fall, especially in the northern areas and the mountains, is brisk and cool, with colorful foliage.

GEORGIA TRIVIA

Georgia has 159 counties, more than any other state except Texas (which is four times larger), and more than twice as many as almost-the-same-size Florida and Alabama. There'd be even more, but two counties went bankrupt in the 1920s and merged with Atlanta's Fulton County.

ELEVATIONS

Georgia's highest point is Brasstown Bald Mountain, 4,784 feet above sea level; lowest point is sea level on the Atlantic coast.

Georgia's hottest recorded temperature was 113 degrees on May 27, 1978, at Greenville; the coldest was 17 degrees below zero in Floyd County (Rome) on January 27, 1940.

INTERESTING INFORMATION

You can travel around the world and never leave Georgia. Towns include Vienna (called VIE-enna), Cairo (KAY-ro), Berlin, Boston, Bremen, Hamburg, Rome, Milan, Athens, Arabic, and Sparta. You can shop at Bloomingdale and try to solve the secret of Enigma. Like Scarlett O'Hara, you'll never be hungry in Peach, Bacon, Baker, and Coffee Counties. Don't stub your toe on The Rock, and don't Bogart that joint, my friend.

Metro Atlanta

Atlanta and Fulton County

With a population of 4.7 million, Metro Atlanta is one of the nation's fastest-growing and most diverse urban centers. New suburbs with cookie-cutter subdivisions and shopping malls, threaded by perpetually clogged freeways, sprawl in all directions. In the city of Atlanta—population 450,000—an energetic young population is busily reviving many older neighborhoods. Downtown is also experiencing rebirth.

Centennial Olympic Park, created for the 1996 Summer Olympic Games, is surrounded by new high-rise condos, hotels, retail shops, restaurants and major new visitor attractions. In the twenty-two-acre park, at Marietta Street and Andrew Young International Boulevard, you can sit in the sunshine and admire downtown's striking skyline. If the weather's warm, shuck your shoes and splash in the park's *Five Rings Fountain* and perhaps look for your name on the 467,000 bricks that pave the walkways. The *Five Quilt Plazas,* made of brick and marble, tell the story of the largest games in Olympics history. You can play on a life-size chessboard and enjoy artworks from quirky to classical.

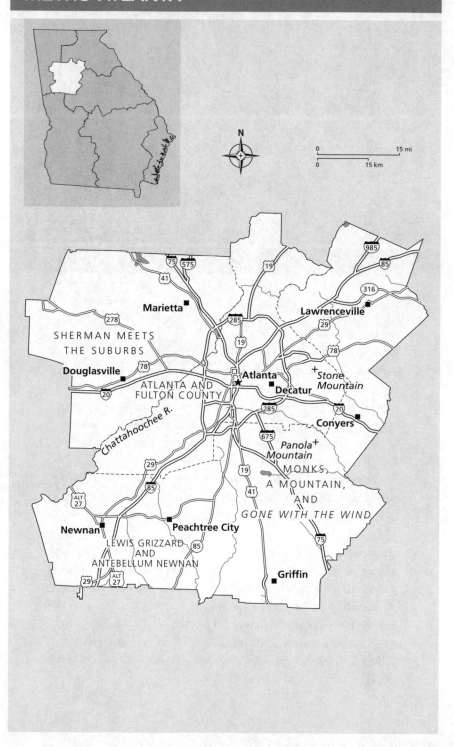

SHERMAN MEETS
THE SUBURBS

Marietta

Lawrenceville

278

Douglasville

78

+ Stone
Mountain

ATLANTA AND
FULTON COUNTY

Atlanta

Decatur

20

Conyers

70

Chattahoochee R.

285

675

Panola+
Mountain

MONKS
A MOUNTAIN,
AND
GONE WITH THE WIND

29

85

ALT
27

Newnan

Peachtree City

LEWIS GRIZZARD
AND
ANTEBELLUM NEWNAN

85

29

ALT
27

Griffin

N

0   15 mi

0   15 km

Attractions include the *Georgia Aquarium,* opened in November 2005. It's the world's largest fish tank, holding some eight million gallons of water. It's home to the world's largest fish, whale sharks named Ralph and Norton, who are destined to reach the size of school buses, and a supporting cast of over 120,000 fish and mammals from around the world. The ark-shaped aquarium is at 35 Baker Street, Atlanta, (404) 581–4000, www.georgiaaquarium.org. Open daily. Adults $22.75, seniors 55 and over $19.50, children ages 3 to 12

METRO ATLANTA'S TOP HITS

Centennial Olympic Park

Georgia Aquarium

Ansley Park

Atlanta Botanical Garden

Piedmont Park

Atlanta History Center

Little Five Points

Zoo Atlanta

Atlanta Braves Baseball

Chattahoochee River National

Recreation Area

Chattahoochee Nature Center

Roswell

Atlanta Preservation Center

Oakland Cemetery

Wren's Nest

Center for Puppetry Arts

Herndon Home

"The Big Chicken"

Michael C. Carlos Emory University Museum of Art and Archaeology

Fernbank Museum of Natural History

Fernbank Science Center

Stone Mountain Village

Norcross's Historic Old Town

Southern Museum of Civil War and Locomotive History

Yellow River Wildlife Game Ranch

High Museum of Art

Imagine It! The Children's Museum

Panola Mountain State

Conservation Park

Antebellum and Victorian

Newnan Driving Tour of Homes

Lewis Grizzard Museum

The Little Manse

National Museum of Patriotism

Sweetwater Creek

Conservation Park

Kennesaw Mountain National

Battlefield Park

Decatur Town Square

Marietta Town Square

Pickett's Mill Battlefield

$17.00, and under 3 free. The nearby *Imagine It! The Children's Museum of Atlanta,* 275 Centennial Olympic Park Drive, Atlanta, (404) 659–5437, www .imagineitcma.org, has scores of interactive ways to keep energetic youngsters busy. Open daily. Age 3 and up $11.00, 2 and under free.

The new *World of Coca-Cola* attraction will open in summer 2007. Get information on area attractions at the Atlanta Chamber of Commerce, on the edge of the park, 235 Andrew Young International Boulevard, (404) 880–9000.

For quick eats, step across Marietta Street to the food court and sit-down restaurants in the *CNN Center* atrium. You can take the *Inside CNN Tour* of the Cable News Network Studios and Turner Broadcasting Network and see news broadcast around the world. Fifty-five-minute tours begin every ten minutes. Adults $12.00, seniors $11.00, ages 4 to 18 $9.00, no one under age 4 admitted. For information and reservations phone (404) 827–2300, www .cnn.com/tour.

Castleberry Hill is an up-and-coming arts district, downtown off the beaten path, but only a short walk west of Centennial Olympic Park and its numerous attractions. The neighborhood, a pie-shaped wedge bounded by Peters, Walker, and Nelson Streets, was once a bustling industrial area with packing plants, warehouses, and livery stables. In the early 1980s artists and other urban pioneers discovered the rundown buildings and commercial storefronts and began converting them into galleries and spacious loft apartments.

Now more than a dozen art galleries and studios call Castleberry home. Loft conversions and new residential buildings are home to more than 600 permanent residences. Among the galleries that keep regular hours are Atlanta Gallery Project, 331 Walker Street, (678) 839–4954, www.westga.edu~artdept; Marcia Wood Gallery, 263 Walker Street, (404) 827–0030, www.marcia woodgallery.com; Krause Gallery, 291 Peters Street, (404) 522–6205; Romo Gallery, 309 Peters Street, (404) 222–9955, www.romogallery.com; Ty Stokes Gallery, 261 Walker Street, (404) 222–9863, www.tystokes.com; and Skot Foreman Fine Art, 315 Peters Street, (404) 222–0440, www.skotforeman.com. It's best to call in advance. Regularly held Friday night and Saturday afternoon *Art Strolls* are the best way to take in all the galleries. Check the Web site, www.castleberryhill.org.

As the number of galleries and residents increases, restaurants and other services are also developing. *Slice,* a pizza joint and martini bar at 259 Peters Street, (404) 588–1820, www.sliceatlanta.com, always attracts a lively, eclectic crowd. Other restaurants and bars are scheduled to open in early 2007.

The food court and tablecloth restaurants in the *Peachtree Center* office building and hotel complex, on Peachtree Street between Andrew Young International Boulevard and Baker Street, have a wide selection of cuisine to

TOP ANNUAL EVENTS

Southeastern Flower Show,
mid-February, City Hall East,
640 North Avenue,
(404) 888–5638

Conyers Cherry Blossom Festival,
late March, Georgia
International Horse Park,
(770) 918–2169

Atlanta Dogwood Festival,
early April, Piedmont Park,
(404) 329–0501

Georgia Renaissance Festival,
April and May,
September and October,
7795 Spence Road, Fairburn,
(770) 964–8575

**Inman Park Spring Festival and
Tour of Homes,**
late April, Euclid and
Edgewood Avenues, no phone

Stone Mountain Village Arts Festival,
mid-June, Main Street,
Stone Mountain,
(770) 498–2097

Peachtree Road Race 10K,
July 4, Peachtree Road–
Peachtree Street,
(404) 231–9064

Christmas at Bulloch Hall,
throughout December,
Roswell, (770) 992–1731

Christmas at Callanwolde,
early to mid-December,
Callanwolde Fine Arts Center,
(404) 872–5338

take out or enjoy in. Pick up a souvenir T-shirt with your burger and fries at the **Hard Rock Cafe,** under the Cadillac over the doorway at Peachtree and International, (404) 688–7625.

Downtown Atlanta's **Woodruff Park** doesn't have a lot of greenery, but on weekdays this open space at Peachtree, Marietta, and Decatur Streets is an A-1 people-watching location. At weekday lunch, the benches and small patches of grass fill up with Georgia State University students, office workers, street preachers, politicians, freelance musicians, and entertainers. Pick up a sack lunch at one of the numerous eateries around the park and sit back and watch the water wall and fountain at the north end of the park. *Phoenix Rising,* the large bronze sculpture at the park's south end, symbolizes Atlanta's rebirth after its Civil War destruction.

North of downtown, the **Midtown neighborhood,** along Peachtree Street between Ponce de Leon Avenue and Sixteenth Street, is one of Atlanta's liveliest and most eclectic areas. Straight and gay bars and dance clubs, restaurants of every stripe, hotels, shops, live theaters, and sleek high-rise condos line Peachtree, Tenth, and Juniper Streets and Piedmont Avenue. *The Woodruff*

Art Center (home of the *Atlanta Symphony Orchestra* and *Alliance Theater*) and *High Museum of Art,* at 1280 Peachtree Street, are the city's cultural temples. In 2005, the High tripled its exhibition space with three new buildings and a central piazza, designed by Italian architect Renzo Piano. Now through fall 2009, the museum will exhibit hundreds of art works from the Paris Louvre. Most have never been out of France, and the High is the only place they will be shown. Mona Lisa and Venus de Milo won't make the trip. Phone (404) 733–4400, www.high.org.

The *Margaret Mitchell House and* Gone With the Wind *Museum,* 999 Peachtree Street, Atlanta, (404) 249–7015, www.gwtw.org, includes two attractions associated with the best-selling novel and 1939 movie. Mitchell wrote her novel on the battered typewriter in her basement apartment in the restored Victorian boardinghouse she called "The Dump." There's a video about her life and her book, as well as letters, photos, and memorabilia. Opened in 1999, the *GWTW* Museum adjacent to the house is devoted to the movie, which premiered in Atlanta in 1939. Exhibits include movie scripts, props, costumes, set design sketches, the front door of the O'Hara family's fictional Tara plantation house, and a portrait of Scarlett O'Hara (Vivien Leigh) in a blue dress, still showing a stain from a whiskey glass an angry Rhett Butler (Clark Gable) threw against it in the second half of the movie.

Although Mitchell wrote only one novel, she was a prolific letter writer. In a letter to her mother-in-law in 1936, she describes the day she frantically gathered the *GWTW* manuscript to deliver to the editor of Macmillan Books: "For years [the manuscript] has been knocking about the house in about twenty very dirty manila envelopes. Some were under the bed . . . some were in the pot and pan closet. I had sixty first chapters, each worse than the other. So, I sat down and took off my garters and tore off a new first chapter. . . . It wasn't until I got to the lobby of [the editor's] hotel that I realized what I looked like, hatless, hair flying . . . my hastily rolled up stockings coming down around my ankles."

The museum is open daily from 9:30 A.M. to 5:00 P.M. Admission for the house and museum is $12.00 for adults, $9.00 for seniors and students, and $5.00 for children ages 6 to 17. Mitchell was struck and killed by a taxi on her beloved Peachtree Street, 4 blocks from the house, in 1949. She's buried under a simple gravestone, with her married name Marsh, in downtown Atlanta's historic Oakland Cemetery.

One of the most interesting ways to delve into the city's history is on a tour led by the *Atlanta Preservation Center* (404–688–3350). The center's half-dozen walking tours from April through October focus on the city's architectural and cultural heritage. The *Fox Theatre* tour takes you backstage at one of America's last surviving 1920s "picture palaces." Adorned with minarets, Moorish arches, Egyptian hieroglyphics, and a blue-sky ceiling that twinkles with electric stars, the Fox (404–881–2100) hosts a full schedule of touring musicals, concerts of all sorts, and a summertime classic movie festival. It's at 660 Peachtree Street at Ponce de Leon Avenue, Atlanta.

MARTA, the Metropolitan Atlanta Rapid Transit Authority, is an up-to-date way to get around the city. The clean, two-line rapid rail system intersects at Five Points Station downtown and is a swift way of getting to the **Woodruff Arts Center/High Museum of Art** and other attractions. The MARTA bus system is a more comprehensive but much slower way of getting about. Fare for both is $1.75 one way, including transfers; for information call (404) 848–4711.

For an ear on what's happening, pick up the "Access Atlanta" section in Thursday's *Atlanta Journal-Constitution,* the alternative weeklies *Creative Loafing* and *Sunday Paper,* and gay-oriented *Southern Voice*, all available in sidewalk boxes free.

Ansley Park, a lovely neighborhood dating to the 1920s, is a quiet place to walk, drive, or ride a bike. On Peachtree Street at the Woodruff Arts Center/ Colony Square area, turn east onto Fifteenth Street and north onto Peachtree Circle and follow the meandering byways past sumptuous lawns and gardens skirting homes in a spectrum of styles. Stop for a picnic, a walk, or a giddy ride on a swing at **Winn Park,** at Peachtree Circle and Lafayette Drive. Follow a street called The Prado to Piedmont Avenue. Cross this busy street and you're at the **Atlanta Botanical Garden** (404–876–5859, www.atlantabotanicalgarden .org). Take your time strolling through thirty acres of formal gardens, rose gardens, a Japanese garden, and a fifteen-acre hardwood forest with a marked walking trail. Many state, regional, and national flower shows are held in the Day Building at the entrance. The Botanical Garden's centerpiece is the Dorothy Chapman Fuqua Conservatory, with 16,000 square feet of tropical, desert, Mediterranean, and endangered plants. The Fuqua Orchid Center displays tropical orchids from around the world in their natural habitat. There's also a gift shop and small restaurant. Open Tuesday through Sunday 9:00 A.M. to 6:00 P.M. Admission is $10.00 for adults, $7.00 for senior citizens, and $6.00 for children 3 and older.

After the Botanical Garden, wander into adjoining **Piedmont Park.** The city's largest park has tennis courts, a swimming pool, softball fields, playgrounds, and paved, auto-free roadways for jogging, hiking, biking, and rollerblading. In summer, the park's lawns and hillsides fill up with tanning bodies. You can rent skateboards, rollerblades, roller skates, and bikes at **Skate Escape** (404–892–1292), across from the park at 1086 Piedmont Avenue, Atlanta.

BILL'S FAVORITES

Atlanta Botanical Garden	Stone Mountain Park
Virginia-Highland neighborhood	Old Norcross
Little Five Points/East Atlanta Village	Old Buford
Chattahoochee River National Recreation Area	Kennesaw Mountain National Battlefield Park
Court Square entertainment area in Decatur	

The ***Virginia-Highland neighborhood,*** about a mile and a half east of Piedmont Park, is one of the city's favorite dining, shopping, and entertainment areas. It's divided into three parts: From Ponce de Leon Avenue, a lively strip of restaurants, bars, coffee shops, and offbeat shops extends about 3 blocks north on North Highland Avenue; after a 3-block residential break, it comes back to life around the Virginia Avenue–North Highland Avenue corner; after another residential break, you'll find more fun stuff at North Highland and Amsterdam Avenues and at another strip at North Highland and Morningside Drive.

The ***Buckhead neighborhood,*** off Peachtree Street/Road about 6 miles due north of downtown, has long been Atlanta's most splendid residential enclave. West of Peachtree Road, follow the green and white SCENIC DRIVE markers past Spanish and Italian villas, French chateaux, Old English Tudor homes, and white-columned Greek Revival, Georgian, and even Japanese-style showplaces that preside over immense lawns and great stands of trees and flowering shrubbery. Some of the most beautiful homes are on West Paces Ferry, Andrews, Habersham, Blackland, Valley, and Tuxedo Roads.

The neighborhood also has some of the city's finest restaurants. Lenox Square and Phipps Plaza, tony malls at the Peachtree Road/Lenox Road intersection, offer the treasures of Gucci, Saks, Neiman Marcus, and other upscale retail chains.

Famous part-time resident Elton John lives in the penthouse at Park Place, a high-rise condo at Peachtree and East Wesley Roads. "Elton-watchers" sometimes see him driving his car around Buckhead and shopping at area stores. Pop singer Janet Jackson also lives in Elton's building.

You'll have a better understanding of what makes Atlanta the kind of city it is after a day at the ***Atlanta History Center*** (404–814–4000, www.atlantahistory center.com). The tree-shaded, thirty-acre sanctuary at 3101 Andrews Drive,

Atlanta, includes three fascinating attractions: the insightful and very well done Museum of Atlanta History; the circa 1836 "plantation plain" Tullie Smith Farmstead; and the Swan House, an opulent Italian-Palladian villa, built in 1926 and appointed with European and Asian furnishings and set among formal gardens and terraced fountains. Open daily. Admission is $12.00 for adults, $10.00 for seniors 65 and older and students 18 and over with ID, $4.00 for children ages 6 to 17; free for children 6 and under.

The *Centennial Olympic Games Museum,* opened in summer 2006, is the History Center's newest attraction. The 27,500-square foot, three-story museum traces Atlanta's dark-horse bid for the 1996 games, the building of venues, and a time table of events at the sixteen-day games. Exhibits include medals dating to 1896, a collection of Olympic torches and gifts to the city from the 197 participating teams. An interactive Sports Lab lets kids and adults test their skills against Olympic athletes.

If you still pine for the flower-child days of the 1960s or feel like dyeing your hair electric blue or orange and skateboarding on the sidewalk, *Little Five Points* is your kind of place. You can be totally mainstream and still enjoy an outing at this Southern-style East Village/Soho area. Around the intersection of Moreland and Euclid Avenues, across Ponce de Leon Avenue from Virginia-Highland and about 3 miles east of downtown, you'll find a cluster of good, inexpensive restaurants—Indian, Caribbean, Mexican, Italian, Cajun—coffee bars, bars with and without music, and funky shops selling vintage clothing, new and used CDs, and books on astrology, herbal medicine, and other esoteric subjects. Just like the good old days, street musicians perform for your pleasure and spare change.

East Atlanta Village, off I–20 and Moreland Avenue about ten minutes south of Little Five Points, is the latest given-up-for-dead old neighborhood to get the Lazarus treatment. Young entrepreneurs have turned vacant storefronts around the Flat Shoals Avenue–Glenwood Avenue intersection into kicky shops with unique and offbeat

howbuckhead gotitsname

Buckhead, Atlanta's most affluent, most fashionable neighborhood, owes its unique name to an early settler. In 1838, Henry Irby paid a few dollars for a small piece of wilderness near the modern-day intersection of Peachtree, Roswell, and West Paces Ferry Roads. He put up a tavern and a general store that became a meeting place for farmers, hunters, and tradesmen. One day while hunting in the dense woods, he shot a buck, posted the deer's impressive head on his door, and christened the establishment The Buck's Head Tavern. In time, the tavern gave its name to the entire neighborhood. Irby Avenue remembers the founding father.

gifts, art, antiques, and imports. The resurgent old neighborhood's new-found diversity is reflected in inexpensive to moderately priced eateries that serve French, vegan, Italian, Australian, Caribbean, and contemporary American fare. Hot local bands draw the young and sleepless to *The Earl,* 488 Flat Shoals Avenue, (404) 522–3950, and *Echo Lounge,* 551 Flat Shoals Avenue, (404) 681–3600. *Mary's,* 1287 Glenwood Avenue, (404) 624– 4411, is a popular gay bar. For a quick pick-me-up, find a sofa at *Joe's East Atlanta Coffee House,* 510 Flat Shoals Avenue, (404) 521–1122. The anti-corporate java and dessert shop is the unofficial "living room" for urban pioneers, who meet for jolts of espresso while they read, study, and revel in the urban slacker lifestyle.

Zoo Atlanta, in Grant Park, 800 Cherokee Avenue, Atlanta, (404) 624–5600, www.zooatlanta.org, a few blocks from the Village and 2 miles from downtown, is a fun place to spend a day. For the next several years, the zoo's stellar attractions will be Lun-Lun and Yang-Yang, a pair of adorable giant pandas on loan from China. They spend a lot of time sleeping and munching bamboo, but when they move around and climb trees in their lavish habitat, you'll wish you could rush in and give them a big bear hug. The zoo's other big attraction is the Ford African Rain Forest, a natural habitat for families of silverback mountain gorillas. In early 2000, Willie B., the zoo's beloved 41-year-old silverback—the king of the zoo since his childhood—died of old age. A life-size statue of the world-famous silverback is at the zoo entrance. Other zoo habitats house more than 1,000 tropical birds, big cats, bears, giraffes, reptiles, and other exotic creatures from around the world. Open daily. Admission is $16.50 for adults, $12.50 for seniors, $11.50 for children 3 to 11.

Also in Grant Park, the Cyclorama is a colossal painting in the round capturing a crucial hour in the Civil War Battle of Atlanta. Open daily. Phone (404) 658–7625. Admission is $5.00 for adults, $4.00 for seniors, $3.00 for children.

Atlanta has many other off-the-beaten-path attractions. Here are a few:

The *Robert C. Williams American Museum of Papermaking,* on the Georgia Tech campus, 500 Tenth Street, (404) 894–6663, www.ipst.edu/amp, takes you on a self-guided tour through thousands of years of paper and paper technology. "Pre-paper" exhibits include tree leaves from India, Egyptian papyrus, Indonesian bark, and other substances that ancient peoples used before the invention of the real thing, in China around A.D. 105. Contemporary exhibits feature North America's first paper mill in 1690 and mills that produce paper in the twenty-first century. Papermaking workshops are held periodically. Open Monday through Friday 9:00 A.M. to 5:00 P.M. Free admission.

William Breman Jewish Heritage Museum, 1440 Spring Street, Midtown Atlanta, (678) 222–3700, www.thebreman.org, explores the history of

Judaism and Atlanta's own rich Jewish history. In addition to two main galleries, the museum offers a genealogy center, extensive archives, a resources library, and changing exhibits such as "Shalom, Y'all," a history of Judaism in the South. Open Monday through Thursday 10:00 A.M. to 5:00 P.M., Friday 10:00 A.M. to 3:00 P.M., and Sunday 1:00 to 5:00 P.M. Adults $6.00, seniors and students $4.00, children 6 and under free.

Children as well as adults will enjoy the **Center for Puppetry Arts** (404–873–3391), on the northern edge of downtown at 1404 Spring Street. The converted redbrick school building houses a fascinating puppetry museum and puts on a year-round program of puppet theatricals, some aimed at youngsters, others tailored for adults.

The **National Museum of Patriotism,** across from the Center for Puppetry Arts, was opened in 2004 to inspire patriotism and love of country. Seven viewing areas include the America Room Theater, a film that ranges from July Fourth parades, flag burnings and panoramic views of American landmarks; Symbols of America includes the Liberty Bell, Washington, D.C., landmarks, Mount Rushmore, the Statue of Liberty, and the Great Seal of the United States; "The Immigrant Experience" highlights our melting-pot population; Hall of Patriots honors recipients of the Congressional Medal of Honor and Presidential Medal of Freedom; World War II Sweetheart Jewelry and Collectibles; and United We Stand, featuring more than 500 magazines dedicated to the flag and American spirit in July 1942. There's also an exhibit on Atlanta's 1996 Summer Olympic Games. It's at 1405 Spring Street, (404) 875–0691, www.museumofpatriotism.org. Open Tuesday through Friday 10:00 A.M. to 5:00 P.M., Saturday 11:00 A.M. to 5:00 P.M., Sunday 1:00 to 5:00 P.M. Adults $12.00, age 65 and over and ages 7 to 18, $10.00.

Oakland Cemetery, 248 Oakland Avenue at Memorial Drive, Atlanta, (404) 688–2107, is a book on Atlanta's past, right behind the ultramodern King Memorial MARTA Station. Established in 1850, Oakland has redbrick walls that enclose a wealth of architectural and cultural heritage. Victorian aristocrats are entombed in templelike mausoleums, embellished with stained glass, gargoyles, and marble busts. You can walk through Confederate and Jewish sections, see the graves of the city's firstborn child and other celebrities, such as *Gone With the Wind* author Margaret Mitchell, golf champion Bobby Jones, governors, mayors, Union spies, and beloved pets, and spread a picnic lunch under the magnolia trees. Open daily. Free tours are conducted on weekends.

A MARTA train to West End Station and a bus connection or 3-block walk will bring you to the **Wren's Nest,** the Victorian home of Joel Chandler Harris, creator of Br'er Rabbit, Br'er Fox, the Tar Baby, and other delightful critters who roam through his 1880s book, *Uncle Remus: His Songs & His Sayings.*

Rooms are filled with furnishings and mementos of Harris and his family, editions of his book in many languages, and re-creations of his beloved characters. The house got its name when a mother wren decided that Harris's wooden mailbox would be perfect for her brood. The mailbox now has an honored place among the Wren's Nest's treasures. Especially if you have children, try to visit when storytelling sessions are scheduled—usually the last Saturday of the month and daily during the summer. Wren's Nest, at 1050 Ralph David Abernathy Boulevard, Atlanta, (404) 753–7735, is open Tuesday through Saturday from 10:00 A.M. to 4:00 P.M. and Sunday from 1:00 to 2:30 P.M. Admission is $7.00 for adults, $6.00 for senior citizens and teens, $4.00 for children ages 4 to 12.

West of downtown, **Herndon Home,** at 587 University Place, Atlanta, is a landmark of Black achievement. The dignified Beaux-Arts style mansion was built in 1915 by Alonzo Herndon, a former slave who founded Atlanta Life Insurance Company, the nation's largest Black-owned insurance firm. The fifteen rooms showcase his remarkable life. Most of the antique furnishings and family photos are original. The Herndon Home is open Tuesday through Saturday from 1:00 to 4:00 P.M. Free admission. For more information call (404) 581–9813.

Georgia's nineteenth-century poet Sidney Lanier sang the praises of the Chattahoochee River in his idyllic "Song of the Chattahoochee." The river rises in the north Georgia mountains and flows through metropolitan Atlanta on its way to the Gulf of Mexico.

The **Chattahoochee River National Recreation Area,** a 48-mile stretch of river and gentle rapids flowing between wooded palisades, is the focus for recreational pursuits of all sorts. From spring through fall, Atlantans love to set

The Wren's Nest

their rafts, canoes, and kayaks loose in the river for a lazy day of relaxation. Sturdy four-, six-, and eight-person rafts may be rented from Chattahoochee Outdoor Center, 1990 Island Ford Parkway, (770) 395–6851. If rafting isn't your pleasure, you can also spread a picnic, hike, bike, jog, bird-watch, and exercise on the twenty-two-station fitness trail. The park's main entrance is at Highway 41 and the Chattahoochee River bridge. Contact the Park Superintendent, 1978 Island Ford Parkway, Atlanta 30350; (770) 399–8070, www.nps.gov/chat.

The river's fauna and flora are celebrated at the ***Chattahoochee Nature Center,*** 9135 Willeo Road, Roswell 30075; (770) 992–2055, www.chattnature center.com. The private, nonprofit natural-science center's exhibits of plants and wildlife, special programs, and workshops are in a tranquil fifty-acre setting by the riverbank, about 25 miles north of downtown Atlanta. Guided walks on Saturday and Sunday at noon and 2:00 P.M. weave through twenty acres of nature trails and along a 1,400-foot boardwalk over the river. You can also pick up a brochure and take a self-guided tour. Make a full day of it with a picnic lunch. The center is open Monday through Saturday from 9:00 A.M. to 5:00 P.M. and Sunday from noon to 5:00 P.M. Adults $3.00, seniors and age 3 to 12 $2.00.

On December 22, 1853, Mittie Bulloch, a ***Roswell*** debutante, married New Yorker Theodore Roosevelt in the dining room of ***Bulloch Hall,*** her family's Greek Revival showplace. The happy couple, of course, had no inkling of the far-reaching consequences of their union. After the nuptials, they moved to New York and in 1858, had a son, Theodore, who became our twenty-sixth president when William McKinley was assassinated in 1901. Their other son, Elliot, had a daughter, Eleanor, who married her cousin Franklin.

In 1905, President "TR" made a sentimental journey to his mother's ancestral home. If he came back today, he'd find Bulloch Hall looking pretty much as it was when his mother was a blushing bride.

Mittie's father, Maj. James Stephens Bulloch, grandson of Georgia's Revolutionary War Gov. Archibald Bulloch, built the house in 1839, the same year Roswell King, a Connecticut Yankee, founded the town and built textile mills on the Chattahoochee River.

One of the South's rare examples of pure temple-form architecture, with a fully pedimented portico, Bulloch Hall is one of more than 100 Roswell structures on the National Register of Historic Places. In 1978, the city of Roswell purchased the house and sixteen acres and opened it to the public. A few of the Bulloch family's original furnishings are complemented by period pieces. Modern brides say their vows in the same dining room where Mittie said hers. A reenactment of Mittie and Theodore's wedding is a highlight of "Christmas in Roswell," which also includes Victorian holiday decorations, high teas, parades, seasonal storytelling and the lighting of the Town Square.

Bulloch Hall, 180 Bulloch Drive, Roswell 30075, (800) 776–7935, (770) 992–1731, is open Monday through Saturday from 10:00 A.M. to 3:00 P.M., Sunday 1:00 to 3:00 P.M. Admission for all ages is $5.00.

Another noteworthy historical site is ***Archibald Smith Plantation,*** an 1845 cotton farm, with twelve original buildings, at 935 Alpharetta Street, Roswell, (770) 641–3978. Open Monday through Friday from 11:00 A.M. to 2:00 P.M., Saturday from 11:00 A.M. to 1:00 P.M. Adult admission $5.00, $3.00 for students.

Teaching Museum North, in a former elementary school at 791 Mimosa Boulevard, Roswell, (770) 552–6339, is a good place to learn about the history of Roswell, the state of Georgia and the United States. The Roswell Room's exhibits depict the town's antebellum homes and other buildings spared by the Civil War. A mural traces the region's history from Native Americans to the present. Georgia's many authors, including Pat Conroy, Flannery O'Connor, Sidney Lanier, Alice Walker, Margaret Mitchell, James Dickey, Eugenia Price and Erskine Caldwell, are honored in the Writers Corner. Other rooms showcase Georgia's economic, political and social history; U.S. presidents; transportation and the changing role of women in America. Open Monday through Friday from 8:00 A.M. to 4:00 P.M.

Roswell King laid out the Town Square in New England fashion, with a park in the center and a bandstand where "TR" spoke to townsfolk in 1905, surrounded by brick shop buildings. An original general store that once sold everything but liquor now houses ***J. Christopher's*** (605 Atlanta Street, 770–640–5548), which serves breakfast, brunch and lunch, and still nothing more potent than sweet tea.

A town as old as Roswell naturally (or supernaturally) has plenty of rumored ghosts. "Ghost Talk, Ghost Walk," (770) 753–0037, every Friday evening takes you on a stroll through the Historic District, where you'll hear legendary tales, ghost stories, scandals and very likely an outright fabrication or two. The biggest mystery is the fate of 400 women and children textile workers, charged with treason by the Union army in 1864 and taken north, most of them never heard from again. The Lost Workers of Roswell Monument, in Old Mill Park on Sloan Street, is their memorial.

Antiques shops and galleries are foremost on many visitors' minds. Canton and Alpharetta Streets are chock-a-block with cozy shops and mammoth collectibles malls. If your art preferences lean in the folk and whimsical direction, stop in ***Matilda's Enchanted Cottage,*** 377 South Main Street, Alpharetta, (770) 754–7831, www.matildascottageonline.com. You'll find a magical complex of imaginatively decorated cottages crammed with folk art, pottery, paintings, hand-painted furniture, quilts, weaving, glassware, etc., made by local and nationally recognized artists.

Where's the Olympic Stadium?

If you'd like to visit Atlanta's Olympic Stadium, you'll have to attend an Atlanta Braves baseball game at Turner Field. The stadium where the 1996 Summer Games opening and closing ceremonies and track and field events were held was ingeniously constructed so that about half of the 85,000 seats could easily be taken out after the games and the stadium converted to a new high-tech, 50,000-seat home for the Braves. If you get bored with the game, the stadium has plenty of other bells and whistles. You can play a host of virtual reality games or Nintendo, shop, visit the Braves Museum, and have dinner and drinks in food courts and the center field restaurant and bar.

TV screens all over the place let you enjoy the game just as you would in the comfort of your own living room. It was renamed for Braves owner Ted Turner, whose TBS Superstation puts the Braves in living rooms from coast to coast.

To arm yourselves with information on what to see and do, stop first at the Roswell Visitors Center on the square, 617 Atlanta Street, Roswell, (800) 776–7935, (770) 640–3253, www.roswell.ga.us for a video overview, historical exhibits and walking/driving maps. Guided walking tours leave from the center at 10:00 A.M. Wednesday and 1:00 P.M. Saturday, $5.00 a person.

With a population of 700,000, **DeKalb County** is the Metro area's second most populous county and Georgia's most ethnically diverse. You'll find many off-the-beaten-path attractions among the county's busy streets and freeways, shopping malls, and Andrew Young subdivisions.

There's an Andrew Young International Boulevard in downtown Atlanta, but the metro area's real "international" boulevard is **Buford Highway** (Highway 23). A 10-mile stretch of multilane urban roadway from Lenox Road in the city of Atlanta north through the DeKalb towns of Chamblee and Doraville to Jimmy Carter Boulevard in Gwinnett County is lined with more than 700 businesses and services run by Asian and Hispanic immigrants. Since the early 1980s, old strip shopping centers and newly built malls have filled up with supermarkets where shoppers come from around the Southeast for Korean, Thai, Chinese, Vietnamese, Caribbean, Mexican, Central American, and South American produce, seafood, rice, spices, and other staples. The area is nicknamed "Chambodia" for Chamblee and Cambodia.

Dozens of restaurants offer a selection of authentic cuisines you might expect to find only in Seoul, Bangkok, and Lima (or in Los Angeles, San Francisco, and New York). Some of the major hubs include Mall Fiesta, a revamped outlet mall at the busy Buford Highway–Clairmont Road intersection, where you can explore the exotic wares in the cavernous Hong Kong Supermarket and visit specialty shops and several restaurants serving Asian, South American, and Central American cuisines. Pho 79, a storefront Vietnamese eatery, serves a variety of pho—hearty soups with beef, pork, and seafood—while you watch Asian music videos on a TV screen; (404) 728–9129.

Farther north, Asian Square, 5150 Buford Highway, is anchored by the mammoth Ranch 99 supermarket stocked with Asian and Hispanic goods and about a dozen Taiwanese, Malaysian, Chinese, and Vietnamese restaurants. Asiana Garden (770–452–1677) has Korean and Japanese food and a sushi bar; Little Malaysia (770–458–1818), Malaysian and Singaporean noodle and rice dishes, curries, and seafood. You can also find jewelry, books, videos, clothes, toys, and gifts, as well as an Asian bank, accountants, and other services.

While you're in northeast DeKalb, you can explore an assortment of antiques shops and flea markets around the Peachtree Road–Broad Street Junction in "old" downtown Chamblee. You're bound to find something you can't resist at *Moosebreath Trading Company* (770–458–7210), *Broad Street Antique Mall* (770–458–6316), and *Whipporwill Co.* (770–455–8357).

Since the Olympics, *Decatur,* the DeKalb County seat, has enjoyed an ongoing renaissance. Vacant storefronts on *Court Square,* across from the historic county courthouse, are now filled with upbeat restaurants, taverns, coffeehouses, and shops.

In a cul-de-sac, off East Ponce de Leon Avenue, there is a choice of popular eateries. You'll probably have to wait for a table on weekends. In warm weather, you can sit at outdoor tables that line the sidewalks. Restaurants are right outside the Decatur MARTA rail station, about a fifteen-minute ride from downtown Atlanta. On summer Saturday nights, Decaturites spread blankets and picnic suppers on the courthouse lawn and enjoy live music at the bandstand.

Emory University's *Michael C. Carlos Emory University Museum of Art and Archaeology,* 571 South Kilgo Street, Atlanta, (404) 727–0516, holds a trove of antiquities from around the world. Treasures in this beautifully planned building on the Emory Quadrangle include Greek and Roman coins, statuary, and amphorae; an Egyptian mummy with a gilded face; and European, pre-Columbian, and Asian art objects. Floors are inlaid with diagrams of ancient temples and palaces. Special exhibitions are held regularly. A $5.00 donation is requested. Open Tuesday through Saturday from 11:00 A.M. to 4:30 P.M. The museum is near the university's main entrance at North Decatur and Oxford Roads. On-campus paid parking is available.

Across from the campus on North Decatur and Oxford Roads, you'll find a row of popular student-oriented eateries, including Everybody's Pizza, Doc Chey's Noodle House, Caribou Coffee, Starbucks, and Burrito Art. If you're into vegetarian and organic foods, check out *Rainbow Grocery,* North

Decatur Plaza, 2118 North Decatur Road, (404) 636–5553. The compact store stocks organic and nonorganic fruits and vegetables, cheese, frozen food, bread and other staples, and herbal remedies. Help yourself to the salad bar and carryout sandwiches, desserts, and prepared dinners. The cafe in the rear of the store serves delicious vegetarian burritos, lasagna, chili, sandwiches, and soups. Open daily.

What can you do on a rainy day in Atlanta? Rain or shine, you can spend all of it at the *Fernbank Museum of Natural History* and the companion *Fernbank Science Center.* The museum's attractions include the hands-on "Walk through Time in Georgia" and "The Maurer World of Shells and Living Coral Reef Exhibits," children's discovery rooms, lifelike dinosaurs, and an IMAX theater. They are located at 767 Clifton Road, Atlanta, between downtown Atlanta and Decatur. The museum (404–929–6400, www.fernbank .edu/museum) is open Monday through Friday from 10:00 A.M. to 9:00 P.M. and Saturday and Sunday from noon to 5:00 P.M. Adults, $12.00; students and senior citizens, $11.00; ages 3 to 12, $10.00. IMAX theater: adults, $10.00; students and seniors, $9.00; ages 3 to 12, $8.00. Combination museum-IMAX: adults, $13.95; students and seniors, $11.95; ages 3 to 12, $9.95.

Fernbank Science Center, in a sixty-five-acre hardwood and pine forest threaded with walking trails, has a 500-seat planetarium offering seasonal looks at the heavens. You can also look at far-flung galaxies through the Southeast's largest telescope. Other exhibits focus on Georgia's varied plant and animal life. Open daily, charges only for planetarium shows: $2.00 for adults, $1.00 for students. Located at 156 Heaton Park Drive, Atlanta, (678) 874–7102, fernbank.edu.

A granite monolith 825 feet high and 6 miles around, with numerous attractions and six million visitors yearly, is hardly off the beaten path. However, many Stone Mountain Park visitors include a visit to *Stone Mountain Village.* Outside the park's gates, the Village's nineteenth-century Main Street is flanked by covered sidewalks and 3 blocks of stores stocked with vintage books, arts and crafts, Civil War artifacts, antiques, geodes, apparel, jewelry, and oddities.

Buster, Hero Dog

Buster, a heroic police dog, is remembered with a granite tribute in front of the Jonesboro police headquarters on North McDonough Street. The inscription reads NOT JUST A DOG, BUT A POLICE OFFICER, A PARTNER, A FRIEND, ONE WHO MADE A DIFFERENCE. Buster's fellow officers put up the monument bearing Buster's image after bad guys brought down the fearless, five-year-old crime fighter in 1990.

You can get a haircut in an old-fashioned barber shop and buy an ice cream, a sandwich, or a full meal at several cafes and restaurants.

If you love to rummage through old bookstores, lose yourself in the crowded aisles of **Memorable Books**, 5380 Manor Drive, (770) 469–5911, a few steps off Main Street. Shelves are stacked to the ceiling with books on Americana, Georgia, and the South. You can also find scholarly books and books on cooking, gardening, medicine, the military . . . you want it, chances are it's in here somewhere, and the owner will know exactly where to find it. Next door to the bookstore, **ART Station,** (770) 469–1105, exhibits paintings, sculpture, and other works by local and regional artists.

Clayton County, south of downtown Atlanta, was the setting for Tara, Twelve Oaks, and other *Gone With the Wind* landmarks. Appropriately, the **Road to Tara Museum,** in Jonesboro's Depot Welcome Center, 104 North Main Street, Jonesboro, (770) 478–4800, (800) 662–7829, www.visitscarlett.com, houses one of the largest collections of *GWTW* memorabilia. Exhibits include re-creations of some of the movie's most famous costumes, first editions of the book in many languages, posters, continuous showings of the film, and souvenir items. If you look closely at a mural, you'll see the familiar face of Elvis Presley, carrying the Confederate battle flag. The mural's artist, Del Nichols, includes Elvis in everything he does. The museum is open Monday through Friday 8:30 A.M. to 5:30 P.M., Saturday 10:00 A.M. to 4:00 P.M. Adults, $5.00, seniors and students, $4.00.

Margaret Mitchell's childhood playhouse is located behind **Pope Dickson & Son Antique Funeral Museum,** 168 North McDonough Street, Jonesboro, (770) 478–7211, www.popedickson.com. The playhouse was originally at the

Nose-to-Nose with Bobby Lee

I'm one of the few people who's actually been close enough to touch the monumental sculpture on the face of Stone Mountain. When the 90-foot-high-by-190-foot-long carving of Jefferson Davis, Robert E. Lee, and Stonewall Jackson was nearly completed in 1970, politicians, VIPs, and news media were invited to a fried-chicken lunch on the scaffolding in front of the figures, which are about halfway up the sheer side of the 825-foot-high, 6-miles-in-circumference chunk of granite. The event commemorated a similar fund-raising lunch during the first attempt at creating the Confederate memorial in the 1920s. I don't remember anything about the fried chicken except feeling queasy at the thought of it. I do remember the awe at actually standing nose-to-nose with the carving and thinking how fine the workmanship was, even at such close range. I only regret not getting a picture of myself standing up there next to Jeff Davis, Stonewall, and Bobby Lee.

Fitzgerald Plantation, which belonged to Mitchell's grandparents. Pope Dickson's Antique Funeral Museum is believed to be America's only drive-by museum of its type. Exhibits in a glassed-in, lighted room include a horse-drawn hearse that led a double life: In 1883, it carried the body of Georgia governor and former Confederate vice president Alexander Hamilton Stephens to his resting place at Crawfordville, 70 miles east of Atlanta. "Little Alex," as he was affectionately known, would have been amazed to learn that during the Civil War, this same hearse smuggled runaway slaves over Northern lines and returned Confederate soldiers across Southern lines. The smugglees hid in a secret compartment and escaped by a trapdoor. Other exhibits include a Civil War iron casket, Victorian funeral jewelry, and embalming equipment. It's lighted until 11:00 P.M. nightly.

Monks, a Mountain, and *Gone With the Wind*

Like other Metro Atlanta counties, Gwinnett (population about 700,000) has grown so rapidly the past twenty-five years, it seems to be one vast, unbroken landscape of mammoth shopping malls, subdivisions, and apartment complexes. But if you peek behind the "new" Gwinnett, you'll find that many of its old towns and cities have become walkable havens with unique shops, restaurants, and art galleries.

Norcross's Historic Old Town is a pleasant throwback to yesteryear a few minutes off traffic-crazy I–85 and Jimmy Carter Boulevard. Take North Norcross-Tucker Road off Jimmy Carter and follow the HISTORIC NORCROSS signs to South Peachtree Street. Antiques and gift shops include *Taste of Britain,* 75 South Peachtree Street, (770) 242–8585, with imported teas, biscuits, jams, china, and gifts. There are also an old-fashioned barber shop, a vintage hardware store, and other small businesses in the well-preserved nineteenth-century buildings grouped around the old wooden train depot.

For more than a century, the small north Gwinnett County town of *Buford* was Georgia's leather-making capital. Leather processed at the town's large Bona Allen tannery was turned into shoes and saddles that were then sold all over the world. When the tannery closed in 1981, most of the businesses on Main Street were forced to close. But thanks to an enterprising small army of artists, Main Street has come back to life.

The *Tannery Row Merchants Association,* (770) 778–2306, www.trma .us, includes nearly two dozen shops and restaurants. Several are inside the historic Bona Allen Tannery building. *Gallery 150,* 150 West Main Street, (770)

271–0188, features a nudes-to-landscapes range of paintings, metal art, steel furniture, and garden sculpture by artists Allen Rodgers and Dennis Primm. *The Purple Iris Tea Shoppe,* in a renovated Victorian cottage at 80 South Alexander Street, (678) 482–6441, serves traditional English tea, with antiques and collectibles for sale. *Saxon's Dogwood Brew House,* 554 South Main Street, (678) 714–9669, complements its microbrews with tasty pub fare. Other shops feature consignment apparel, photography, pottery, interior design, woodwork, and glassware. Shops are open Monday through Saturday. From Atlanta, take I–85/985 to Highway 20 and follow South Lee Street to Main Street.

Not to be outdone by other Gwinnett County cities, *Lawrenceville,* the county seat, has done a vibrant renovation of its Courthouse Square. The centerpiece is the majestic 1885 redbrick courthouse with the tall white turret and clock tower. No longer the seat of county government since a modern courthouse was built in the early 1990s, the historic building, with its manicured lawns, brick-paved sidewalks, benches, retro street lights, and memorials to soldiers who died in the Civil War and Creek Indian War, has historical displays and meeting rooms. Around it is a lively mix of shops, galleries, and eateries. Shoppers have a choice of Scotland Yard gifts and accessories, (678) 407–1010; the Paper Fairy, (770) 513–0400; and NanTiques, with one of north Georgia's biggest selection of Red Hat Society accessories, (770) 682–7992. Just What I Like! is a jumble of contemporary watercolors, acrylics, prints, metal wall sculptures, wood furniture, and accessories, (678) 985–5506.

The food is as much fun as the shops. Choices include Flying Saucer Retro Cafe and Bakery, with sandwiches, salads, soups, and delectable sweets, (770) 339–9930; and Lil' River Grill, with a fine-dining menu, a large wine list and live music in a restored nineteenth-century mercantile building, (770) 995–1183, www.lilrivergrill.com.

For a look at Gwinnett County "when," take a walk through the *Lawrenceville Female Seminary.* Built in the 1850s after the original burned, the two-story brick Greek Revival building was a finishing school that tutored antebellum young ladies in reading, writing, and etiquette. Over the years the old school building taught boys and hosted civic clubs, the United Daughters of the Confederacy, and a radio station. In the 1970s, when Dairy Queen coveted the site, the county government purchased it, had it placed on the National Register of Historic Places, and made it the home of the Gwinnett County History Museum's collections of farm implements, textiles, historic photos, and exhibits on schools, religion, music, and other aspects of the county's life. Imagine the blushing bride coming down the aisle in a wedding gown fashioned of cotton and flour sacks. It's at 455 South Perry Street, in downtown Lawrenceville. Open daily. No admission charge. Phone (770) 822–5178, www.gwinnettparks.com.

In the mood for authentic Mexican tacos and *moles,* Ecuadorean and Salvadorean empanadas, *pad Thai,* Korean barbecue, Cantonese dim sum, fiery Szechuan, Vietnamese *pho,* Indo-Pak curries and *dosai,* and the ingredients to make your own? Georgia's most ethnically diverse county, Gwinnett, has scores of restaurants, food markets, and other services catering to large communities from Asia, Mexico, Central and South America, and homegrown Anglos and others looking for some adventure for their palates.

For information contact the Gwinnett Convention & Visitors Bureau, 6500 Sugarloaf Parkway, Duluth 30097. Phone (770) 623–3600, (888) 494–6638, www.gcvb.org.

Yellow River Wildlife Game Ranch is a peaceful place in the woods in the midst of south Gwinnett County's suburban explosion. Just off very busy Highway 78, 3 miles east of Stone Mountain Park, the twenty-four-acre privately owned nature preserve is home for dozens of free-roaming brown deer, huggable bunnies, goats, sheep, coyotes, ducks and geese, pigs and porcupines, foxes, wolves, donkeys, a skunk named William T. Sherman, and a spring-forecasting groundhog named Gen. Beauregard Lee.

Deer are Yellow River's self-appointed reception committee. You're no sooner on the tree-shaded walking trail than whole families of gentle does, bucks, and fawns are ambling up for handouts of bread and crackers and a scratch behind the ears. During summer, fragile newborn fawns are an especially appealing sight. Lambs, piglets, baby ducks, and goat kids are also very much in the spotlight.

Young children get a kick out of the Bunnie Burrows, an enclosed area where rabbits of all sizes and colors seem to enjoy being petted and hand-fed raw carrots and celery.

What's purportedly the largest herd of American buffalo east of the Mississippi roams a back meadow. Black bears, bobcats, mountain lions, foxes, and wolves are secured in open-air enclosures, out of the reach of little fingers. If you spread a picnic lunch in a grove by the Yellow River, expect some "deer" friends to drop by for a treat.

You may reserve Yellow River's *Birthday House* for your youngster's special day or for a family reunion or other group activity. Yellow River Wildlife Game Ranch, at 4525 Highway 78, Lilburn, (770) 972–6643, www.yellow rivergameranch.com, is open daily from 9:30 A.M. to 5:00 P.M. Admission is $8.00 for adults, $7.00 for children 3 to 11; free for children 2 and under.

The *Sugar Hill Municipal Golf Course* (8 miles north of the Suwanee exit off I–85), (770) 271–0519, is a sweet layout for those who'd like to play like the pros but have an amateur's budget. Spread over 300 acres at the north Gwinnett County town of Sugar Hill, the well-maintained par-72, 18-hole

I'll Have a Co-coler

For millions of people around the world, Atlanta is synonymous with Coca-Cola. The soft drink was created in a Peachtree Street pharmacy in 1886. Dr. John Stith Pemberton, originally from Columbus, Georgia, was seeking a nonalcoholic cure for the common headache. He blended coca leaves, African kola nuts, and other ingredients into an elixir he called Coca-Cola. It was first sold as a heavy syrup diluted with water. But one day the clerk substituted soda water for tap water, and voilà, Coke was on its way around the world.

Headquartered in Atlanta, the company closely guards its secret formula. If you visit the World of Coca-Cola, a colorful three-story museum, 55 Martin Luther King Drive, near the Georgia State Capitol, (404) 676–5151, you can see videos and films on Coke's history, as well as hundreds of exhibits and souvenir items, and enjoy free samples of Coke and soft drinks the company makes for specialized markets around the world. It's open for self-guided tours Monday through Saturday from 9:00 A.M. to 6:00 P.M., Sunday from 11:00 A.M. to 6:00 P.M. Admission is $7.00 for adults, $5.00 for seniors 55 and over, $4.00 for children 6 to 11.

course offers plenty of challenges as it swoops up and down hills and around six lakes and forty-five traps.

The **Southeastern Railway Museum** in Duluth, 25 miles northeast of downtown Atlanta (3395 Peachtree Road, Duluth), honors the golden age of passenger trains. Owned and operated by the Atlanta Chapter of the National Railway Historical Society, the thirty-acre indoor and outdoor museum invites train buffs to sit in red cabooses, hauled around the yards by vintage diesel loco-motives. On the third Sunday of the month, the cabooses are hooked to huffing, puffing steam locomotives. Before and after the ride, there's time to look at more than ninety pieces of rolling stock, exhibits, and displays. One of the showpieces is "Superb," the 1911 Pullman car that carried President Warren G. Harding across the country in the early 1920s. When Harding died in San Francisco in 1923, "Superb" carried him back to Washington and then to burial in Ohio. Army chefs prepared meals for the troops in a military kitchen car parked nearby. You can walk through locomotives, passenger coaches, dining cars, a railway post office, and Pullman sleeper cars. Kids and grown-up "kids" who enjoy the sport of model railroading can see the miniature train in the exhibit hall. From down-town Atlanta, take I–85 North to exit 104/Pleasant Hill Road and follow the signs. Trains roll April through November every Thursday, Friday, and Saturday, 10:00 A.M. to 5:00 P.M.; the third Sunday April to November, noon to 5:00 P.M.; Thursday, Friday, and Saturday in December, 10:00 A.M. to 4:00 P.M.; and Saturday January through March, 10:00 A.M. to 4:00 P.M. Unlimited rides are $7.00 adults; $5.00 age

65 and over; $4.00 ages 2 to 12. The complex is available for birthdays, meetings, and other events. Phone (770) 476–2013, www.srmduluth.org.

Amid the burgeoning suburbs of Rockdale County, a short drive off the busy lanes of I–20, about 25 miles east of downtown Atlanta, the **Monastery of the Holy Ghost** is a place of inordinate peacefulness. Since the late 1940s, Benedictine Trappist monks have dwelt and prayed in this cloistered sanctuary at 2625 Highway 212, Conyers, (770) 483–8705. The Spanish Gothic–style buildings, even the stained glass in the main church, are all products of their labors.

welikeitsweet

Georgians, like their fellow Southerners, are addicted to iced tea. We drink gallons of it summer, winter, fall, and spring. And the sweeter, the better. Real Southern iced tea has the sugar brewed in; adding it later doesn't have the same effect. When you order, you'll usually be asked, "Sweet or unsweetened?" If you want it sugarless and aren't asked for a preference, you're liable to get a glassful so syrupy it will make your teeth and gums ache.

Men and women can attend Sunday morning Mass in the church, which is highlighted by the monks' chants and prayers. Men may make retreats at the modern guest house nearby. A small shop sells bread, cheese, jam, religious items, and produce and herbs grown in the monastery's fields. You may also bring a picnic lunch to tables that sit by a lake beside the cloister.

The abbey does not observe a strict rule of silence, and most monks can converse with visitors.

Just east of Conyers on I–20 is Covington in Newton County. Fans of TV's *In the Heat of the Night* will recognize many of the show's locations around the **Covington** courthouse square. Many beautiful white-columned homes are on the tree-shaded streets radiating from the square.

You'll also find a trove of antebellum treasures around nearby Oxford College of Emory University, which welcomed its first freshman class in 1839.

Twenty miles southeast of downtown Atlanta, via Highway 155, **Panola Mountain State Conservation Park** is a peaceful 585-acre day-use park where you may have a walk in the woods, enjoy a picnic, and wonder at a one hundred–acre granite outcropping that's been part of the Henry County landscape for about a million years. The lichen-covered monadnock is part of a major belt of granite, most dramatically evidenced by Stone Mountain, a few miles away.

Stop first at the park's Nature Center for information on trails leading through the woodlands and around the mountain. Meandering through hardwood and pine forests, the 1¼-mile Microwatershed Trail is a moderately strenuous course. Several stations along the way have benches and markers describing the park's fauna and flora. At the base of Panola Mountain, a three-acre pond is alive with turtles, frogs, fish, and small reptiles.

The ¾-mile Rock Outcrop Trail takes you through the woods to an overlook on one of the mountain's major outcroppings. On Saturday and Sunday afternoon, park naturalists conduct walks and give talks at the small amphitheater close to the Nature Center. Picnic tables are located near restrooms and soft drink machines. Pets on leashes may be walked in the picnic area but aren't allowed on the nature trails.

The park is open daily from 8:00 A.M. to sundown. There is a $2.00 parking fee. Contact the superintendent, Stockbridge 30281, (770) 389–7801, (800) 864–PARK, www.gastateparks.org.

If you didn't surmise it while battling the perpetual traffic on **Henry County**'s streets and highways, the south suburban metro county is the third-fastest-growing county in Georgia and fifth-fastest in the entire United States. So it's a pleasant surprise to drive into the courthouse square in **McDonough,** the county seat, and wonder if you haven't drifted plum out of Henry into some rural place far from Metro Atlanta.

With a population of about 14,000, tidy, compact McDonough (pronounced "Mcdunnah") is a throwback to calmer, less frantic small-town times. Stop first at the McDonough Hospitality and Tourism Bureau in a regeared 1920s Standard Oil station on the square, pick up a map and helpful pointers, and start poking around the antique malls, "attics," flea markets, gift and specialty shops: the **Geranium House** (monogramming and gifts, 770–610–6060), **Bell, Book and Candle** (used books, gifts and jewelry, 770–957–1880); **The Antique Mall** (thousands of antiques and collectibles, 770–954–1196) and **Beth's Bargains** (home accessories and eclectic pieces at wholesale prices, 770–320–7982) are good places to start.

Dining on the square includes **Truman's,** a white-tablecloth restaurant in an early 1900s home serving pastas, seafood, steaks, and great desserts, (770) 320–8686; **Gritz,** serving Southern-style breakfast and lunch, (770) 914–0448; **PJ's Cafe,** American cuisine and a popular bar, (770) 898–5373; and the **Koffee Klutch,** coffee and pastries, (678) 432–4499.

Scarlett's Retreat and Day Spa, in a historic house just off the square, offers the full range of body treatments, (678) 432–7474.

"The Geranium City" lives up to its nickname during late January's **Geranium Festival.** Blooming with thousands of the colorful plants, the park in the square features music, entertainment, food, and more than 300 craftspeople selling their wares.

For information contact McDonough Hospitality and Tourism Bureau, 5 Griffin Street, McDonough 30253, (770) 898–3196, www.tourmcdonough.com.

Bargain lovers should put the Spalding County seat of *Griffin* high on their shopping lists. The textile town of 20,000, on Highways 19/41, 40 miles south of Atlanta, has some especially tempting values in antiques and socks.

Spalding Hosiery Shoppe (770–227–4362) has the answer to virtually all your hosiery needs. Aisles are jammed with colorful argyles, athletic socks, dress socks, and heavy-duty work socks, as well as pantyhose, sweatshirts, and other items made by major manufacturers. Irregulars, with all but impossible to discern blemishes, go for at least half the price you'd normally pay. First-run items are more expensive, but still very much a bargain. It's open Monday through Saturday from 8:30 A.M. to 5:30 P.M. No credit cards accepted, 432 East Broad Street, across from the redbrick Spalding Mills, a block from the center of town.

The *Antique Griffin at Dovedown,* 315 West Solomon Street, (770) 227–7708, displays the treasures of more than three dozen dealers in a 4,500-square-foot former textile mill in downtown Griffin. Take your pick of china, old coins, Civil War relics, vintage toys, country primitive and Victorian furniture, decorative accessories, jewelry, and folk art. *Aging Gracefully Antiques,* 10 North Hill Street, (770) 233–9000, has eclectic selections of pottery, furniture, quilts, and oil, gas, and kerosene lamps.

Architecture buffs can stroll downtown Griffin and see a range of styles surviving from the late 1800s to the 1930s. Most of the downtown commercial buildings, on Broad, Solomon, and Taylor Streets, are two stories high, constructed of brick, with wood or cast-iron storefronts and plate glass display windows. Many of the old buildings have been adapted for contemporary use.

Lewis Grizzard and Antebellum Newnan

Coweta and Fayette Counties, on Metro Atlanta's southwest periphery, are perfect for a one-day getaway from the big city, and they have more than enough to keep you happily occupied for much longer than that.

Take I–85 exit 47, 40 miles south of Atlanta, and follow Bullsboro Drive/Highway 34 into downtown *Newnan.* First stop is the Coweta County Welcome Center, 100 Walt Sanders Memorial Drive, Newnan, 1 mile off I–85 exit 47. Phone (770) 254–2627, (800) 826–9382, www.coweta.ga.us. They'll fill you in on every place to see, do, eat, and sleep in and around the city of 15,000. Open Monday through Saturday, 9:00 A.M. to 5:00 P.M. Be sure to pick up an *Antebellum and Victorian Newnan Driving Tour of Homes* guide, which describes twenty-three pre–Civil War landmarks. Many of the homes welcome visitors during the annual *Tour of Homes and Arts and Crafts Show* the third week of April. Before your driving tour, park around the majestic old

judgelandis

In the wake of the Chicago "Black Sox" betting scandal during the 1919 World Series, Judge Kenesaw Mountain Landis was named major league baseball's first commissioner. He is credited with restoring the game's integrity and saving it from self-destruction. He was named for Marietta's Kennesaw Mountain, where his father was wounded during the Civil War. His father spelled the name with only one n instead of two.

courthouse in the center of the square and browse the many antiques, gift, and bookshops that lure locals away from the ubiquitous malls on the outskirts. The Alamo Gift Shop used to be Newnan's first-run movie house. Owner Elizabeth Crain spent many childhood hours in the old theater, and she's left the Alamo's stage and balcony for old-time's sake.

If you're a fan of the late syndicated humor columnist Lewis Grizzard—a Coweta native son— you'll find all his books and tapes at *Scott's Books,* (770) 253–2960. Owner Earlene Scott was a close friend of Grizzard's, and she's always happy to share her memories. A Grizzard museum, described below, is in the small community of Moreland, south of Newnan.

Male Academy Museum, 30 Temple Avenue, Newnan, (770) 251–0207, www.nchistoricalsociety.org, is a must for Civil War enthusiasts. The historic school building displays a major collection of uniforms, weapons, artifacts, and soldiers' personal effects. You'll also find clothing, furniture, and photographs from the mid-nineteenth to the early twentieth centuries and an 1890s classroom. Open Tuesday through Thursday from 10:00 A.M. to 3:00 P.M. and Saturday and Sunday from 2:00 to 5:00 P.M. Admission is $3.00, children $1.00.

Lewis Grizzard wrote fondly about growing up in tiny Moreland (population 450). In appreciation, townsfolk have opened The *Lewis Grizzard Museum* on Highway 29 (770–254–2627, 800–826–9382, www.coweta.ga.us). The small museum displays his many books, photos, battered manual typewriters, and memorabilia. If you're a true fan, be here the first Saturday of April when thousands of his friends and fans come for the Annual Lewis Grizzard Storytelling and Barbecue. The museum is open Thursday through Saturday from 10:00 A.M. to 5:00 P.M. Admission is $1.00 for adults, free for children.

Coweta Countians have restored *"The Little Manse,"* birthplace of novelist Erskine Caldwell. The author of *God's Little Acre* and *Tobacco Road* was born in The Manse in 1903 when his father was a Presbyterian pastor here. The family left when Caldwell was 5 years old, and he never lived here as an adult. But the simple frame house is very much as he knew it. Biographical exhibits, personal items, copies of his books in several languages, and a video trace the career of the author, who died in 1987. The house is on Moreland's Town Park, off Highway 29; open by appointment. Admission is $2.00 for adults, $1.00 for children 6 to 12. Call Winston Skinner at (770) 254–8657 for more information. You can go directly to Moreland from I–85 exit 41 and driving south on Highway 29.

Senoia, a drowsy little Coweta County town on Highway 85, 40 miles south of Atlanta, is like a delightful trip through Norman Rockwell–land.

On Main Street, **Hutchinson Hardware** (770–599–3414) is a revered Senoia institution of long standing. Painted bright blue, with a parade of tall arched windows and doors, the building started out as a Ford dealership in the 1920s and became a hardware store early in World War II, when the Hutchinson's supply of Fords went dry. The aisles are stacked with anything you'd want for fishing, hunting, canning, serious farming, and hobby gardening, or building a house or barn and keeping them in proper order. Owner Jimmy Hutchinson is used to hearing townspeople say: "I know what I need is in here somewhere" and "If Hutchinson ain't got it, I don't need it."

The **Culpepper House** dates to 1871, when it was built by Dr. John Addy, a returning Civil War veteran. Innkeepers Suzanne and Sam Helfman have three guest rooms with private baths and furnished with Victorian antiques. Public areas shine with gingerbread trim, stained glass, and pocket doors. A full Southern breakfast is included in the inexpensive to moderate rate for a double with private or shared bath. Write to 35 Broad Street, Senoia 30276, or call (770) 599–8182, www.culpepperhouse.com.

Four miles north of Senoia, at the junction of Highways 85 and 74, stands **Starr's Mill,** one of Georgia's most photographed landmarks. One look at the

Starr's Mill

200-year-old red frame mill, by a pond and waterfall, and you'll be rushing for your camera, too. When you go, be sure to bring along a blanket and picnic.

Melear's (770–461–7180), on Highway 85 at Fayetteville's southern limits, has been serving delicious barbecue and Brunswick stew for more than thirty years. A big plateful costs under $6.00. During the short wait, amuse yourselves with the owner's collection of pig pottery and portraits. Open for lunch and dinner Monday through Saturday.

Sherman Meets the Suburbs

Since 1968 the picturesque rapids of Sweetwater Creek and the adjacent hardwood and piney woodlands have been the heart of *Sweetwater Creek Conservation Park,* a peaceful day-use state park. A short drive off I–20, 15 miles west of downtown Atlanta, the park serves the populace of rapidly growing Douglas County and many others who find it a delightful retreat from the hurly-burly of big-city life.

The ghostly ruins of the *New Manchester Manufacturing Company,* a Civil War–era enterprise torched by General William T. Sherman's troops, stands by the churning rapids, which provided the company with power to produce uniforms for the Confederate army. During the summer, kick off your shoes and join others wading in the swift, cool waters. Be careful of the slick patches of moss covering the rocks.

Five miles of nature trails lead you through the woods beside the creek. A 250-acre reservoir is stocked with bass, catfish, and bream, which you can fry in a pan and serve on one of the park's picnic tables. The park is open daily from 8:00 A.M. to sundown. There is a $2.00 parking fee. Contact the superintendent, Lithia Springs 30057, (770) 732–5871, (800) 864–PARK, www.gastate parks.org.

With more than 600,000 residents, affluent *Cobb* is one of the nation's fastest growing counties and the northwest flagship of the Atlanta metropolitan area. Off the well-beaten paths of freeways and around the corner from high-rise hotels, glitzy shopping galleries, and trendy eateries, you'll find fascinating historic sites, charming town squares, and outdoor recreation.

Acworth, in northern Cobb County, is one of Metro Atlanta's newest and most successful turnaround stories. An influx of domestic and overseas newcomers has transformed the once-sleepy little town by the train tracks into a buzzing hub of contemporary dining and shopping.

Along two blocks of Main Street, just off busy I–75, exit 277, diners choose from an eclectic array of cuisines. At *Red Peppers,* (770) 529–3636, Elias and Marta Endara prepare "downhome" Cuban- and South American–style cooking.

Their specialties include an Incan-inspired dish of roasted pork with hominy and sweet potatoes, and *ropa vieja,* a classic Cuban favorite of shredded beef and olives. **Seasons de Provence,** (678) 574–7188, serves country French bistro fare. On the floor above, **Teacup Cottage,** (678) 574–6011, pours international teas with soups, salads, sandwiches, and desserts in a delightful gift shop. Other options include **Henry's Louisiana Grill,** (770) 966–1515; **Fusco's Via Roma,** (770) 974–1110; and **Charlie's Original Oyster King,** (770) 917–1707. Antiques shops, book, jewelry, clothing, housewares, garden accessories and wine shops, an ice cream store, and a repertory theater are spaced among the restaurants. For information: Acworth Area Visitors Bureau, 4415 Senator Russell Avenue, Acworth 30101, (770) 974–8813, www.acworth.org.

After the fall of Chattanooga in late 1863, the Confederates grudgingly fell back to Kennesaw Mountain, 25 miles north of Atlanta and the site of **Kennesaw Mountain National Battlefield Park.** For two weeks in June 1864, 60,000 soldiers dug into the wooded flanks of the 1,808-foot mountain. When a series of assaults failed to dislodge the Southerners, Union commander General William T. Sherman executed a flanking strategy, which forced the Confederates to leave the mountain and retreat to Atlanta.

Stop first at the National Park Service Visitors Center and view the slide presentation and exhibits. Outside are some of the cannons that took part in the battle. From Monday through Friday you may drive your car up a paved road to a parking area 200 yards below the summit. From there take an easy walk through the woods studded with cannons, earthworks, and markers telling the story of the battle. On Saturday and Sunday the mountain road is open only to a free shuttle bus that makes the trip every half hour. In fair weather many visitors hike at least one way on an easy 1-mile trail. If you've the stamina, you can extend your hike from the Kennesaw summit 4 miles to **Cheatham Hill** and 7 miles to **Kolb's Farm,** other principal battlegrounds in the Kennesaw theater. The two areas are also accessible by car.

Picnic tables, grills, and restrooms are in a grove of trees near the visitors center parking area. The park, about 4½ miles west of I–75 exit 269 (Barrett Parkway) in Kennesaw, is open Monday through Friday from 8:30 A.M. to 5:00 P.M., Saturday and Sunday to 6:00 P.M. Free admission. Contact the superintendent, P.O. Box 1167, Marietta 30061, (770) 427–4686, www.nps.gov/kemo.

Civil War and old-time train buffs can have a great day exploring the **Southern Museum of Civil War and Locomotive History** in Kennesaw. The celebrated steam locomotive "General" is the centerpiece of the new 40,000-square-foot, Smithsonian-affiliated museum. In April 1862, Union raiders hijacked the engine and several cars at the Kennesaw depot and drove it north toward Chattanooga. The train's crew, breakfasting at a trackside hotel during the heist, pursued the hijackers by foot, platform car, and locomotive for 87 miles. When the "General" ran out of fuel, twenty-two raiders were captured and eight were hanged as spies. Six received the Congressional Medal of Honor. In 1956 Walt Disney Pictures dramatized the episode in *The Great Locomotive Chase*, starring Fess Parker. With eight wheels, a barrel-shaped smokestack, and a bright red cowcatcher, the "General" sits on original track in its own spacious exhibit hall. The museum's other displays include a history of Southern railroading, Civil War weapons, uniforms, and soldiers' personal items. A large wing re-creates the Glover Machine Works, a foundry in nearby Marietta where 300 locomotives were built during the early 1900s. Special exhibits from the Smithsonian are held all year. The museum is at 2829 Cherokee Street, Kennesaw, off I–75 exit 273, about 25 miles north of down-town Atlanta. Open Monday through Saturday 9:30 A.M. to 5:00 P.M., Sunday noon to 5:00 P.M. Adults, $7.50; age 60 and over, $6.50; children, $5.50; under age 5, free. Phone (770) 427–2117, www.southernmuseum.org.

For more train memorabilia, and big helpings of Southern comfort food, step across the street to the **Whistle Stop Cafe,** open every day, (770) 794–0101.

Londoners rendezvous by Big Ben, New Yorkers under the Grand Central Station clock. Since the early 1960s, motorists navigating the highways of Marietta and Cobb County have set their sights by **The Big Chicken,** a 56-foot red-and-white sheet-metal rooster that preens on the façade of a KFC outlet on busy U.S. 41/Cobb Parkway. The Big Chicken was "hatched" in 1963 by S.R. "Tubby" Davis, who wanted a really big sign to ballyhoo his fast-food restau-rant. In the 1970s, KFC bought out Tubby and reluctantly retained the Chicken, which had become a landmark and popular icon. When it was severely dam-aged by a 1993 tornado, KFC bowed to public demands and spent "buckets" on a makeover.

The Chicken's flapping beak and rolling eyes point travelers a mile west to Marietta's lovely old courthouse square. Something of an anomaly in a city of nearly 60,000, seat of 700,000-strong Cobb County, the square's centerpiece, **Glover Park,** is a peaceful Victorian throwback, with big trees, flowering plants, a gazebo, a bandstand, benches, and kids' play areas.

Low-rise late nineteenth- and early twentieth-century buildings on three sides of the square house a slew of antiques shops and others with clothing, jewelry, gifts, stationery, toys, garden accessories, folk art, and a pet bakery. Restaurants cover the map, with Turkish, Slovakian, Italian, Mexican, Australian, Irish, and American cuisines. Pubs and music clubs feature live music. **Theatre in the Square** is one of Metro Atlanta's finest professional companies.

Before ducking into any of the above, stop in the Marietta Welcome Center, in the 1898 Western & Atlantic railroad depot, 4 Depot Street, Marietta 30060,

(800) 835–0445 and (770) 429–1115, www.mariettasquare.com, for maps, information on museums and walking and driving tours of the city's five National Register historic districts.

A few steps from the welcome center, the *Marietta* **Gone With the Wind Museum's** Scarlett On the Square exhibit tells you all about Atlanta author Margaret Mitchell's all-time best-selling novel and the 1939 film. Several hundred pieces collected by Dr. Christopher Sullivan of Akron, Ohio, include costumes, conceptual artwork, rare press and publicity books, film posters, editions of the novel in many languages, programs from the 1939 Atlanta movie premiere, contracts, promotional items, and much more. One of the most valuable artifacts is the bengaline silk gown that Vivien Leigh, as Scarlett O'Hara, wore on her New Orleans honeymoon with Rhett Butler/Clark Gable. Other exhibits highlight Mitchell's life and a tribute to Hattie McDaniel, the first African American to receive an Oscar, for her role as "Mammy."

The museum is at 18 Whitlock Avenue, a block from the Marietta Square, (770) 794-5576, www.gwtwmarietta.com. Open Monday through Saturday 10:00 A.M. to 5:00 P.M. Adults $7.50, seniors 65 and over, and children 8 and older, $6.00; and $5.00 per person for groups of fifteen or more.

The adjacent *Marietta Museum of History* is located in a historic landmark, 1 Depot Street, Marietta, (770) 528–0431, www.mariettahistory.org, open Monday through Saturday 10:00 A.M. to 4:00 P.M., Saturday 1:00 to 4:00 P.M., adults $5.00, seniors ages 55 and up, and students $3.00. In its original life as the Kennesaw Hotel, the building housed James Andrews and his Union raiders the night before they train-jacked the locomotive "General" from the depot in nearby Kennesaw, an event immortalized in the Disney film *The Great Locomotive Chase*.

Cinch up your hiking shoes, pump up your bike, and head for a blissful day on the *Silver Comet Trail*. The tree-shaded, 38-mile paved path takes you from suburban Smyrna into northwest Georgia's peaceful rural countryside. As you head for the Alabama border, you'll cross a towering 500-foot-long railroad trestle, over streams, around rock formations, through tunnels, pine forests, modest hills, and farmlands. Mavell Road in Smyrna, the trail access closest to Atlanta, is the busiest, but once you're free of the suburbs, it's just you and your fellow travelers, with no hassles from trucks and cars. The Silver Comet will eventually extend 60 miles to the Alabama border, where it will connect with the Chief Ladiga Trail, providing a 101-mile trail from Atlanta to Anniston, Alabama. It's part of a metro-wide greenways system being developed by the nonprofit PATH Foundation. In the city of Atlanta, 3 miles east of downtown, the *Freedom Park Trail* is a 6-mile, two-trail system in a grassy, moderately hilly residential park with a trailhead near the Carter Presidential

Center. For information on the Silver Comet and other pathways, phone (404) 875–7284, www.pathfoundation.org.

Pickett's Mill Battlefield Historic Site, 5 miles northeast of Dallas, should be high on Civil War buffs' "must-do" list. The battlefield is much as it was when blue and gray troops fought here during the Battle of Atlanta campaign. Living-history programs demonstrate cooking, weapons firing, and military drills of the Civil War era. Artifacts and exhibits are in the interpretive center/visitor center. The battlefield is at Mt. Tabor Road, Dallas, (770) 443–7850, (800) 864–PARK, www.gastateparks.org. Admission is $2.00 for adults, $1.00 for students. Open Tuesday through Sunday.

Places to Stay in Metro Atlanta

DOWNTOWN ATLANTA

The Glenn Hotel,
110 Marietta Street,
(404) 521–2250,
(866)–40GLENN,
www.glennhotel.com
Downtown Atlanta's first boutique hotel is a hip makeover of a 1920s office building. Close to the new Georgia Aquarium, CNN Center, and other attractions, the Glenn has ninety-three guest rooms and sixteen suites, with deluxe furnishings and accessories. Its signature feature is BED (for Beverage, Entertainment, Dining), a two-level clone of the successful South Beach and Manhattan celebrity hot spots. Guests in robes and PJs enjoy drinks and eats on bedlike platforms that seat up to ten. Traditional seating is also available. A rooftop terrace overlooks the downtown skyline. Expensive.

MIDTOWN/VIRGINIA/ HIGHLAND/LITTLE FIVE POINTS AREA

Ansley Inn,
253 Fifteenth Street,
(404) 872–9000,
(800) 446–5416,
fax (404) 892–2318,
www.ansleyinn.com
Twenty-two guest rooms in an Ansley Park Tudor mansion have cable TV, direct-dial phone, individual heat and AC controls, and whirlpool baths. Close to Woodruff Art Center/High Museum of Art, restaurants, shops; moderate to expensive, including breakfast.

Gaslight Inn,
1001 Saint Charles Avenue,
(404) 875–1001,
fax (404) 876–1001,
www.gaslightinn.com
Six rooms with private bath are in this delightful craftsman-style bed-and-breakfast within walking distance of the Virginia-Highland action. Guests can relax in the Southern-style walled garden; moderate to expensive, including breakfast.

King-Keith House Bed & Breakfast,
889 Edgewood Avenue,
(404) 688–7330,
(800) 728–3879,
fax (404) 584–0730,
www.kingkeith.com
The spectacular Queen Anne–style "painted lady" mansion is on a tree-shaded street in Inman Park, a regentrified Victorian neighborhood 2 miles east of downtown. Jan and Windell Keith have five guest rooms with antiques and modern amenities. Close to shops, restaurants, live theater, entertainment, and the Inman Park MARTA rapid rail station; moderate to expensive, includes full breakfast.

If you'd like to stay at a homey bed-and-breakfast inn and meet some engaging Atlantans, contact Bed-and-Breakfast Atlanta, 790 North Avenue, #202, Atlanta 30306, (404) 875–0525, (800) 967–3224, fax (404) 876–1001, www.bedandbreakfast atlanta.com

Accommodations are in beautiful private homes, and rates usually include a full breakfast and the opportunity to meet Atlantans on an informal basis.

DECATUR

Sycamore House,
624 Sycamore Street,
(404) 378–0685,
fax (404) 373–6631.
Judy and Ren Manning's beautiful home, in one of Decatur's historic neighborhoods, is within walking distance of shops and restaurants and the MARTA rail station. A first floor suite has a queen bed and bath. Two upstairs rooms have a queen bed and twins and their own baths. You can unwind in the heated pool and hot tub in their secluded garden. Full breakfast included. Moderate.

GRANTVILLE

Bonnie Castle Bed & Breakfast,
2 Post Street,
(770) 583–3090,
(800) 261–3090,
www.bonnie-castle.com
This brick Romanesque-Revival Victorian is a startling contrast to Newnan's white columns. Built in 1896 by a wealthy Coweta County family, the turreted mansion, with a slate roof and wraparound porch, has been updated by new owners James and Dee Latimone, who invite guests to relax in the romantic ambience of antique furnishings, regional art collections, hardwood floors, gilded ceilings, and stained glass. Off I–85, 15 minutes south of

Newnan. Inexpensive rates include full Southern breakfast and evening refreshments.

KENNESAW

Hill Manor Bed & Breakfast,
2676 Summers Street,
(770) 428–5997,
www.hillmanor.com
Two large guest rooms in Paul and Kelly Ewing's 1890 Victorian home have antique furnishings, private bath with Jacuzzi tub, and access to gardens and verandas. Southern Museum of Civil War & Locomotive History, antiques shops, restaurants, and Kennesaw Mountain National Battlefield Park are close by. Moderate rates include huge Southern breakfast.

MARIETTA

Sixty Polk Street, A Bed & Breakfast,
60 Polk Street,
(770) 419–1688,
(800) 845–7266,
www.sixtypolkstreet.com
Four guest rooms in Joe and Glenda Mertes's 1872-era French Regency showplace are furnished with antiques and private baths. Full Southern breakfast is served in the grand dining room. Take a short walk to the antiques shops, restaurants, and other attractions around the square. Inexpensive to moderate.

Whitlock Inn Bed & Breakfast,
57 Whitlock Avenue,
(770) 428–1495,
fax (770) 919–9620,
www.whitlockinn.com
Innkeeper Alexis Edwards has five guest rooms with private baths in her Victorian mansion a block from the Marietta square. The spacious public rooms are popular for weddings, corporate gatherings, and other special events. Moderate rates include continental breakfast.

ROSWELL

Ten-Fifty Canton Street Bed & Breakfast,
1050 Canton Street,
(770) 998–1050,
www.bandbfinder.com
The Victorian cottage in downtown Roswell's historic district is close to the town square, Bulloch Hall, restaurants and scores of antiques shops and collectibles malls. Three cozy guest rooms with private baths, full breakfast. Moderate to expensive.

STONE MOUNTAIN

The Village Inn Bed & Breakfast,
992 Ridge Avenue,
(770) 469–3459,
(800) 214–8385,
fax (770) 469–1051,
www.villageinnbb.com
Has six guest rooms with private baths and antiques. Some have two-person whirlpool baths and fireplaces. Just outside Stone Mountain Park, within walking distance of Village shops and restaurants. Moderate. Includes full breakfast.

Places to Eat in Metro Atlanta

DOWNTOWN

Max Lager's American Grill and Brewpub,
320 Peachtree Street,
(404) 525–4400.
A variety of house-brewed beers, wood-fired cuisine, and great views of downtown. Inexpensive to moderate.

Mick's,
557 Peachtree Street,
(404) 875–6425.
Old-fashioned soda fountain eatery, with hefty hamburgers, sandwiches, pasta dishes, and desserts. A good place to fill up the kids. Inexpensive.

Pleasant Peasant,
555 Peachtree Street,
(404) 874–3223.
Pressed tin ceilings, black-and-white tile floor, an Atlanta mainstay for innovative beef, chicken, pastas, and great desserts. Dinner daily. Moderate to expensive.

The Varsity,
61 North Avenue,
near Georgia Tech,
(404) 881–1706.
May or may not be the "World's Largest Drive-In," as its motto proclaims, but this mammoth emporium of chili dogs, hamburgers, french fries, onion rings, ice cream, and other short-order treats that might not be so good for the waistline, but are mighty satisfying all the same, is where thousands go every day to get their "grease fix." Enjoy it in your car or in one of the rooms, with TVs tuned to sports events and other popular shows. Open 24–7. Inexpensive.

LAWRENCEVILLE

Lil' River Grill,
176 East Crogan Street,
(770) 995–1183,
www.lilrivergrill.com
In a restored early 1900s mercantile building, across from the historic courthouse on the Lawrenceville Square, Lil' River's menu is American contemporary, with French and Southwestern influences. The wine list is extensive, and there's live music most nights. Lunch and dinner Monday through Saturday. Moderate.

ROSWELL

Fratelli di Napoli,
928 Canton Street,
(770) 642–9917.
Bring along a mob of friends and family and dive into large platters of richly sauced southern Italian cuisine. Dinner daily. Moderate to expensive.

Greenwood's,
1087 Green Street,
(770) 992–5383.
Only truly prodigious appetites finish the huge servings of meat loaf, fish, chicken, duck, pork chops, fresh vegetables, and desserts in this former country home. Dinner Wednesday through Sunday. Inexpensive.

Mittie's Tea Room Cafe
1619 Canton Street, Roswell
(770) 594–8822,
and 62 North Main Street,
Alpharetta,
(770) 772–0850,
www.mitties.com
Mittie Bulloch would feel right at home in these cozy cafes, serving Southern-style breakfast, lunch, and tea. *Southern Living* magazine proclaims, "The chicken salad is wonderful."

The Swallow at the Hollow,
1072 Green Street,
(678) 352–1975,
www.swallowatthehollow.com
Sauce-smeared patrons gorge on heaping plates of barbecue and ribs, with Brunswick stew, mac 'n' cheese and the joyful noise of loud, lively music. Lunch and dinner Wednesday through Sunday. Inexpensive.

MIDTOWN/VIRGINIA/HIGHLAND/LITTLE FIVE POINTS AREA

American Roadhouse,
892 North Highland Avenue,
(404) 872–2822.
Busy family-friendly neighborhood eatery. Terrific breakfasts, also great for lunch and dinner sandwiches, salads, fresh vegetables, chicken, fish, meat loaf, and pasta plates. Breakfast, lunch, dinner daily. Inexpensive.

Blind Willie's,
828 North Highland Avenue,
(404) 873–2583.
Some of the country's best-known blues rockers come close to blowing the roof off this popular storefront club, which packs in the crowds every night of the week. Inexpensive.

Doc Chey's Noodle House,
1424 North Highland Avenue,
(404) 888–0777.
Pan-Asian noodle house is a beehive-busy place to enjoy huge, cheap helpings of Vietnamese soup and other noodle- and rice-based dishes. Lunch, dinner daily. Inexpensive.

Eats,
600 Ponce de Leon Avenue,
(404) 888–9149.
Another perpetually packed "filling station." Students, families, and business types stand in usually long cafeteria lines for pasta, jerk chicken, and fresh veggies at rock-bottom prices. Lunch, dinner daily. Inexpensive.

George's Restaurant,
1041-A North Highland Avenue,
(404) 892–3648.
Longtime neighborhood tavern hasn't changed in more than forty years. Some of the best hamburgers in town. Open daily. Inexpensive.

Limerick Junction,
824 North Highland Avenue,
(404) 874–7147.
Rollicking Irish pub has Guinness and Harp on tap, musicians from Dublin and Belfast (and Limerick), and plenty of hearty pub-style eats. Dinner and entertainment nightly. Inexpensive.

Manuel's Tavern,
602 North Highland Avenue,
(404) 525–3447.
Atlanta's best neighborhood saloon. Generations of journalists, politicians, and just-plain folks have whiled away their days and nights at the worn wooden booths and long bar festooned with photos of JFK, Hubert Humphrey, and other Democratic icons. Put away chili dogs, burgers, BLTs, onion rings, and steak fries while you sip beer and spirits and watch sports on big-screen TVs. Like Cheers, after a couple of visits, they'll know your name and your poison. Open daily. Inexpensive.

Mary Mac's Tea Room,
224 Ponce de Leon Avenue,
(404) 876–1800.
Two blocks east of Peachtree Street, this maze of a cheerful dining room has served celestial fried chicken, turnip greens, squash soufflé, biscuits, and cornbread to several generations of Atlantans and out-of-towners seeking the truth in Southern home cooking. Lunch, dinner Monday through Saturday. Inexpensive.

Son's Place,
100 Hurt Street at DeKalb Avenue, across from the Inman Park MARTA rail station,
(404) 581–0503.
The answers to all your soul food needs are on the cafeteria line of this plain but friendly diner, where the spectrum of society comes to fill up on top-grade fried chicken and fish, chitterlings, cornbread, vegetables, and homemade pies and cakes. Breakfast and lunch weekdays. Inexpensive.

Surin of Thailand,
810 North Highland Avenue,
(404) 892–7789.
Spicy Thai curry, noodle, rice, seafood, meat, and chicken dishes make this spacious restaurant one of Viriginia-Highland's mainstays. Lunch, dinner daily. Inexpensive to moderate.

The Vortex,
438 Moreland Avenue,
(404) 688–1828 and 878 Peachtree Street,
(404) 875–1667.
Don't let the laughing-skull front door scare you away from some of the best burgers and zaniest surroundings in town. Top your whopper with blue cheese, pimiento cheese, bacon, or jerk sauce, and sit back and enjoy the experience and big-time attitude. Lunch, dinner daily. Inexpensive.

DEKALB COUNTY'S LITTLE ASIA

Machu Picchu,
Northeast Plaza Shopping Center, 3375 Buford Highway,
(404) 320–3326.
A delightful little Peruvian entry into Buford Highway's ethnic stewpot. Decorated with colorful woven tapestries, with weekend music by an Andean flute and guitar combo, the restaurant's specialties include several varieties of ceviche (slices of raw fish "cooked" in lime juice acid, with cilantro) and large plates of seafood, chicken, and pork mixed with rice and potatoes. Lunch, dinner daily. Inexpensive to moderate.

Pung Mie,
5145 Buford Highway,
(770) 455–0370.
A large, bright, and shiny Chinese restaurant with a distinctly Korean spin. Complimentary bowls of kimchee, mung beans, pickled and dried fish, and other appetizers precede your lunch and dinner. Don't miss the steamed dumplings! Lunch, dinner daily. Inexpensive to moderate.

Seoul Garden,
5938 Buford Highway,
(770) 452–0123.
A large, friendly restaurant in a former chain steak house is one of the best of numerous Korean eateries. Kimchee, seafood pancake, barbecued meats, and rice and noodle dishes are excellent. There's also a sushi bar. Lunch, dinner daily. Inexpensive to moderate.

DECATUR
The Brick Store Pub,
125 East Court Square,
(404) 687–0990.
A cleverly revamped brick-walled former mercantile store that now dispenses a global variety of bottled and draft beers and ales, over a dozen single-malt scotches, and other spirits. The pub fare menu includes fish and chips, burgers, sandwiches, and salads. You can toss darts in the upstairs den. Families are welcome. Lunch, dinner daily. Inexpensive.

Cafe Alsace,
121 East Ponce de Leon Avenue,
(404) 373–5622.
A cozy, charming French Alsatian bistro with quiches, seafood, salads, sandwiches, and soups. Lunch Monday through Friday, dinner daily. Moderate.

Taqueria del Sol,
359 West Ponce de Leon Avenue,
(404) 377–7668.
Soft tacos with spicy fillings and potent margaritas in a retuned service station. Lunch, dinner Monday through Saturday. Inexpensive.

Wahoo! A Decatur Grill,
1042 West College Avenue,
(404) 373–3331,
www.wahoogrilldecatur.com
The quintessential neighborhood bistro, with comfortable ambience, feel-good food and moderate prices. Located in a brick storefront near downtown Decatur, Wahoo's menu focuses on seafood with a Southern flair—shrimp and creamy grits, Georgia rainbow trout and namesake wahoo, a meaty, warm-water ocean fish—as well as chicken, beef, pasta, and duck. The European-aura main dining room features an open

HELPFUL WEB SITES

Georgia Tourist Division,
www.georgia.org and
www.gastateparks.org
(Both sites have information on all the state's regions.)

Atlanta Convention & Visitors Bureau,
www.acvb.com

Atlanta Braves baseball,
www.atlantabraves.com

High Museum of Art,
www.high.org

DeKalb County Convention & Visitors Bureau,
www.dcvb.org

Southern Off-Road Bicycle Association,
www.sorba.org

Historic Roswell Convention & Visitors Bureau,
www.cvb.roswell.ga.us

Georgia State Parks,
www.gastateparks.org

kitchen and a long bar. Many diners prefer the outdoor garden patio. Dinner daily. Inexpensive to moderate.

Watershed,
123 406 West Ponce de Leon Avenue,
(404) 378–4900
Emily Saliers, half of the folk rock duo Indigo Girls, is the guiding light and part-time bartender at this handsomely retuned service station, which prepares sophisticated New Southern and American cuisine, deluxe sandwiches, and salads, and carries an extensive wine selection for patrons who come to downtown Decatur from all over Metro Atlanta. Lunch and dinner daily and Sunday brunch. Moderate to expensive.

NEWNAN

The Redneck Gourmet,
11 North Court Square,
(770) 251–0092,
www.redneckgourmet.com
Downtown Newnan's "Cheers" kind of place for breakfast, lunch, dinner and small-town hospitality since 1991, Redneck Gourmet's menu features traditional Southern breakfast and a full array of sandwiches, salads, soups and light meals. Local favorites include the Redneck Club, with ham, turkey, American cheese, lettuce, tomato, bacon, and mayo on three slices of honey wheat bread; the Redneck Dawg, a beef hot dog with chili, cheese, onion and slaw; and the Scrambled Dawg, the "Redneck" without the bun. Breakfast, lunch, dinner, Monday through Saturday. Inexpensive.

10 East Washington
10 East Washington Street,
(770) 502–9100.
Czech native George Ravosky and his wife, Carmela, oversee Newnan's most stylish restaurant. Their urbane dining room delights lunch and dinner guests with everything from hamburgers and Reubens to pastas, crab cakes, steaks, lamb tenderloin, seafood, and European-style desserts. Excellent wine list. Dinner Tuesday through Saturday. Moderate to expensive.

NORCROSS

Dominick's,
95 South Peachtree Street,
(770) 449–1611.
Proclaims, "Little Italy, Lotta Food," and they're not kidding. The handsomely redone nineteenth-century mercantile building, with brick walls, wooden floors, and original tin ceilings, serves platters of every kind of pasta, seafood, chicken, and veal dishes ample enough for two or three major appetites. It's fun to come with a large group and pass the platters Italian-family style. You can also get half-portions, which are still big enough to share. Open for lunch Monday through Saturday, dinner daily. Moderate.

Norcross Station Cafe,
in the refashioned depot,
40 South Peachtree Street,
(770) 409–9889.
The eclectic menu includes shrimp, steak, baby-back ribs, pastas and other Italian dishes, quesadillas, quiches, sandwiches, soups, salads, and kids' plates. Open for lunch and dinner Monday through Saturday. Moderate.

Southwest Georgia

Chattahoochee Trace

LaGrange, a pretty town of 30,000 near the Georgia–Alabama border, was named in honor of the Marquis de Lafayette's French estate, which accounts for the bronze likeness of the marquis in the center of downtown Lafayette Square. Away from the square, regal white-columned mansions preside over well-tended lawns, gardens, and tree-shaded streets.

Bellevue Mansion, 204 Ben Hill Street, LaGrange, (706) 884–1832; www.lagrangechamber.com, was the stately Greek Revival home of U.S. senator and acclaimed orator Benjamin Harvey Hill. Built in the early 1850s, the home is an architectural treasure inside and out, filled with magnificent furnishings and artwork. It's the LaGrange area's favorite wedding venue. Open Tuesday through Saturday from 10:00 A.M. to noon and 2:00 to 5:00 P.M. Admission is $4.00 adults, $2.00 children.

Lamar Dodd Art Center (706–880–8211, www.lagrange .edu), on the neighboring LaGrange College campus, LaGrange 30240, is a strikingly modern museum displaying changing regional and national exhibitions and a permanent collection of Native American art. It is open Monday through Friday from 8:30 A.M. to 4:00 P.M. Free admission.

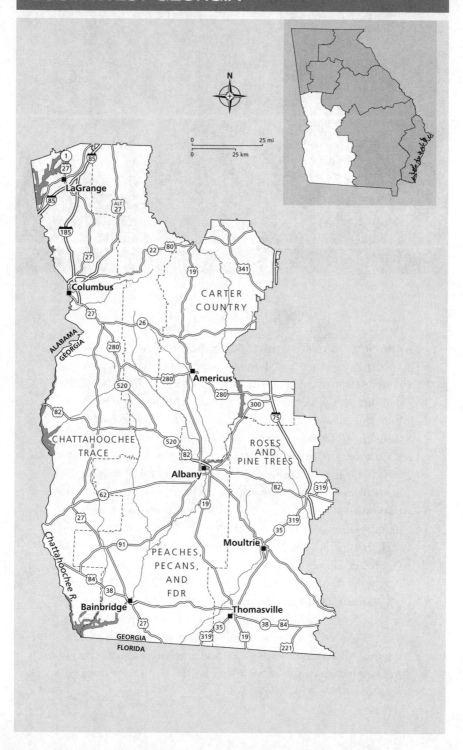

The ***Chattahoochee Valley Art Museum*** (706–882–3267, www.lagrange chamber.com), near Lafayette Square at 112 Hines Street, LaGrange, displays paintings, sculpture, and decorative arts in a restored 1890s jail building. It's open Tuesday through Friday from 9:00 A.M. to 5:00 P.M., Saturday 11:00 A.M. to 5:00 P.M. Free admission.

In 1841, Sarah Ferrell created a formal boxwood garden in west Georgia wilderness that only a few years earlier had been part of Creek and Cherokee lands. Nearly 170 years later, Sarah Ferrell's garden is the centerpiece of ***Hills & Dales Estate.*** The home of two generations of the Callaway family, the estate, opened to the public in 2004, is one of west Georgia's newest attractions.

Sarah Ferrell's garden was actually begun in 1832 by her mother. When she inherited it nine years later, Sarah expanded it into one of the Southeast's

SOUTHWEST GEORGIA'S TOP HITS

Bellevue Mansion	Pasaquan Folk Art Compound
Hills & Dales Estate	Chehaw Wild Animal Park
Chattahoochee Valley Art Museum	"Swamp Gravy"
West Point Lake	Climax Swine Time
Day Butterfly Center	Rattlesnake Roundup
Callaway Gardens	American Camellia Society
Chattahoochee Riverwalk	Albany's Flint RiverQuarium
National Infantry Museum	Andersonville National Cemetery and Historic Site
Port Columbus National Civil War Naval Museum	Windsor Hotel
Providence Canyon State Park	Jimmy Carter National Historic Site
Florence Marina State Park	Georgia Rural Telephone Museum
Westville	Georgia Veterans Memorial State Park
George T. Bagby State Park	Georgia Agrirama
Kolomoki Mounds State Historic Park	Downtown Tifton
Lake Seminole	Lapham-Patterson House
Little White House	Pebble Hill Plantation
Franklin D. Roosevelt State Park	Thomasville Rose Garden

most acclaimed gardens. Deeply religious, she planted an area called "The Sanctuary," with religious symbols sculpted in boxwoods. A harp, a circular boxwood bed planted with yellow flowers, symbolized an offering plate full of coins. A nearby boxwood topiary is shaped like a church organ.

The "God" topiary, planted at the formal entrance to the garden, was a reference to the Genesis passage, "In the beginning, God created the heavens and earth." On the upper terrace near the house, she planted "God Is Love," and for her husband, a judge and Mason, she created the Masonic emblem and *Fiat justitia* ("Let Justice Be Done").

Sarah continued working her garden until her death in 1903. In 1908, the property was purchased by Fuller E. Callaway and his wife, Ida Cason Callaway, who renamed the estate Hills & Dales.

A wealthy west Georgia textile manufacturer, Callaway commissioned renowned Atlanta architect Neel Reid to design an opulent Georgian-Italianate villa. Completed in 1916, the thirty-room house was furnished with American and European antiques and family keepsakes.

The Callaways restored Sarah Ferrrell's gardens and installed classical statuary, sunken gardens, terraces and fountains to complement the Italian character of their house. They added greenhouses and herb gardens, and thousands of trees, flowers, and shrubs.

When Fuller Callaway died in 1928, followed by Ida in 1936, the estate was inherited by Fuller Callaway Jr. and his wife, Alice Hand Callaway. They enhanced the beauty of the house and gardens until their deaths in 1992 and 1998, respectively, after which the estate was granted to the Fuller E. Callaway Foundation and opened to the public. Cason Callaway, who created nearby Callaway Gardens, was Fuller Jr.'s older brother.

Tours of the estate begin at the Hills & Dales Visitor Center. Designed in classical style and inspired by Neel Reid's Italianate villa, the center includes an exhibit gallery, an orientation film, and a gift shop.

A motorized tram takes visitors to the villa on a hill overlooking the gardens. Guests enter the home under four Doric columns, which support a covered two-story porte cochere and red tile roof.

Guided tours begin in the library, the Callaways' favorite room. Reminiscent of an English drawing room, the room is paneled in Circassian walnut, with American and English furnishings and family portraits. Although additions to the library and adjoining living room and dining room were made over the years, the house has retained the comfortable ambience of a fine country estate, in accordance with Fuller Callaway Sr.'s wishes for "a home in the real sense, to express, inside and outside, grace, naturalness and cheery friendliness."

Hills & Dales Estate is on the edge of the LaGrange College campus, a few blocks west of Lafayette Square, in downtown LaGrange. Open Tuesday to Saturday from 10:00 A.M. to 6:00 P.M., Sunday 1:00 to 5:00 P.M. Adults and seniors $10.00; age 7 to college students with ID, $6.00. For information: Hills & Dales Estate, P.O. Box 790, LaGrange 30241, (706) 882–3242, www.hillsand dalesestate.org.

West Point Lake, a mammoth 26,000-acre inland sea a few minutes from downtown LaGrange, offers plenty of opportunities for fishing, boating, swimming, waterskiing, and sunbathing. Contact the West Point Lake Resource Manager, P.O. Box 574, West Point 31833, (706) 645–2937. The lake's commercial outlets include Highland Marina Resort, P.O. Box 1644, LaGrange 30241, (706) 882–3437, where you can rent fishing boats and go after the lake's channel catfish and white and largemouth bass. Also at the marina, you can rent a houseboat or stay in a campground or furnished cottage. The lake is a U.S. Army Corps of Engineers impoundment of the Chattahoochee River, which forms most of the Georgia–Alabama border.

In the mood for a hot dog? *Charlie Joseph's* has been serving them up, and Troup Countians have been gobbling them up, since 1920 when Charlie's opened as a fruit stand in downtown LaGrange. It's been at 128 Bull Street, (706) 884–5416, since 1946. You can have your dog with just plain mustard and onions, or dressed up with slaw, chili, cheese, relish, and other fixin's. Or try the hamburgers and breakfast-time egg-and-cheese sandwiches. Charlie's second location, 2238 West Point Road, (706) 884–0379, serves breakfast, lunch, and early dinner. Both are open Monday through Saturday.

Butterflies—thousands of them, in all sizes and colors, from exotic places around the world—are free and on the wing at the *Day Butterfly Center* at Callaway Gardens in Pine Mountain. Opened to visitors in September 1988, America's first such natural attraction was inspired by similar preserves in Europe and Asia, with some distinctive Georgia touches. Named in honor of Cecil Day, late founder of the Days Inns of America motel corporation, it's a year-round, indoor-outdoor experience.

As you walk into an 8,000-square-foot, glass-enclosed "rain forest," you're suddenly caught in clouds of feathery giant swallowtails *(Papilio cresphontes),* Paris peacock swallowtails *(P. paris),* green-banded swallowtails *(P. palinurus),* owl butterflies *(Caligo sp.),* passion flower butterflies *(Helinconius sp.),* and a rainbow of other iridescent beauties from Asia, the Andes, and the South Pacific. Butterflies and tropical birds perch side by side on exotic plants. A waterfall gently spatters. Bleeding-heart doves hide in the thick tropical foliage. Indoors, you'll find educational displays and a theater with a film all about the remarkable lives of butterflies.

Outside, the native butterfly garden is cunningly designed to lure home-grown butterflies to ***Callaway Gardens,*** Pine Mountain, (800) 225–5292, fax (706) 663–5083, www.callawaygardens.com. If you'd like to have your own butterfly center, Callaway's horticulturists will show you how to plant a "tender trap" in your backyard.

While you're at Callaway Gardens, you can also take a driving tour of the 2,500 acres of gardens planted with 700 varieties of azaleas and more than 450 types of holly, mums, mountain laurel, rhododendron, dogwood, and wild-flowers. These may be viewed in their natural habitat along 13 miles of roads and walking trails, and inside the ***John A. Sibley Horticultural Center,*** a stunning indoor-outdoor conservatory with pools, cascades, and scores of floral displays that change with the season.

Callaway's 14,300 rolling, wooded acres also embrace thirteen lakes for swimming, fishing, boating, and waterskiing. Golfers may play sixty-three picturesque holes and sample from a recreational smorgasbord that includes tennis, skeet shooting, biking, and a summertime big-top circus. A half-dozen restaurants range from candlelight to casual.

The Virginia Hand Callaway Discovery Center and the Callaway Brothers Azalea Bowl are the gardens' newest attractions. Opened in early 2000, the Discovery Center overlooks Mountain Creek Lake, at the end of a scenic 2½-mile drive through woodlands and meadows. Guests reach the Discovery Center from the gardens' new main entrance at Highways 18 and 354. (The former main entrance on Highway 27 is closed.) Named for founder Cason Callaway's late wife, the 35,000-square-foot, $14 million center includes an information desk, a hundred-seat orientation theater, interpretive exhibits, a gift shop, a lakeside restaurant, and interactive kiosks about the gardens' flora and fauna. A 3,000-square-foot museum displays late Italian artist Athos Menaboni's collection of bird paintings. From the Discovery Center, visitors can explore the gardens' many other attractions by foot, bike, tram, or water taxi.

The forty-acre Azalea Bowl, purportedly the world's largest azalea garden, contains more than 5,000 of the colorful shrubs in numerous domestic and exotic

Callaway Gardens

varieties. Set among streams, arched bridges, and wide, curving trails, the azaleas burst into banks of radiant, multicolored blooms in March and April. All-inclusive admission to most attractions is $13.91 for adults, $11.50 for seniors, $6.96 for children 6 to 12; 5 and under free.

Lodgings range from rooms at the Gardens Inn to deluxe villas and cottages. Callaway Gardens lies 12 scenic miles from Warm Springs and Franklin D. Roosevelt's Little White House.

At *Pine Mountain Wild Animal Safari,* 1300 Oak Grove Road, Pine Mountain, 2 miles north of the town of Pine Mountain, (706) 663–8744, (800) 367–2751, www.animalsafari.com, you can drive your own car or take the Safari Bus through a 500-acre preserve populated by zebras, giraffes, camels, axis deer, gnus, antelopes, water buffalo, and other wild, nonpredatory creatures. Also visit the petting zoo, monkey house, and serpentarium. Open Monday through Friday from 10:00 A.M. to 5:30 P.M. and Saturday and Sunday from 10:00 A.M. to 6:30 P.M. Admission is $13.95 for adults, $12.95 for children 10 to 16, $11.95 for children 3 to 9; free for children under 3.

Blanton Creek Park, I–185 exit 11, is a nicely kept Georgia Power Company recreation area on 5,800-acre Lake Harding. The park features fifty-one RV and tent camping sites ($10 a night), which have electrical and water hookups. The park also has boat ramps, picnic pavilions, and playgrounds. Call (706) 643–7737.

If shopping's your favorite sport, indulge to your heart's content on *Pine Mountain's Main Street* (U.S. Highway 27). More than a dozen shops on both sides of the street have antiques and fine art, collectibles, handcrafted pottery, paintings, designer jewelry, books, toys, glass, and furniture. Nearly a century old, *Kimbrough Brothers General Store* (706–663–2528) knew the area when Callaway Gardens was still a gleam in Cason Callaway's eye. Before you begin, stop by the Pine Mountain Tourism and Welcome Center (800–441–3502, www.pinemountain.org) in the center of town.

A number of moderately priced motels, bed-and-breakfasts, cottages, and chalets are around Pine Mountain, Hamilton, and Warm Springs. Contact the Pine Mountain Tourism Association, (706) 663–4000, www.pinemountain.org.

Columbus is Georgia's third largest city. To get your bearings in the city of 300,000, stop by the *Columbus Convention and Visitors Bureau* (706–322–1613 and 800–999–1613, www.visitcolumbusga.org) at 900 Front Avenue, Columbus 31901, facing the Chattahoochee Riverwalk.

The *Chattahoochee Riverwalk,* a wide brick pathway with trees, benches, and attractive lighting, meanders 14 miles along the Chattahoochee and in the downtown historic district. It's adorned with lots of ornamental brick and iron-work, flowers and landscaping, and steps that lead right to the river's edge.

TOP ANNUAL EVENTS

Thomasville Antiques Show and Sale,
early March, Exchange Club
Fairgrounds,
(912) 225–3919

Thomasville Rose Festival,
late April,
(800) 704–2350

Callaway Gardens Spring Celebration,
mid-April,
(800) 282–8181

Riverfest Weekend,
late April, Columbus Riverwalk,
(706) 322–0756

Cotton Pickin' Country Fair,
early May, Gay,
(706) 924–2558

Andersonville Spring Fair,
late May,
(912) 924–2558

Indian Battle Reenactment,
late May, Westville,
(888) SEE–1850

Watermelon Festival,
first week July, Cordele,
(912) 273–1668

Christmas in Thomasville,
early December,
(912) 226–2344

Voices of Christmas,
early December, Albany,
(912) 787–1008

Christmas Festival of Lights,
Callaway Gardens,
(800) 282–8181

Close to the Riverwalk, ***Heritage Corner Tours,*** sponsored by the Historic Columbus Foundation, takes you through four homes at the corner of Broadway and Seventh Street. They include an early 1800 pioneer log cabin; an 1828 Federal-style cottage; the Victorian cottage of Dr. John Stith Pemberton, a Columbus pharmacist who left here for Atlanta, where he invented Coca-Cola in 1886; a mid-nineteenth-century farmhouse that now houses the Period Pieces Gift Shop; and the Victorian townhouse at 700 Broadway that serves as the Historic Foundation's headquarters. Tours begin at the headquarters for an all-inclusive $3.00. Phone (706) 323–7979, www.historiccolumbus.com.

If it's open—or holding one of its many regular stage productions—don't miss a chance to see the restored ***Springer Opera House*** (706–327–3688, 888–332–5200, www.springeroperahouse.org), built in 1871, which has hosted such illuminati as Oscar Wilde, Will Rogers, and Edwin Booth.

You can also take a walking/driving tour of numerous historic homes, churches, and public buildings with an illustrated brochure called ***"Original City Tours,"*** available at the Historic Columbus Foundation.

The ***Coca-Cola Space Science Center,*** 701 Front Avenue, Columbus, (706) 649–1470; www.ccssc.org, is one of Riverwalk's most exciting attractions. Developed in conjunction with Columbus State University, its components include the Mead Observatory, which captures high-detail images of far-flung celestial bodies (you can take a space flight and land on the moon); the Challenger Learning Center, an interactive, hands-on experience that helps sharpen science, math, team-building, and communications skills for school-children and other groups; and the Omnisphere Theater, which projects laser shows, science and science fiction movies, concerts, and theatrical perform-ances onto a giant domed ceiling. An accurate replica of the Apollo space cap-sule is one of the many permanent exhibits. Special events include "Night Out Under the Stars," an overnight campout at the Space Center that includes a Challenger Center Mission, the Omnisphere Theater, construction and launch of a model rocket, a laser concert, and a science fiction movie. Open Tuesday through Friday from 10:00 A.M. to 4:00 P.M., Saturday from 1:30 to 9:00 P.M., Sunday from 1:30 to 4:00 P.M.

The ***Columbus Black Heritage Tour*** is a self-guided tour of more than two dozen sites that played vital parts in the city's rich African-American cul-ture. The tour begins with the last home of legendary blues singer Gertrude "Ma" Rainey (1886–1939) and includes churches, schools, theaters, businesses, and landmarks that showcase achievements of the city's Black community. Pick up the free brochure at the Convention and Visitors Bureau.

Oxbow Meadows Environmental Learning Center, South Lumpkin Road, north of the Fort Benning Military Reservation, Columbus 31906, (706) 687–4090, is a fun and fascinating place to get out in the countryside and learn something about the world around you. Start your visit to the 1,600-acre site in

Trade Ya My Apple for That Baloney Sandwich

If you're old enough to remember when you took your sandwiches and cookies to school in a metal lunch box, take a trip down memory lane at Allen Woodall's collection of thousands of metal, plastic, and vinyl boxes with images from the A Team to Zorro, and scenes from popular radio and TV shows like *Hopalong Cassidy, Howdy Doody, The Green Hornet, Lost in Space, Little Lulu,* and *The Jetsons.* Originating in the 1890s, metal boxes were replaced with plastic and vinyl in the 1980s, when parents argued that the metal type were potential weapons. Woodall's 2,000 lunch boxes, and collections of furniture, glassware, military items, and other collectibles, are displayed at ***River Market Antiques and Art Center,*** 3226 Hamilton Road, Columbus. Phone (706) 653–6933, www.rivermarketantiques.com.

the Chattahoochee River flood plain in a 2,000-square-foot building where you can observe live, mounted, and re-created plant and animal life. Two nature trails will let you stretch your legs in the wetlands and woodlands and come face to face with the creatures that live there. Open Tuesday through Friday from 10:00 A.M. to 5:00 P.M., Saturday and Sunday from noon to 4:00 P.M. Free admission.

Even if you're staunchly antiwar, don't miss the **National Infantry Museum,** 101 Fourth Avenue, Columbus, (706) 545–2958, www.infantry .army.mil/museum, on the mammoth Fort Benning Army compound. The museum's three floors and twelve spacious galleries exhibit more than 6,000 items from the French and Indian War and the American Revolution, through the world wars, to Vietnam and the Persian Gulf conflict. You'll see a porthole from the battleship *Maine,* sixteenth-century English armor, the wing of a WWII Japanese Zero, ancient Korean and Chinese weapons and armor, gas masks worn by WWI horses, and wartime documents signed by twenty U.S. presidents. Open Monday through Friday from 10:00 A.M. to 4:30 P.M. (except for major national holidays), Saturday and Sunday from 12:30 to 4:30 P.M. Free admission.

Opened in 2001, the **Port Columbus National Civil War Naval Museum,** 1002 Victory Drive, Columbus, (706) 327–9798, www.portcolumbus.org, covers the war on the high seas, from blockade runners to conventional wooden gunboats, the new age of ironclads and Union and Confederate amphibious operations. Visitors to the $8 million, 40,000-square-foot museum witness simulated battles from inside an ironclad and view naval artillery pieces, weapons, uniforms, personal effects, flags, interpretive exhibits, and artwork. The Confederate iron ram CSS *Jackson* is the museum's star attraction. Built at the Columbus Shipyards, less than a mile from the museum, the Jackson was within a few of weeks of completion when Union raiders crossed the Chattahoochee River from Alabama in December 1864, and burned it to the water line. The hull drifted 30 miles downriver and sank to the bottom, where it was salvaged in the 1960s. Visitors view the *Jackson's* 225-foot hull from a platform above the bow and at floor level. A steel "ghost" superstructure over the hull helps viewers appreciate the ship's enormous size. Fully operational, it would have been sheathed in two layers of iron plate, been armed with six big cannons weighing about 700,000 pounds, and would have sat only 7 feet deep in the water. Other exhibits include a partial replica of the USS *Hartford,* the flagship that Union Admiral David Farragut rode into Mobile Bay, shouting, "Damn the torpedoes, full speed ahead!" Inside the *Hartford,* mannequins of enlisted sailors lie in hammocks and pass the time playing harmonicas and banjos, writing letters, and embroidering. In the officer's ward room, the ship's only table did double duty. When the medical officer wasn't suturing and sawing, it was wiped down and set for dinner. An 87-foot reconstruction of the ironclad CSS *Albermarle* gives visitors an "inside" audiovisual look at a Union surprise attack. A little-known fact: During the Civil War, a young man named Isidor Strauss was the overseas agent for a Columbus group, which financed construction of Confederate blockade runners in England. After the war, Strauss went to New York, where he built Macy's Department Stores; he died on the *Titanic* in 1912. Open daily except Christmas, 9:00 A.M. to 5:00 P.M. Admission is $4.50 for adults, $3.50 for active military and age 65 and older, $3.00 for students.

The **RiverCenter for the Performing Arts**, 900 Broadway, Columbus, (706) 653–7993, www.riverarts.net, is a spectacular new $75 million downtown Columbus cultural complex, with five interconnected buildings, joined by a dramatic four-story atrium lobby and glass curtain exterior wall. Its components include the 150-seat Studio Theater; 450-seat Legacy Hall, with a 4,000-pipe organ; and 2,000-seat Heard Theater. Performances range from classical and country music to touring Broadway musicals, ballet, and contemporary dance. It also houses Columbus State University's Schwob School of Music.

The **Columbus Museum** is a peaceful place to spend a few hours browsing. Permanent exhibits include a hands-on discovery gallery for youngsters and adults, a fine arts decorative gallery, a regional history gallery, and changing exhibits of regional art. Located at 1251 Wynnton Road, Columbus, (706) 649–0713, www.columbusmuseum.com, the museum is open daily except Monday. Donations are invited.

Providence Canyon State Park, near the small town of Lumpkin, south of Columbus, preserves the scenic beauty of an area often referred to as "Georgia's Little Grand Canyon." More than a dozen canyons in the 1,108-acre park have been chiseled out over the past 150 years by the slow, relentless process of soil erosion. As deep as 150 feet, the canyons offer a geological primer and a stunning visual display of stratified soil layers. Many fascinating formations stand alone in the midst of the canyons.

During spring and fall, those making the easy hike to the canyon floor are rewarded by multicolored wildflowers, which complement the pinks, purples, and whites of the Providence soils. From July to September, the rare plumleaf azalea blooms in shades from light orange to salmon and various tones of red and scarlet.

Stop first at the park's interpretive center (229–838–6202, 800–864–PARK, www.gastateparks.org) for an overview. A day-use park, Providence has picnic tables, shelters, and restrooms. It's on Highway 39C, Lumpkin, 7 miles west of Lumpkin, and is open daily from 7:00 A.M. to dark. There is a $2.00 per visit parking fee.

BILL'S FAVORITES

Lamar Dodd Art Center and
Chattahoochee Valley Art Museum

Day Butterfly Center, Callaway
Gardens, Pine Mountain

Chattahoochee Riverwalk

National Infantry Museum

Providence Canyon State Park and
Westville 1850s Village

FDR's Little White House

Chehaw Wild Animal Park

National Prisoner of War Museum,
Andersonville National Cemetery and
Historic Site

Jimmy Carter National Historic Site

Georgia Agrirama

Pebble Hill Plantation

You can stay overnight and fish and boat in the Chattahoochee River at *Florence Marina State Park,* Route 1, Box 36, Omaha 31821, (229) 838–4244, (800) 864–PARK, www.gastateparks.org. Campgrounds have electricity, water, restrooms, and showers. Furnished efficiency apartments, sleeping up to five, with kitchenettes are available. Six new two-bedroom cabins are completely furnished and have fully equipped kitchens. Call (800) 864–PARK, www.gastate parks.org, for rates and reservations. The park also has a swimming pool, tennis courts, a playground, and a small grocery store. It is on Highway 39C, 10 miles west of Providence Canyon. There is a $2.00 per visit parking fee.

If *Westville* were near an interstate highway, more than a million visitors a year would enjoy it. As it is, far from major thoroughfares at the tiny Stewart County seat of Lumpkin, Georgia's "Village of the 1850s" is appreciated by only a fortunate 50,000 or so. Forty miles southeast of Columbus, 25 miles west of Jimmy Carter's Plains, this Williamsburg-style re-creation includes more than two dozen authentic nineteenth-century homes, public buildings, and craftspeople's shops lining the hard-packed clay streets.

As you walk about the town, you'll be treated to a symphony of workaday sounds: the blacksmith hammering nails, horseshoes, farm implements, and household utensils; the cobbler tapping together a pair of fine riding boots; the schoolmarm calling her charges to class. Elsewhere, townsfolk make their own soap, furniture, and candles; hand-stitch quilts; and cook corn breads, stews, and gingerbread over an open hearth. A mule plods in stoic circles, turning an enormous round stone that grinds sugarcane into thick, amber syrup.

Lifestyles range from the rich and famous at the Greek Revival McDonald House to the cottages of the working folk. Every season has its special events: the Spring Festival in early April; May Pole Dances, May 1; Early American

Festival, July 4; the Fair of the 1850s, late October–early November; and, at Christmas, strolling carolers and yule log lighting.

Westville, P.O. Box 1850, Lumpkin 31815, (229) 838–6310, (888) 733–1850, www.westville.org, is open Tuesday through Saturday from 10:00 A.M. to 5:00 P.M., Sunday from 1:00 to 5:00 P.M. Admission is $10.00 for adults, $8.00 for senior citizens 65 and over, college students, and military personnel, and $4.00 for other students.

With its redbrick courthouse, granite Confederate soldier, and one-story buildings flanking the quiet square, **Lumpkin** could be moved, intact, into a museum as an exhibit of nineteenth-century Americana. The **Bedingfield Inn on the Square** (229–838–6419, www.bedingfieldinn.org) was built in 1836 as a doctor's residence and stagecoach inn. This museum is open Tuesday through Saturday from 10:00 A.M. to 5:00 P.M.

George T. Bagby State Park, fronting the Chattahoochee River's 48,000-acre Lake Walter F. George, is a resort-style getaway. The thirty-room Walter F. George Lodge has all the modern comforts and a full-service restaurant. Call (800) 864–PARK for lodge and cottage rates and reservations. Around it you'll find boat ramps and marinas, swimming pools, tennis courts, an 18-hole golf course, and hiking and picnic areas. You can also stay in furnished cottages. There's a $2.00 per visit parking fee. Contact Box 201, Fort Gaines 31751, (229) 768–2571. Phone (800) 864–PARK, www.gastateparks.org, for lodge, cottage, and campsite reservations.

At **Frontier Village** in neighboring Fort Gaines, a one-third-scale replica of the original fort, built in 1814, has Civil War cannons and authentic log cabins that reflect the area's frontier heritage. Phone (229) 768–2248.

Kolomoki Mounds State Historic Park, Route 1, Blakely, (229) 724–2150, (800) 864–PARK, www.gastateparks.org, is an important archaeological site, as well as a recreation area. Within the 1,293-acre park you can climb some of the seven burial mounds and temple mounds built by Creek Indians in the twelfth and thirteenth centuries. The small museum has artifacts unearthed from the mounds and the excavated burial mound of a tribal chief. Also in the park, you're invited to swim in two pools, fish and boat in a pair of lakes, have a picnic, and play miniature golf.

The park's thirty-five camping sites have water and electricity, hot showers, and restrooms.

Driving around the **Early County Courthouse** in Blakely, look for the monument to the peanut.

If ever a body of water were created with anglers in mind, it's got to be **Lake Seminole.** Formed by an impoundment of the Chattahoochee and Flint Rivers, the 37,500-acre lake, with a 250-mile shoreline, is especially bountiful grounds for bass fishing. Largemouth routinely weigh in at upwards of fifteen pounds. Anglers also snare a wealth of bodacious black bass, white bass, hybrid bass, and stripers, as well as bream, chain pickerel, catfish, yellow perch, and many other varieties.

Yet the marshy, reedy lake—afloat with thousands of acres of grass beds and lily pads and spiked with the ghostly trunks of cypress and live oak trees— is so far off the beaten path, down where Georgia's southwestern corner bumps against Alabama and Florida, that when more than fifty boats appear on a single day, old-timers grumble that "Ol' Sem" is turning into a waterbound I–75.

The lake's largest public recreational area is **Seminole State Park,** off Highway 39, 16 miles south of Donalsonville (229–861–3137, www.gastate parks.org). Activities include fishing, boating, swimming, waterskiing, picnicking, and camping; furnished cottages are available. Call (800) 864–PARK for camping and cottage rates and reservations. There is a $2.00 per visit parking fee.

Peaches, Pecans, and FDR

President Franklin Delano Roosevelt left his everlasting imprint on the hills and piney woodlands of Meriwether County. The future president first came to this isolated rural county, 85 miles southwest of Atlanta, in 1924 to immerse his polio-afflicted limbs in the mineral waters of Warm Springs. His **Little White House,** secluded in a wooded grove, became his sanctuary from the monumental pressures of World War II. Now maintained by the Georgia Department of Natural Resources, the comfortable little house remains as he left it when he died there on April 12, 1945.

In the kitchen, simple dishes, pots and pans, a hand-cranked ice-cream maker, and other utensils are neatly stacked. In the woodwork, FDR's cook penciled this touching message: "Daisy Bonner cooked the first meal and the last one in this cottage for President Roosevelt."

Dedicated in 2004, the **FDR Memorial Museum** emphasizes Roosevelt's life at Warm Springs and his impact on Georgia, the South, and the rest of Depression-ravaged rural America. Connected to the entrance plaza and visitor center, the $5-million, 12,000-square-foot museum's hundreds of exhibits include his 1938 Ford convertible equipped with hand controls; his wheelchair, leg braces and canes; photos of his life at Warm Springs; a 1930s kitchen with his "Fireside Chats" playing on a radio; and displays featuring the Rural Electrification Administration, the Tennessee Valley Authority, and other New Deal programs, which brought modern conveniences into millions of homes for the first time.

FDR's Favorite

Ms. Bonner left another legacy. Her recipe for Chicken Country Captain was one of FDR's favorites. It's still served in middle and southwest Georgia restaurants and homes.

DAISY'S CHICKEN COUNTRY CAPTAIN

1 hen or 2 fryers

2 or 3 chopped green peppers

2 or 3 cloves garlic

2 chopped onions

1 can whole tomatoes

1 teaspoon curry powder,

or more to taste

2 cups rice, boiled until dry

1 teaspoon thyme

¼ cup raisins to garnish top

¼ cup almonds or other nuts for sauce

¼ cup almonds or other nuts for garnish

¼ can sliced mushrooms, or equivalent fresh sliced mushrooms

Salt and pepper to taste

Boil chicken until done, then debone. Make the sauce of cut green peppers, onions, tomatoes, mushrooms, almonds, raisins, thyme, salt, pepper, garlic, and curry powder. Add chicken, let simmer on top of stove or in a casserole for one hour, until sauce is thin. Serve over rice. Garnish with cut green peppers, raisins, and nuts.

Daisy usually accompanied her Country Captain with baked grapefruit, French-cut green beans, salads, rolls, and chocolate soufflé.

A film narrated by Walter Cronkite includes historic footage of FDR swimming in the Warm Springs pools, visiting with neighbors, having picnics, playing with his Scottie dog, Fala; and his funeral procession, when he left his Little White House for the last time. While posing in the living room for a portrait by Madame Elizabeth Shoumatoff on April 12, 1945, he suffered a stroke and died. The famous "Unfinished Portrait" is in the museum, with a "Finished Portrait" Madame Shoumatoff painted after World War II. FDR's Little White House State Historic Site, U.S. Highway 27-A, Warm Springs, (706) 655–5870, www.fdr-little whitehouse.org, is open daily. Adults $7.00, ages 62 and over $6.00, ages 6 to 18 $4.00, 5 and under free. Special observances on April 12 commemorate FDR's extraordinary presidency.

The adjacent village of **Warm Springs** (population 450) has been revived with visitors in mind. More than sixty stores along the main street are stocked with antiques, collectibles, and Georgia-made arts and crafts.

The **Warm Springs Welcome Center** (800–FDR–1927, 706–655–3322, www .warmspringsga.ws), on the village's main street, is open every day for information and brochures.

The **Hotel Warm Springs Bed & Breakfast Inn,** 47 Broad Street, Warm Springs, (800) 366–7616, fax (706) 655–2114, (800) 366–7616, www.hotelwarm springsbb.org, once housed the press, Secret Service, and visitors to FDR's Little White House. Now the three-story, 1907 hotel receives bed-and-breakfast guests who come here to see the FDR shrines and shop at Warm Springs' dozens of handicraft stores. Fourteen guest rooms with two full beds are furnished with original oak Val-Kill Furniture. The Presidential Suite has two separate rooms with a connecting bath. The lobby has original ceramic tile floors, a vintage Stromberg-Carlson cord switchboard, stenciled walls, and 16-foot ceilings. The hotel has a restaurant and an old-fashioned soda shop with ice cream (homemade Georgia peach is innkeeper Lee Thompson's special treat). A bountiful Southern "Breakfast Feast" is included in the inexpensive to moderate rates.

Franklin D. Roosevelt State Park, about 5 miles west of Warm Springs, on Highway 190, is ideal for a minivacation. On the wooded crest of Pine Mountain, the 9,480-acre park has a lake for swimming, fishing, and boating; hiking trails; horseback riding; and picturesque picnic spots. Roosevelt's favorite was Dowdell's Knob, with sweeping views of the Pine Mountain Valley. Many of the fieldstone buildings in the park were the product of the Depression-era Civilian Conservation Corps. Campsites ($10 a night) have water, electricity, hot showers, and restrooms. Cottages have fireplaces and fully equipped kitchens for standard state fees. Call (800) 864–PARK or log on to www.gastateparks.org for rates and reservations. There is a $2.00 per visit parking fee. The park office, Box 749, Pine Mountain 31822, (706) 663–4858, is open daily from 8:00 A.M. to 5:00 P.M.

Hikers in your crowd can lace up their boots and hit the scenic 23-mile **Pine Mountain Trail.** Starting at the Callaway Gardens Country Store on Highway 27, the trail winds past rock formations, waterfalls, big stands of trees, and lush vegetation on its way to its terminus at the TV tower on Highway 85W near Warm Springs. One of the country's southernmost mountain trails, it has twelve access points, so you can get on and off with ease. Pick up a trail map at the FDR Park office.

If you'd like to spend some time canoeing on a scenic, unspoiled river, get in touch with **Flint River Outdoor Center,** 4429 Woodland Road, Thomaston, (706) 647–2633, www.flintriverfun.com. Guided and self-guided trips on the river begin at Highway 36, 15 miles south of Warm Springs. You pass through mostly mild rapids, waterfalls, hills and valleys, wildflowers, ferns, and animal habitats. Canoe, kayak, and equipment rentals are available. You can overnight at a seven-room lodge and five RV hookups.

The *Pasaquan Folk Art Compound* would probably seem extraordinary even in the Land of Oz. In rural Marion County, near the tiny county seat of Buena Vista, this outdoor ensemble of toothy totem faces, smiling snakes, whirling pinwheels, suns, moons, and stars—all painted in brilliant primary colors—is positively otherworldly. It was the product of the late Eddie Owens Martin, who was born here in 1908, traveled to New York and abroad, and returned in 1950 to create this fabulous

Pasaquan Folk Art Compound

legacy. To finance his creativity, Martin came to town in a turban and robes and told fortunes and sold jewelry around the courthouse.

Since Martin's death in 1986, his "Land of Pasaquan" has been meticulously restored and opened to the public by appointment. For information phone the Buena Vista–Marion County Chamber of Commerce, (229) 649–2842, (800) 647–2842.

The *Sign of the Dove Bed and Breakfast and Restaurant,* 108 North Church Street, Buena Vista, (888) 690–3363, (229) 649–3663, www.sign-of-the-dove.com, has three large guest rooms in a 1905 neoclassical home and a four-bedroom cottage. The restaurant serves Southern food, steaks, and seafood. Inexpensive to moderate.

Approaching *Albany* from any direction, you'll pass symmetrical groves of papershell pecan trees. Pecans are available year-round, still in the paper-thin shell or roasted and boxed. Some groves invite you to come in and pick your own. The attractive city of 100,000 has other pleasant surprises as well.

While Atlanta boasts the world's largest aquarium with the world's largest fish, Albany is just as proud of its *Flint RiverQuarium.* Although the 175,000-gallon RiverQuarium would be a drop in the fish tank compared to the eight-million-gallon Georgia Aquarium in downtown Atlanta, it's a symbol of rebirth in the city Albanians call "All-benny" that has had its share of watery woes.

In 1994, a month of torrential rains overwhelmed the Flint River and kept much of the city under water for several weeks. In the disaster's wake, the Downtown Riverfront Plan was conceived and a new nonprofit organization, Albany Tomorrow, was created to implement a revival of the neglected riverfront.

The Flint RiverQuarium was the linchpin in the redevelopment plan, which also includes an IMAX-style theater, the first new downtown hotel in a half-century and parklands, play areas, and plazas.

As visitors enter the lobby, they go up a ramp to a room called Skywater, the Creek Indian name for Blue Hole Springs. A re-creation of a natural river spring, the 22-foot-deep hole is open to the outside. Viewed through a 25-foot window, the Blue Hole teems with life. Snapping turtles, sliders, cooters and other turtles swim though the clear water and sun themselves on logs that jut above the spring. Largemouth bass, five-foot-long gar, fifty-pound catfish, and dozens of other species drift through underwater caves and partially submerged cypresses and live oak trees, whose above-water branches house native birds, herons, and egrets. Juvenile and six-foot-long gators have their own portioned-off habitat. Divers go into the Hole every day to feed the fish and amphibians.

A large tank in the gallery area showcases the sometimes ornery Flint River, which is born in a spring near Atlanta's Hartsfield-Jackson International Airport and twists more than 300 miles across middle and southwest Georgia, through Albany down to Lake Seminole. There it joins the Chattahoochee to form the Apalachicola, which flows through the Florida Panhandle into the Gulf of Mexico.

Buster, a ninety-year-old, ninety-pound alligator snapping turtle with a big beak and signature overbite, is the king of the first exhibit gallery and the aquarium's mascot. His lovably homely image graces mugs, T-shirts, and other souvenir items. Big Al, a mere fifty-pound alligator snapping turtle, shares the Spring Run Creek Gallery with Elliott, an adult male gator, and a female named Sheila.

Fish, reptiles, and other creatures from the Amazon, Ganges, and other world rivers populate the "World of Water" exhibit.

In Discovery Caverns, kids can play interactive games that focus on stewardship of natural resources. They make their own weather, change a river's flow, and crawl through a cave to find creatures that live underground.

Across a plaza from the RiverQuarium, the Imagination Theater is a large-format movie theater, with a screen three stories high and four stories wide. Playgrounds, benches, and picnic tables are in Riverfront Park outside the aquarium. Festively decorated fiberglass turtles are goodwill ambassadors. Visitors can stay at the new *Hilton Garden Inn.*

The Flint RiverQuarium is at 117 Pine Avenue, Albany. Open daily. Adults RiverQuarium admission, $8.50, Imagination Theater, $8.00, combo $14.00; seniors, $7.50, $7.00, $12.50; youth, $6.00, $6.00, $10.00. Phone (877) 463–5468, www.flintriverquarium.com.

At **Parks at Chehaw,** on Highway 91, Albany, 2½ miles northeast of the city, (229) 430–5277, www.parksatchehaw.org, African elephants and giraffes, Andean llamas, North American black bears, bobcats, elk, bison, and deer roam in natural habitats designed by Jim Fowler, former naturalist with TV's *Wild Kingdom*. You view the animals from protected, elevated walkways. Admission is $3.00 for adults, $2.00 for senior citizens, children 3 to 11, and military personnel. An additional $2.00 a carload lets you in the companion recreational park with play areas, jogging, hiking, and biking trails, a re-created Creek Indian village, miniature train rides, a boat dock, and picnic areas. The **Chehaw National Indian Festival,** held in the park the third weekend of May, is one of the Southeast Tourism Society's top twenty yearly events. The park is open from 9:00 A.M. to 5:00 P.M. daily.

Thronateeska Heritage Foundation, 100 Roosevelt Avenue, Albany, (229) 432–6955, is a delightful time-trip through the nineteenth and early twentieth centuries. The complex includes an early 1900s "prairie style" train depot, a 1910 steam locomotive, an 1840s house, and a planetarium and science center in a vintage Railway Express Co. office. It's open Thursday through Saturday noon to 4:00 P.M., closed Sunday. Adults $4.25, children $3.25.

The **Albany Museum of Art,** 311 Meadowlark Drive, Albany, (229) 439–8400, has both permanent and changing displays of regional and national artists. The African Art Center collection is one of the nation's most outstanding. Open Tuesday through Saturday from 10:00 A.M. to 5:00 P.M. Admission is $4.00 for adults, $2.00 for seniors and children.

albany'sraycharles

American music icon Ray Charles, who died in 2004, was born Ray Charles Robinson in Albany. Blind at age 7 and orphaned at 15, he forged an incredible career as a pianist, singer, songwriter, and bandleader. He earned gold and platinum records for such worldwide hits as "What'd I Say," "I Can't Stop Loving You," "Hallelujah, I Love Her So," and "Georgia on My Mind," Georgia's official state song.

Albany Civil Rights Museum, 326 Whitney Avenue, Albany, (229) 432–1698, is the restored Mount Zion Baptist Church, where Dr. Martin Luther King Jr. preached during the 1961 civil rights demonstrations. Photos and exhibits illustrate Dr. King's pivotal part in the "Albany movement." He was arrested and jailed for his civil disobedience activities, and freed through the intervention of U.S. Attorney General Robert Kennedy. Open Wednesday through Saturday, 10:00 A.M. to 4:00 P.M., Sunday 2:00 to 5:00 P.M. Adults $3.00, children $2.00.

Contact the Albany CVB & Welcome Center, 225 W. Broad Avenue, Albany 31701, (800) 475–8700, www.albanyga.com.

Every spring in the swamps and bogs of southwestern Georgia, a thorny, scrubby, rather homely tree called the mayhaw produces an applelike fruit prized by gourmets and homemakers. The small, coral-hued fruit is gathered in fishing nets and by hand, then turned into a delectable sweet-tart jelly that's sold in stores around the small Miller County seat of *Colquitt*. The fruit is the star of Colquitt's early April *Mayhaw Festival.*

While you're in the Colquitt area, try to catch a performance of *"Swamp Gravy,"* an entertaining folklife play about the comedies and tragedies, tall tales, music, dance, and songs of Miller County and rural Georgia. Sponsored by the Colquitt/Miller Arts Council, it's performed in March, April, October, and November. Call (229) 758–5450 for more information.

"If walls could talk" isn't wishful thinking in Colquitt. Walk around the town square and five bigger-than-life murals, created by the Colquitt/Miller County Arts Council's Millennium Mural Project, "speak" about events that shaped the lives of the peanut farming community of 2,500. The four panels of *Saturday On the Square*, by Alabama artist Wes Hardin, capture the excitement when "The Circus Comes to Town"; when a runaway "Bull Comes to Colquitt"; "When A Young Soldier Leaves Colquitt"; and "Hanging Out on the Square." Other murals depict neighbors helping neighbors; Saturday morning in Colquitt's Black community; and the story of the South's three dominant cultures: Native American, Black, and White. Contact Colquitt/Miller County Chamber of Commerce, 166 South First Street, Colquitt, (229) 758–2400.

The Tarrer Inn, 155 South Cuthbert Street, Colquitt, (229) 758– 2888 and (888) 282–7737; www.tarrerinn.com, is another welcome newcomer to downtown Colquitt. Built in 1861 as a boardinghouse, the inn has been refurbished as a comfortable small hotel. Twelve guest rooms are decorated with antiques

Grits Is Groceries

The National Grits Festival, held in mid-April at the little Worth County town of Warwick, 17 miles north of Albany, celebrates "The Official Processed Food of Georgia." Imaginative cooks gussy up the humble cornmeal porridge with everything from apples to zucchini, pizza, pineapple, peach pie, and chocolate. The one-day event includes a corn-shucking contest, arts festival, antique tractor show, a beauty contest, and the tour de force—a group wallow in the Grits Pit, a cattle trough filled with cold cooked grits. First prize goes to the contestant who comes out with the greatest quantity of the white stuff stuck to himself or herself. If you'd like to take the plunge, phone (229) 535–6670, www.gritsfest.com.

and modern amenities. Lunch is served Wednesday, Thursday, Friday, and Sunday, dinner on Friday and Saturday. Inexpensive to moderate rates include full Southern country breakfast.

If you're a fan of country fairs and enjoy good, old-fashioned fun, put *Climax Swine Time* (229–246–0910) on your post-Thanksgiving calendar. Held the Friday and Saturday after Thanksgiving in the Decatur County community of Climax, many of the activities are pig-related: a hog-calling contest, best-dressed pig competition, a greased-pig chase, and a "chitlin" (chitterling) eating contest. Also on the agenda are country and gospel music, a 10K race, cane grinding and syrup making, and barbecue and fried chicken for those who care not for "chitlins." Contact Bainbridge/Decatur County Chamber of Commerce, (229) 246–4774, (800) 243–4774, www.bainbridgega.com/chamber.

The *Rattlesnake Roundup,* the last weekend of January, is the social event of the year at the small Grady County town of *Whigham,* 6 miles east of Climax. The event began a couple of decades ago when Whigham residents, tired of being accosted by the hissing reptiles every time they walked through their fields and farms, decided to do something about it and have some sport at the same time. On the big day, visitors pack tiny downtown Whigham as snakes by the hundreds are brought in and displayed. Contact Bainbridge/Decatur County Chamber of Commerce, (229) 246–4774, (800) 243–4774, www.bainbridgega .com/chamber.

Carter Country

Peach County leaves little doubt that it's the heart of Georgia's most luscious industry. Traveling on I–75 at night, you can't miss "The Big Peach," an enormous illuminated rendition of the fruit on a 100-foot-pole at the Byron/Fort Valley exit. During the summer, visitors have plenty of opportunities to go into the orchards and pick their own or to buy fresh peaches at packing houses and roadside stands. The Byron/Fort Valley exit 49 is the northern end of the Andersonville Trail, which leads through Fort Valley to Plains on Highways 49 and 280.

In mid-June you're invited to the *Georgia Peach Festival* in Byron and Fort Valley. This weeklong event includes parades, street dances, peach pie cookoffs, peach-eating contests, and a king-and-queen coronation.

Six miles south of Fort Valley, at the Peach/Macon County line, look for a left turn off Highway 49 into Massee Lane Gardens, home of the *American Camellia Society.* Between November and March, pink and white blossoms in every known variety bloom in the society's nine-acre gardens. Year-round, you're invited to the society's Williamsburg-style headquarters to admire the

170 porcelain birds and flowers created in the studios of the late American artist Edward Marshall Boehm. The pieces are so lifelike they appear to be on the verge of flight. Some were created as gifts for state presidents and kings.

Contact the American Camellia Society, 100 Massee Lane, Fort Valley 31030, (478) 967–2358, www.camellias-acs.com. Open from January through March, camellia blooming season, Monday through Saturday from 9:00 A.M. to 5:00 P.M.; Sunday from 1:00 to 5:00 P.M.; April to December, Monday to Friday from 9:00 A.M. to 4:00 P.M. Admission is $5.00 for adults and children 12 and older; seniors $4.00; free for children under 12.

Part of the Andersonville Trail, **Macon County** is the home of Georgia's largest Mennonite community. You can admire antebellum white columns in the small towns of Marshallville and Montezuma.

The Macon County seat and a thriving Mennonite community, **Montezuma** was named by returning Mexican War veterans. The area has made a remarkable recovery from the devastating Flint River floods that occurred in 1994. Nearly one hundred Mennonite families give the little town some of the appearance of the Pennsylvania Dutch country. Drive east of Montezuma on Highway 26 past the neat barns and silos and the contented herds of the Mennonite dairy farms. Three miles from Montezuma—and 14 miles west of I–75 exit 127—look for a black buggy parked in front of **Yoder's Deitsch Haus** (478) 472–2024, www.montezuma-ga.com, a sparkling clean cafeteria where Mennonites in traditional dress prepare truly admirable Southern cooking, spiced with such Pennsylvania Dutch specialties as shoofly pie and pot roast. Before leaving, stop by the bakery for a sackful of cakes, cookies, breads, and strudel. It's open for breakfast, lunch, and dinner Tuesday through Saturday. Handmade Mennonite dolls, afghans, coverlets, garden ornaments, and other items are on sale in the adjacent gift shop.

At **Kauffman Strawberry Farm,** 1305 Mennonite Church Road, (478) 472–8833, www.kauffmanstrawberries.com, you can pick your own berries off the vine and buy already-picked berries in the farm store. It's open Tuesday through Saturday. The berries are at their luscious strawberry shortcake peak in mid summer.

Pick up a driving tour map from the Macon County Chamber of Commerce, P.O. Box 308, Montezuma 31063, (478) 472–2391, www.maconcountyga.org.

Sumter County, the epicenter of Georgia's peanut industry, is home of the world's most famous peanut farmer, our thirty-ninth president, Jimmy Carter. The southern anchor of the Andersonville Trail, Sumter is also the site of the Civil War's most notorious prisoner-of-war camp.

These days, all is green and peaceful at the **Andersonville National Cemetery and Historic Site,** Highway 49, Andersonville, (229) 924–0343, www.nps.gov/ande. Stop first at the National Park Service Visitors Center to view the film and exhibits, then take the self-guided driving tour.

Built in 1864 as confinement for 10,000 Union prisoners of war, the 26½–acre stockade soon became a charnel house for upwards of 33,000 captives. With the Confederacy barely able to feed and clothe its own forces, about 12,000 of the Andersonville inmates perished of disease and starvation. As park rangers point out, however, Southern prisoners in the more well-off North often fared no better than the Union prisoners at Andersonville.

After the war, the camp commander, Swiss-born Captain Henry Wirz, was found guilty of war crimes and hanged. The self-guided tour leads you past thousands of graves and impressive memorials erected by states whose sons died here. Tunnels testify to the prisoners' usually failed attempts to escape the horrors.

The *National Prisoner of War Museum,* www.nps.gov/ande, opened on the Andersonville Grounds in spring 1998, honors the 800,000 American solidiers, sailors, and airmen who've endured the horrors of capture and imprisonment from the American Revolution to the Persian Gulf conflict. The 10,000-square-foot museum was built in partnership by the American Ex-Prisoners of War (AXPW), a national organization of 20,000 former POWs, and Friends of the Park, local citizens who support the National Park Service at Andersonville. Funds were raised by the sale of 270,000 commemorative coins created by the U.S. Mint. More than 10,000 donors and corporations gave about $700,000, and the Georgia Department of Transportation built a new entrance road and parking areas. Andersonville was chosen for the museum in recognition of the site's tragic history as the nation's most infamous POW camp. During the tour, you "experience" the terror of being captured by enemy troops and taken to prison. One room highlights the horrors of World War II's Bataan Death March and the forced marches to North Korean POW camps. Another room displays drawings, poetry, carvings, and clandestine radios POWs created to help them keep their sanity. The tour ends with a full-scale replica of POWs digging an escape tunnel under a Nazi prison camp. The museum's courtyard opens onto the remains of the Civil War Andersonville stockade. A fountain gushing water into a stream symbolizes the lack of fresh water prevalent in most POW camps.

A granite springhouse marks the site of *Providence Spring,* which legend says flowed from barren ground in answer to prisoners' prayers.

Across Highway 49, the village of *Andersonville* (population 250, 229–924–2558, www.andersonvillega.freeservers.com) has been returned to its 1860s appearance. At the Train Depot–Welcome Center, you'll be greeted by Peggy Sheppard, a live wire transplanted from Yonkers, New York. She'll direct

pea-nuts!fresh roastedpea-nuts!

Jimmy Carter, Georgia's peanut farmer–president, drew the world's attention to the state's most bountiful crop. His native southwest Georgia is the heart of this tasty industry, and it produces most of the more than two billion pounds of goobers grown in the state every year.

Breaking it down, there are about 200 peanut pods to a pound, and usually two peanuts per pod. They would make a mountain of about 800 billion peanuts. Laid end to end, they'd extend for more than 6 million miles, about twenty-five times the distance from the Earth to the Moon. "Goober" is believed to come from an African word, *nguba*, which, of course, means "peanut."

you to the village's antiques and crafts shops, picnic groves, and antebellum churches and homes. The ***Drummer Boy Museum*** (open by appointment) houses an extensive collection of guns, swords, battle flags, and documents signed by Jefferson Davis and Abraham Lincoln. The village's major yearly happenings are the ***Great Southern Carriage and Wagon Auction*** in early April, the ***Andersonville Antiques and Civil War Artifacts Fair*** Memorial Day weekend, and the ***Andersonville Historic Fair*** in early October, which features battle reenactments and scores of craftspeople and musicians.

Peggy Sheppard runs a charming country bed-and-breakfast called ***A Place Away.*** The two bedrooms in the comfortable, rustic-looking cottage have private baths, refrigerators, and coffeemakers. Guest rooms and a sitting room are decorated in kick-off-your-shoes casual country style. The inexpensive rate comes with a bountiful Southern breakfast. Contact Anderson-ville Welcome Center, Andersonville 31711, (229) 924–2558.

At nearby ***Americus,*** stop at the Americus/Sumter County Tourism Council Welcome Center, 123 West Lamar Street, (229) 928–6059, (888) 278–6837, www .therealgeorgia.com, for a driving guide to the historic showplaces around the pleasant city of 20,000. Memorabilia of our thirty-ninth president are displayed at the ***James Earl Carter Library*** of Georgia Southwestern University.

After leaving the presidency in 1980, Jimmy Carter received worldwide acclaim for his efforts on behalf of Habitat for Humanity International. Since 1976, when it was founded in Americus as a nonprofit housing ministry, Habitat for Humanity has partnered with more than 70,000 families to build simple, affordable houses in every state and more than sixty countries. ***Habitat's Tour Center and Museum*** in downtown Americus has model homes and exhibits about the organization's history. It's open Monday through Saturday. Admission is free. Habitat for Humanity International, 322 West Laman Street, Americus 31709, (229) 924–6935, (800) HABITAT, www.habitat.org.

If you love old movie palaces, try to be in Americus for a performance at the gorgeously restored **Rylander Theater.** Opened in 1921, the ornate theater was the setting for thirty years of vaudeville, silent movies, stellar attractions like bandmaster John Philip Sousa, the Ziegfeld Follies, political speeches, graduations, dance recitals and concerts, and films from Hollywood's golden era. The theater closed in 1950 and was forgotten until 1992, when a restoration movement began. Reopened in 1999, the venerable house, with 630 seats on three levels and a "Mighty Mo" Moller pipe organ, hosts touring musicals, plays, concerts, and festive events of all sorts. It's at 310 West Lamar Street, next to Habitat for Humanity. Phone (229) 931–0001, www.rylander.org.

In 1923, four years before he captured the world's imagination with his historic trans-Atlantic solo flight, an unheralded barnstormer named Charles A. Lindbergh made his first-ever solo flight at Souther Field, a U.S. Army aviation training camp at Americus. "The Lone Eagle" made his flight in the first plane he ever owned, a single-engine WWI surplus, *Jenny.* It was obviously love at first flight. His feat is remembered on a plaque at what's now Americus Airport: "I had not soloed up to the time I bought my *Jenny* at Americus, Georgia [signed] Charles A. Lindbergh." Contact the Americus Welcome Center, 123 West Lamar Street, Americus 31709, (229) 928–6059, (888) 278–6837, www.thereal georgia.com.

For contemporary comforts wrapped in a splendid turn-of-the-century package, check into the **Windsor Hotel** in downtown Americus. Built in 1896, the redbrick, turreted-and-towered Italianate landmark reopened in 1991 to rave reviews. The fifty-three large guest rooms are beautifully furnished and decorated. The Grand Dining Room serves high-Southern and continental cuisine, and there's a full bar and an open veranda with wicker rockers. The private Lindbergh Dining Room was named for "Lucky Lindy," who purchased his first plane and made his first solo flight from nearby Souther Field. Some old-timers remember him playing pool across the street from the hotel. The Windsor is at 125 West Lamar Street, Americus. Call (229) 924–1555, (888) 297–9567, www.windsoramericus.com. Inexpensive to moderate.

More than two decades after Jimmy Carter left the White House, the thirty-ninth president's sleepy little Sumter County hometown of Plains treasures the legacy of the quiet-spoken peanut farmer who made it world-famous. Visitors still come to town to visit the simple, unassuming places included in the *Jimmy Carter National Historic Site.* The National Park Service Visitor Center in the former Plains school is the best place to start. In the late 1930s and early 1940s, when Carter sat in the classrooms, and walked its corridors, the brick school housed grades 1 through 11. There was no twelfth grade in those days. Today the school is a museum, showcasing life in the rural South during the Great

Depression. Stiff-backed wood and metal school desks are lined up like rows of peanuts in a red clay field. On an audiotape, today's Carter talks fondly of Julia Coleman, his teacher and school principal, who advised him and fellow students to "accommodate changing times, but cling to unchanging principles." When students got out of hand, a wooden paddle, legal in those days, was there to get them back in line. Wouldn't Julia Coleman be proud to know her former pupil became president and won the 2002 Nobel Peace Prize? The Visitor Center is open daily from 9:00 A.M. to 5:00 P.M. Admission is free.

Elsewhere in town, the old railroad depot, made famous by the 1976 presidential campaign, is now the **Depot Museum,** dedicated to that historic campaign.

Also part of the National Historic Site, the **Jimmy Carter Boyhood Home,** in the Archery community, 2 miles from Plains, includes the farmhouse, barns, outbuildings, and the farm store where Carter grew up in the 1930s. In push-button audios around the site, Carter describes the no-frills life on his father's farm. The house had no electricity until the early 1940s, and the family's day usually began before dawn and ended not long after dark. A battery-operated radio with newscasts and popular shows like *Amos 'n Andy* and *Fibber Magee and Molly* was one of the family's few sources of entertainment.

Opened in May 2002, the **Plains Inn and Antique Shop** is the town's newest attraction. The two-story building on Main Street has a twenty-four-booth antiques mall on the street floor and seven luxury suites on the second floor, each decorated in the style of a decade from the 1920s to the 1980s. Inexpensive to moderate. Phone (229) 824–4517, www.plainsgeorgia.com.

A peanut with a famous toothy grin welcomes visitors to Plains. Made of wooden hoops, chicken wire, aluminum foil, and polyurethane, the 13-foot-tall goober was a gift to the town from Carter's friends. When termites took a liking to "Mr. Peanut" a few years back, townsfolk came to the rescue with patches of cement.

The Carters' current home, a modest ranch-style house, will eventually be included in the National Historic Site. Carter and his wife, Rosalynn, can often be seen around town when they're taking time out from their services with Habitat for Humanity International and their peacemaking efforts around the world. Visitors are welcome when the former president teaches Sunday school at Maranatha Baptist Church. For information about the National Historic Site, write National Park Service, Plains 31780, (229) 824–4104, www.nps.gov/jica. All sites are open daily, and admission is free. Plains is on Highway 280 about 40 miles west of I–75 exit 101. Shops on Plains's main street are stocked with Carter memorabilia and peanuts in many different guises.

Hello, Central! The *Georgia Rural Telephone Museum* in the small Sumter County town of Leslie recalls the bygone era when the telephone was a friend, not an impersonal convenience and telemarketing nuisance. Tommy Smith, who owns the local Citizen's Telephone Company, opened the museum in 1995 in a 1911 cotton warehouse he saved from destruction. His 2,000 pieces of telephonia include hand-cranked wooden voice boxes, early telephones of every size and description, and lifesize dioramas of switchboard operators in period dress. You'll also see a re-creation of Alexander Graham Bell's workshop, phone booths, and an early 1900s Model A Ford service truck. The museum is located on Highway 280 west, 135 Bailey Avenue, Leslie, 22 miles off I–75 exit 101 (Cordele). Open Monday through Friday from 9:00 A.M. to 3:00 P.M. Adults $5.00, seniors $4.00, children $3.00. Phone (229) 874–4786, www.grtm.org.

Like many rural towns, tiny *Parrott* on GA 520 in Terrell County, southwest of Plains, has been trying to reinvent itself as an antiques and flea market mecca. Shops come and go, and currently there are four or five on the 1-block main street selling antiques, art, gifts, collectibles, and oddities. *The China-berry Cafe,* 120 Main Street, Parrott, (229) 623–2233, is a delicious constant. Shoppers and nonshoppers fill the homey cafe's dozen or so tables for barbecue, beef tips, fried chicken, fish, and a choice of vegetables, salads, and homemade pies and cakes. Open Tuesday, Thursday, and Sunday, 11:00 A.M. to 3:00 P.M., and Friday and Saturday, 11:00 A.M. to 9:00 P.M.

Georgia Veterans Memorial State Park is a tranquil haven 9 miles west of Cordele and the racetrack lanes of I–75. A museum and vintage aircraft honor the state's military veterans. The park sits on Lake Blackshear, an 18-mile-long waterway renowned for catfish, black bass, bream, pickerel, and other delicious catches. Visitors can also enjoy boating, an 18-hole golf course, swimming in a freshwater pool, and a nature interpretive center and playground. The one hundred camping and trailer sites have electricity, water, restrooms, and hot showers. Ten two- and three-bedroom cottages, with fireplaces and fully equipped kitchens, are available. There is a $2.00 per visit parking fee. The park office, on Highway 280, Cordele, (229) 276–2371, (800) 864–PARK, www.gastateparks .org, is open daily from 8:00 A.M. to 5:00 P.M. The *Lake Blackshear Resort & Golf Club* is a deluxe resort inside Georgia Veterans Park. Looking more like a modern art museum than a state park lodge, the Retreat's eighty-eight smartly furnished guest rooms and villas are moderately priced. Amenities include an upscale Italian/American restaurant, full bar, indoor and outdoor pools, fitness center, conference center, golf, fishing, and water sports. Moderate to expensive. Phone (800) 459–1230, www.lakeblackshearresort.com.

Daphne Lodge, on Highway 280 near the park entrance, (229) 273–2596, is a pleasantly rustic, family-owned restaurant famous for its fried catfish and hush puppies. They also serve shrimp, steaks, and fried chicken at dinner Tuesday through Saturday.

If you're down this way the first week of July, join in the fun of Cordele's annual *Watermelon Festival.*

Calling all train nuts! The *Savannah-Americus-Montgomery Shortline* is now accepting passengers for its 36-mile daily run between Cordele and Plains. Opened in late 2002, the state-operated excursion train, dubbed "The Rolling State Park," glides through pecan groves, peanut fields, and small towns and makes a scenic crossing of Lake Blackshear. It stops at the Jimmy Carter National Historic Site and the Georgia Rural Telephone Museum and also gives riders time to tour Habitat for Humanity's Tour Center and Museum in Americus. The SAM Shortline gets its name from a historic route and goes nowhere near Savannah. Passenger car fares are adults $22.99, ages 62 and over and military, $19.99, ages 3 to 12, $12.99. Premium car with chairs and tables, adults $29.99, children $17.99. Phone (229) 276–0755, (877) GA–RAILS, www.samshortline.com.

Roses and Pine Trees

The *Georgia Agrirama* is an off-the-beaten-path experience less than ¼-mile off the well-beaten path of I–75 exit 63B. About three dozen vintage farm buildings make up the state's agricultural heritage center. Inside the gates of this nineteenth-century time warp, youngsters may go nose to nose with friendly farmyard animals and take a trip on a steam-powered logging train. Cotton is planted in the old-fashioned way by a farmer in bib overalls commanding a mule and a plow. The village blacksmith hammers out nails and utensils over a white-hot forge. Sugarcane is harvested by hand and ground into syrup and corn into grits and meal at a picture-postcard gristmill. A country store sells handmade quilts, preserves, cookbooks, toys, and corn shuck dolls.

The Agrirama, P.O. Box Q, Tifton 31793, (229) 386–3344, (800) 767–1875, www.agrirama.com, is open year-round Tuesday through Saturday, 9:00 A.M. to 5:00 P.M. All-inclusive admission is $10.00 for adults, $8.00 for senior citizens 55 and over, $4.00 for children 4 to 16; free for children under 4.

Downtown Tifton has been revitalized thanks to the Georgia Main Street Program. About thirty shops and eateries are now attracting visitors to a complex of restored nineteenth- and early twentieth-century buildings. The 1906 Myon Hotel now houses City Hall, a permanent collection of regional art, shops, offices, and a restaurant. Contact the Tifton/Tift County Tourism Association, 100 South Central Avenue, Tifton 31794, (229) 382–6200, (800) 550–8438, www.tiftonchamber.org.

From 1870 to the turn of the new century, *Thomasville* was a Southern Newport, the forefather of Palm Beach and Miami. Encouraged by reports of the area's healthy climate, wealthy Northerners came by private train to spend the winter at grand hotels, which brought chefs and orchestras all the way from New York and Europe. Many regular visitors built their own lavish homes and purchased surrounding plantations for grouse and quail hunting. In the early 1900s, the rich and famous discovered Florida, and Thomasville's "Golden Age" was over. Left behind was a remarkable heritage. Presidents, aristocrats, and "commoners" still flock to the city of 20,000 to hunt game birds and antiques, tour homes and plantations, and participate in late April's Thomasville Rose Festival.

Stop first at the Thomasville/Thomas County Convention and Visitors Bureau, 401 South Broad Street, Thomasville, (229) 228–7977, (866) 577–3600, www.thomasvillega.com, where you can load up on maps, brochures, and self-guided walking and driving tour information. Guides can be arranged for tour groups. The Welcome Center is open Monday through Friday from 9:00 A.M. to 5:00 P.M. and Saturday from 10:00 A.M. to 3:00 P.M.

On your own, stop at the *Thomas County Historical Museum,* 725 North Dawson Street, Thomasville, (229) 226–7664, where you'll see hundreds of photos and souvenirs of the "Golden Age." It's open daily 2:00 to 5:00 P.M. Admission for adults is $4.00, for students $1.00.

Nearby, the *Lapham-Patterson House State Historic Site,* 626 North Dawson Street, Thomasville, (229) 225–4004, (800) 864–PARK, www.ga stateparks.org, is an outlandish Victorian mansion built for Chicago shoe man-ufacturer C.W. Lapham. Maintained as a state historical museum, the tri-winged, mustard-yellow mansion is highlighted by cantilevered interior

Lieutenant's Scrambled Dogs

Lieutenant Stevens, who prepared them for many years, has retired from active duty. Fortunately for those who can't get through a day without a Scrambled Dog, he passed on his recipe to the staff at Columbus' Dinglewood Pharmacy. They still prepare it by splitting and splaying two hot dogs on a bun in a banana split dish and dressing them with cheese, mustard, pickles, and a rich coating of Lieutenant's secret-recipe chili, topped with a shower of oyster crackers. Betcha can't eat more than one! Incidentally, Lieutenant is Stevens' real name. He was born on Armistice Day, 1931, and his parents wanted their son to honor America's armed forces. Dinglewood Pharmacy is at 1939 Wynnton Road, near downtown Columbus, (706) 322–0616.

balconies, double-flue chimneys, and fish-scale shingles. It's open Tuesday through Saturday from 9:00 A.M. to 5:00 P.M., Sunday from 2:00 to 5:00 P.M. Admission is $3.00 for adults, $1.00 for children 6 to 18; free for children 5 and under.

Pebble Hill Plantation (229–226–2344, www.pebblehill.com) is a "must-see." The twenty-eight-room Georgian and Greek Revival main house and the gardens, stables, and kennels were left as a museum by the late Pansy Ireland Poe. Inside the house are thirty-three original John James Audubon bird prints and extensive collections of silver, crystal, and antique furnishings. Five miles southwest of Thomasville, on Highway 319, Thomasville, it's open Tuesday through Saturday from 10:00 A.M. to 5:00 P.M. and Sunday from 1:00 to 5:00 P.M. Adult admission fee is $3.00 to the grounds, $7.00 to the main house; children under 6 not permitted in main house.

Melhana The Grand Plantation, 301 Showboat Lane, Thomasville, (888) 920–3030, www.melhana.com, is a nineteenth-century hunting plantation transformed into a five-star quality country inn. The 1825 Greek Revival manor house has eight guest rooms and suites tastefully furnished with antique repro-ductions, imported linens, fresh flowers, and private baths with whirlpool tubs for two. Other deluxe accommodations are in the former Williamsburg-style carriage house and dairy barns.

The dining room serves three daily gourmet meals, and room service is available twenty-four hours. Guests can swim in the heated, enclosed, Olympic-size pool, play tennis, and enjoy horsedrawn carriage rides around the forty-acre grounds. Quail hunting and horseback riding can be arranged. Doubles are expensive.

The *Thomasville Black Heritage Trail* was created by retired Air Force officer James "Jack" Hadley to give visitors an opportunity to learn about the city's rich African-American history. The two-and-a-half-hour "step-on, step-off" tour includes churches, historic sites, schools, cemeteries, businesses, parks, and a Black-owned bed-and-breakfast. More than a half dozen sites focus on the life of Lt. Henry Ossian Flipper, who was born a slave on a Thomasville area plantation in 1856 and twenty-one years later became the first Black grad-uate of the United States Military Academy at West Point. For information: Thomasville Black Heritage Tour, (229) 228–6983, www.rose.net/flipper.htm and www.thomasvillega.com/black_history.htm.

Several of Thomasville's most beautiful old homes welcome bed-and-breakfast guests. All take pride in their antique furnishings and traditional south Georgia hospitality. They include the AAA Four Diamond 1884 Paxton House, 445 Remington Avenue, (800) 278–0138, (229) 226–5797, www.paxtonhouse

inn.com; 1854 Wright House, 415 Fletcher Street, (229) 225–9922, www.wright house.com; Dawson Street Inn, 324 W. Dawson Street, (229) 226–7515; Evans House, 725 South Hansell Street, (229) 226–1343; The Magnolia Leaf, 501 East Washington Street, (229) 226–4499, www.magnolialeaf.com; Mitchell-Young-Anderson House, 319 Oak Street, (229) 226–3463; Cottage on the Park, 801 South Hansell Street, (229) 227–6327; and Serendipity Cottage, 339 East Jefferson Street, (229) 226–8111, (800) 383–7377, www.serendipitycottage.com. All have private baths, antiques, and personable hosts. Rates range from inexpensive to expensive. All are located in zip code 31792.

If you'd like to enjoy a bit of Thomasville's sporting life, shoot some skeet, and hunt birds and game, contact *Myrtlewood Plantation,* P.O. Box 32, Thomasville 31799, (229) 228–6232, www.myrtlewoodplantation.com.

Thomasville's really big annual event is the late-April *Rose Festival,* a week of parades, pageantry, home tours, and rose judgings that attracts visitors from many countries. In the good-news-bad-news category, the renowned Thomasville Rose Test Garden has closed, but it's been replaced by the *Thomasville Rose Garden,* which displays scores of varieties of blooming plants around the shores of Cherokee Lake, at the corner of Covington and Smith Avenues. Admission is free.

Places to Stay in Southwest Georgia

ALBANY

Hilton Garden Inn,
101 South Front Street,
(229) 888–1590,
www.albanygardeninn
New in 2005, the 125 room hotel, on the downtown riverfront near the Flint RiverQuarium, has a fitness center, pool, full-service restaurant and bar, business center and in-room high-speed Internet connections. Moderate to expensive.

BUENA VISTA

Sign of the Dove Bed & Breakfast and Restaurant,
Church Street and Fourth Avenue,
(229) 649–3663,
(888) 690–3663,
www.sign-of-thedove.com
Donna and Ray Armer's 1905 neoclassical home has three guest bedrooms and a guest cottage, near the Pasaquan attraction and Buena Vista's ("Bew-na Vista") courthouse square. The restaurant serves steaks and seafood on Friday nights and Sunday Southern buffet, with fried chicken, salad bar, veggies and desserts. Inexpensive to moderate.

LAGRANGE AREA

The House on Seventh,
311 East Seventh Street,
West Point,
(706) 645–2064.
The Queen Anne–style cottage was built in the early twentieth century in the small textile town of West Point, on the Georgia-Alabama border. Ira and Emily Culpepper have three guest rooms with private baths and period antiques, and serve a generous country breakfast. Inexpensive.

Thyme Away Bed and Breakfast,
508 Greenville Street,
LaGrange,
(706) 885–9625.
The imposing Greek Revival

house in downtown LaGrange has been returned to its 1840s elegance. Guest rooms are furnished with antiques, TV, phone, refrigerator, and private baths with whirlpool tubs and gas fireplaces. You can relax in the parlor, play the piano, and use the fax and modem services. Inexpensive rates include full breakfast.

COLUMBUS

Gates House,
737 Broadway,
(800) 891–3187,
fax (706) 324–2070.
A short walk from Riverwalk, Carolyn and Tom Gates's 1880 Colonial Revival house is a time-trip to the elegance of Victorian America. Guest rooms have family antiques, private baths, and queen or twin beds. You can have breakfast in the dining room, Victorian garden, or front porch. Inexpensive.

Marriott Columbus,
800 Front Avenue, at the Riverwalk,
(888) 228–6290
(706) 324–1800
The former Columbus Hilton is now flying the Marriott flag. Built partially in a nineteenth-century ironworks, the 177-room hotel has an outdoor pool, restaurant and bar, and meeting rooms. Located across from the Columbus Convention Center, a short walk from the Rivercenter for Performing Arts and downtown restaurants. Moderate.

Rothschild-Pound House,
201 Seventh Street,
(800) 585–4075,
fax (706) 322–4075,
www.thepoundhouseinn.com
Built in the 1870s, the

Second Empire–style showplace has ten guest suites with private baths, some with Jacuzzi. Original art and antiques are throughout the house. Innkeepers Mamie and Garry Pound offer full breakfast and evening cocktails. Moderate to expensive.

AMERICUS

The 1906 Pathway Inn,
501 South Lee Street,
(229) 928–2078 and
(800) 889–1466,
www.1906pathwayinn.com
Chuck and Angela Nolan's turn-of-the-century Victorian showplace is among the mansions and old trees in Americus's most beautiful residential neighborhood. Five guest rooms have private baths with whirlpools and king or queen beds. Inexpensive to moderate rates include full breakfast, wine, and refreshments.

Americus Garden Inn,
504 Rees Park,
(229) 931–0122,
(888) 758–4749,
www.americusgardeninn.com
Built between 1847 and 1848, Kim and Susan Egelseer's 5,000-square-foot home is set in an acre of walkways and gardens. Eight guest rooms have plush antique furnishings, large private baths, phone, TV, and ceiling fan. Three have tubs large enough for two, 12-foot ceilings, and original fireplace mantels. "Scarlett's Room" has an optional adjoining room that makes a two-bedroom suite. Well-mannered pets are welcome. Inexpensive to moderate.

CHULA

Hummingbird's Perch Bed & Breakfast,
I–75 exit 23, 5 miles north of Tifton, Route 1,
Box 1870, Chula,
(229) 382–5431.
Gracious country living, with bird-watching and fishing around a small lake. Three guest rooms, with private or shared bath. Inexpensive.

HAMILTON

Magnolia Hall Bed & Breakfast,
127 Barnes Mill Road,
(706) 628–4566,
www.bbonline.com/ga/magnoliahall
A grand 1890s Victorian mansion in the little Harris County town of Hamilton, 5 miles south of Callaway Gardens. Dale and Ken Smith's five large guest rooms have private baths and antiques. Full Southern breakfast is served in the formal dining room. Moderate.

Places to Eat in Southwest Georgia

COLUMBUS

The Cannon Brewpub,
1041 Broadway,
(706) 653–2337.
Pizza, pasta, burgers, steaks, and house brews in a lively pair of vintage downtown storefronts. Look for the Civil War cannon parked on the sidewalk. Open daily. Inexpensive.

Country's BBQ,
1329 Broadway,
(706) 596–8910.
Chattahoochee Valley-style
'cue—ribs, chopped pork,
chicken, and beef grilled over
green saplings—is served by
the big, saucy platesful in a
former Trailways bus depot in
downtown Columbus. Eat in
the station or an adjoining
old road warrior. Open daily.
Inexpensive.

**Minnie's Uptown
Restaurant,**
104 Eighth Street,
(706) 322–2766.
If you can't find Minnie's, just
follow your nose and look for
the crowds lining up out the
doors of the green cinder
block building near down-
town Columbus. Fried
chicken, fried fish, meat loaf,
turnip greens, stewed corn,
black-eyed peas, corn bread,
and cobblers, with big
glasses of sweet tea, keep
the place packed every day
but Sunday. Inexpensive.

Miriam's Cafe and Gallery,
1350 Thirteenth Street,
(706) 327–0707.
Enjoy fine American and continental cuisine in a cozy cafe
brightened by work of local
artists. Specialties include

seafood, filet mignon, pastas,
and chicken dishes. Lunch
Friday only, dinner Friday and
Saturday, Sunday brunch.
Moderate.

**The Olive Branch Cafe
& The Loft,**
1032 Broadway,
(706) 596–8141.
Columbus's choice for continental and American fare,
with some Greek flourishes
to its lamb loin with spinach
and olives, fried goat cheese,
salad, and moussaka. Other
house specialties include
steaks, seafood, and pasta.
Dinner Monday through
Saturday. After dinner go
upstairs to The Loft for jazz
and other live entertainment.

GEORGETOWN

Michelle's of Georgetown,
Highway 82,
(229) 334–5912.
Southern homecooking in all
its glory is on the daily
$6.75-all-you-can-eat break-
fast, lunch, and dinner buf-
fets at this popular dining
room on the Chattahoochee
River, across from Eufaula,
Alabama. Fresh vegetables,
fried chicken, chicken and
dumplings, barbecue, corn
bread, biscuits, sweet potato

soufflé, squash casserole,
homemade pies, and cakes
don't get any better than
this. On Sunday morning,
church-goers on both sides
of the Chattahoochee pray
for a short sermon so they
can beat their neighbors to
the serving line. Open daily.
Inexpensive.

PARROTT

The Chinaberry Cafe,
120 Main Street,
(229) 623–2233.
While exploring the antiques
and gift shops on tiny
Parrott's 1-block Main Street
(GA 520/280, between
Columbus and Albany), take
a break for delicious southwest Georgia homecooking
at The Chinaberry Cafe.
Lunch Tuesday through
Sunday and dinner Friday
and Saturday. Inexpensive.

PINE MOUNTAIN

**Chipley's Family
Restaurant,**
U.S. Highway 27,
(706) 663–2640.
Grits, biscuits, sausage, and
eggs for breakfast, and buffet lunch and dinner with
fried chicken, fish, meat loaf,
pork chops, vegetables, and

HELPFUL WEB SITES

**Americus-Sumter County
Tourism Council,**
www.gomm.com/americus

Pebble Hill Plantation,
www.webvista.com/sghtsee/pebble/

**Columbus Convention
& Visitors Bureau,**
www.columbusga.com/ccvb

**Massee Lane Camellia
Society Gardens,**
www.peach.lib.ga.us/ACS/acs.htm

desserts make this friendly, family-owned place a popular stop for Pine Mountain locals and Callaway Gardens visitors.

Cricket's Restaurant,
State Highway 18,
(706) 663–8136.
Features jambalaya, crawfish, blackened fish, oysters, shrimp, gumbo, and other Louisiana Cajun and Creole favorites.

Mandella's Italian Restaurant,
U.S. 27,
(706) 663–7736.
Pastas, pizza, parmagianas, beer, and wine in downtown Pine Mountain's shopping area. Lunch and dinner Tuesday through Saturday.

Rose Cottage,
111 East Broad Street,
(706) 663–7877.
English tea, sandwiches, soup, salads, desserts, wine. Lunch daily.

WARM SPRINGS

The Bulloch House,
on Highway 27 just off Warm Springs's main street,
(706) 655–9057.
Really big appetites should check out the buffet line. Inexpensive.

The Victorian Tea Room,
Broad Street,
Highway 27, downtown
(706) 655–3508.
A 1906 mercantile store has been turned into a cozy dining room specializing in soups, salads, sandwiches, and Southern home cooking. It's open for lunch Tuesday through Sunday and for dinner Friday only. Inexpensive.

THOMASVILLE

The Billiard Academy,
South Broad Street,
(912) 226–9981.
Thomasvillians can't seem to get through a day without chowing on Joe Kirkland's hot dogs, dressed in his special chili sauce. Out-of-towners drive miles for their daily fix. Folks in a hurry get 'em to go at the sidewalk window. If you've a little more time, step inside for a friendly game at the billiard tables and have a cool brew and a chat with the boys at the lunch counter/bar. Dogs and billiards are available from early morning to late at night, Monday through Saturday. Inexpensive.

Dunbar's BBQ,
1984 Smith Avenue,
(229) 225–1085.
Dunbar's all-you-can-eat lunch buffet, under $10, includes ribs, pork barbecue, fried chicken, a half-dozen vegetables, and desserts. Dinner plates include barbecue, chicken, and fish. Lunch, dinner Monday through Saturday. Inexpensive.

George & Louie's,
217 Remington Avenue,
(912) 226–1218.
Fresh seafood plates, channel catfish, snapper, broiled and fried shrimp and oysters, scallops, burgers and shish kebab, steaks, and sandwiches draw big crowds for dinner Monday through Saturday.

The Homecoming,
1164 Myrick Road,
(912) 226–1143.
A short drive out of town, this former country cabin with a big front porch is a nostalgic old-timey place for all-you-can-eat catfish and quail, and fried, boiled, and grilled shrimp, oysters, scallops, fried chicken, and Delmonico steak. A kids-under-12 menu has smaller portions of catfish, shrimp, and chicken, as well as hot dogs, hamburgers, and PB&J sandwiches. Dinner Monday through Saturday. Inexpensive to moderate.

Melissa's,
134 Madison Avenue,
(912) 228–9844.
Cleverly redone laundry warehouse does a great job with beer-battered shrimp, quesadillas, chicken tarragon, black bean cakes, pastas, grilled double-cut pork chops, and chicken tacos. Lunch and dinner Monday through Saturday. Inexpensive to moderate.

Mom & Dad's Italian Restaurant,
1800 Smith Avenue,
(912) 226–6265.
Traditional Italian pastas, seafood, chicken, veal, steak, and other American fare. Dinner Tuesday through Saturday. Moderate.

The Plaza,
217 South Broad Street,
(912) 226–5153.
An old, old favorite, The Plaza has served steaks, seafood, prime rib, and Greek dishes for nearly eighty years. Breakfast, lunch, and dinner Monday through Saturday. Moderate.

Southeast Georgia

BBQ and Harness Horses

The **New Perry Hotel** has been a beacon for middle Georgia travelers since the 1920s, when it replaced a circa-1854 country inn. In bygone days, when Highway 41 funneled Florida-bound vacationers through the center of Perry, the New Perry's cheerful guest rooms—and especially its dining room—were a command performance. Even now, with most of the traffic a mile away on I–75, weary motorists still find their way to this surviving vestige of small-town hospitality.

Set among trees and gardens, across from the Houston (pronounced HOUSE-ton) County Courthouse, the New Perry has twenty-six rooms in its main building and seventeen more in a modern motel-type addition by the swimming pool. They're nice, comfortable, air-conditioned, and inexpensive, but the dining room is the main attraction.

With its starched white tablecloths, fresh flowers, and bird and floral prints, this is the genteel Southern dining room personified. The menu is the chapter-and-verse Sunday Southern dinner: fried chicken, broiled Spanish mackerel and perch, baked ham, turkey and dressing, stewed corn, turnip greens, yams, green beans, congealed salads, shrimp cocktail, and

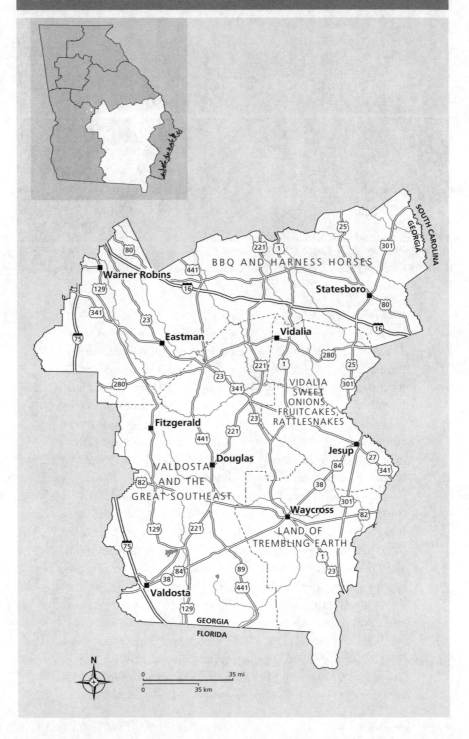

SOUTHEAST GEORGIA

SOUTH CAROLINA
GEORGIA

BBQ AND HARNESS HORSES

Warner Robins

Statesboro

Eastman

Vidalia

VIDALIA
SWEET
ONIONS,
FRUITCAKES,
RATTLESNAKES

Fitzgerald

Jesup

Douglas

VALDOSTA
AND THE
GREAT SOUTHEAST

Waycross

LAND OF
TREMBLING EARTH

Valdosta

GEORGIA
FLORIDA

N

0   35 mi
0   35 km

pecan and peach pies. Breakfast is also the full Southern board of grits, hot biscuits, sausage, ham, and eggs.

Breakfast, lunch, and dinner are served daily, at prices that are inexpensive to expensive. The Tavern Pub has a full bar and a casual menu. Contact the New Perry at 800 Main Street, Perry, (478) 987–1000 or (800) 877–3779, www.newperryhotel.com.

Henderson Village, a luxurious country inn and restaurant 10 miles south of Perry, is an Old South dream come true for German electronics manufacturer Bernard Schneider. As a youngster in postwar Munich, Schneider was fascinated by *Gone With the Wind* and other movies depicting the romanticized antebellum South. In the 1980s Schneider bought 8,000 acres of farmland, began restoring vintage Southern country houses, and created Middle Georgia's nicest resort.

Guests stay in twenty-eight designer-decorated rooms and suites with deluxe private baths, feather beds, fireplaces, stereos, TVs, and CD players. In

SOUTHEAST GEORGIA'S TOP HITS

New Perry Hotel	Okefenokee Swamp Park
Museum of Aviation	Laura S. Walker State Park
Big Pig Jig	Suwannee Canal Recreation Area
Georgia Cotton Museum	Stephen C. Foster State Park
Harness Racing Festival	Valdosta
George L. Smith State Park	The Crescent
Magnolia Springs State Park	Hahira Honeybee Festival
Statesboro	Reed Bingham State Park
University Museum	Jefferson Davis Memorial State Historic Site
Center for Wildlife Education and Lamar Q. Ball Jr. Raptor Center	General Coffee State Park
Vidalia Sweet Onion	Douglas's public golf courses
Rattlesnake Roundup	Blue and Gray Museum
Lake Grace	Statue of Liberty
Edwin L. Hatch Nuclear Plant Visitors Center	Little Ocmulgee State Park

the dining room, in the early 1900s Langston House, the European chef prepares upscale American and continental cuisine, with a full bar. Things to do include horseback riding, swimming in the outdoor pool, skeet shooting, fishing, and quail hunting. You can help feed sheep, goats, llamas, and other tame creatures in the barnyard. Take I–75 exit 127 and go 1 mile south to Highway 26 in the unincorporated community of Henderson. Moderate to expensive double occupancy rates include full breakfast. Phone (478) 988–8696 or (888) 615–9722, www.hendersonvillage.com.

The **Museum of Aviation and Georgia Aviation Hall of Fame** (478–926–6870, 888–807–3359, www.museumofaviation.org), 2 miles south of Warner Robins Air Force Base, is a tribute to our winged military might. In two huge buildings you can admire more than ninety American and foreign military aircraft. You can also see a film on the history of the Air Force and numerous exhibits and displays. The Aviation Hall of Fame honors men and women who have made significant contributions to aviation in Georgia. Take I–75 exit 146 (Centerville/Warner Robins) and follow the signs through the city of Warner Robins. Open daily from 10:00 A.M. to 5:00 P.M. Free admission. P.O. Box 2469, Warner Robins 31099.

After touring the Museum of Aviation, tuck into a hearty, perfectly cooked sirloin or T-bone with sautéed mushrooms, vegetables, and baked potato at **Montana's** (478–929–9555), 2212 Watson Boulevard, Warner Robins, and enjoy it with beer or wine. Dinner is served Monday through Saturday.

Barbecue is dear to Georgians' hearts, celebrated in song and story, and exalted at annual festivals such as the **Big Pig Jig** the second weekend of October at the little middle-Georgia town of Vienna (pronounced VIGH-enna). Dubbed the "Cadillac of Barbecue Contests" and proclaimed the state of Georgia's official barbecue cooking contest by the state legislature, this is serious

BILL'S FAVORITES

New Perry Hotel Dining Room	Suwannee Canal Recreation Area
Museum of Aviation	Stephen C. Foster State Park
Big Pig Jig	Lamar Q. Ball Jr. Raptor Center
Harness Racing Festival	Blue and Gray Museum
Okefenokee Swamp Park	

business indeed. The winning team takes home prize money, trophies, bragging rights, and the honor of representing Georgia at the annual International Pig Cook-off in Memphis, Tennessee—and just maybe coming back as world champion of the barbecuing arts.

Of course, there's a fun side to all this serious business. Judges sample the secret sauces, which, according to the rules, may include "any nonpoisonous substances" and the flavors and textures of ribs, shoulders, and other succulent portions of the porkers. Famished festivalgoers also get their chance to savor the entries in a "People's Choice" competition and take part in a host of other activities. There's always plenty of bluegrass and country music, square dancing and clog dancing, arts and crafts, a 5-kilometer "Hog Jog," and a "Whole Hog Parade," featuring handsome porkers, still not ready for the grill, decked out in all manner of zany costumes.

For information, contact Dooly County Chamber of Commerce, 117 East Union Street, Vienna 31092, (229) 268–8275, www.doolychamber.com and www .bigpigjig.com.

Cotton may no longer be king, but it's still important to the economy of Dooly and other southeastern Georgia counties. At harvest time in September and October, the white bolls cover the ground like fresh-fallen snow. The **Georgia Cotton Museum,** I–75 exit 109, Vienna, (229) 268–2045, created by farmers and other Dooly Countians, looks at "white gold's" past, present, and future with artifacts, displays, and tools that planted, plowed, and harvested the cotton in the days before mechanized farming. It also looks at the dark side, the slave labor that was vital to its production. It's at 1321 East Union Street, Vienna. Open Monday through Saturday from 9:00 A.M. to 4:30 P.M. Admission is free.

Hawkinsville, the Pulaski County seat, is Georgia's harness racing capital. The **Harness Racing Festival,** the first weekend of April, celebrates this sport, which has been a part of Pulaski County's life since the late 1800s, when the county's mild climate made it a popular winter training grounds for harness horses from the Midwest, the Northeast, and Canada.

Nowadays, more than 350 of the sleek, high-stepping trotters and pacers come to the town of 4,000 between October and April. On the two-day festival weekend, more than 10,000 spectators crowd the grandstand at the festival grounds to watch the races and enjoy the country fair atmosphere that surrounds the red clay track. For those not familiar with the sport, the horses have two decidedly different gaits. Pacers wear plastic leg hoops (called hobbles) that cause the legs on each side of their body to move in tandem: left front and left rear, right front and right rear. Trotters navigate with a diagonal gait: left front and right rear legs move together, likewise right front and left rear. They seem to effortlessly pull the colorfully silked jockeys riding behind them in light two-wheeled sulkies.

After the festival the horses pack up and head for the big-money tracks up north. One thing missing from the event is parimutuel betting. Georgia law prohibits it, but that doesn't mean you can't find some friendly unofficial wagers around the track. For information, call the Lawrence Bennett harness training facility at (478) 892–3240. It's on Highway 129, Hawkinsville.

Away from the track, Hawkinsville's main attraction is its restored early-twentieth-century opera house. Built in early 1907 as a stop on the vaudeville circuit between New York and New Orleans, the **Old Opera House** was abandoned in the 1950s and was about to fall totally into ruins when a group of Pulaski County businesspeople came to its rescue a few years ago. Now it hosts touring concerts and local productions. If you're here when an event is scheduled, come and spend a nostalgic evening in the restored horseshoe-shaped auditorium, 100 North Lumpkin Street, Hawkinsville, (478) 783–1884, www .hawkinsville.org.

Several antiques shops are on Broad Street, Hawkinsville's main street. For other information call **Hawkinsville-Pulaski County Chamber of Commerce,** 108 North Lumpkin Street, Hawkinsville 31036, (478) 783–1717.

Lovers of finely crafted cemetery art should have a "Kodak moment" at **Orphans Cemetery** in Eastman. It's the legacy of the late Albert G. "A.G." Williamson. Born in North Carolina in the mid-1800s, Williamson and his five brothers were orphaned by the Civil War and moved to Dodge County, where they were collectively known as "The Orphans." A.G., the oldest, became a wealthy landowner. In 1887 he learned of the untimely death of a neighbor's 3-year-old son and deeded land for Orphans Cemetery, across from Orphans Christian Church. He planted a magnolia tree by the boy's grave that still blooms every summer. Before his own death, Williamson commissioned a sculptor in Carrara, Italy (where Michelangelo found the right stuff for "David"), to carve the cemetery's masterpiece, a marble-columned canopy with life-size statues of himself, his wife, and nephew for the family mausoleum. The sculptor created the realistic images with only photos to work from. Eastman is on Highway 341, between McRae and Hawkinsville. Contact the Eastman/Dodge County Chamber of Commerce Welcome Center, 116 Ninth Avenue, Eastman 31023, (478) 374–4723, www.eastman-georgia.com.

Jaybird Springs, a recreation area in the small community of Chauncey, 4 miles south of Eastman, owes its beginnings to an accident that became a legend. In the 1800s a logger who injured his leg allegedly followed a blue jay to a natural spring bubbling from the ground. He bathed his leg in the spring's mineral waters and was healed. When word got around, people came to test the waters for themselves. Sensing an opportunity, the landowner built a 60-foot-by-100-foot spring-fed swimming pool, and people still come to heal their weary spirits, if not their ailing bodies. Around the pool they can enjoy a water slide and roller skating rink, ball fields, picnic grounds, putt-putt golf, and campgrounds. The park is off Highway 341, at 1221 Jay Bird Springs Road, Chauncey, (229) 868–2728.

That wonderful but sadly fading American landmark, the small-town cafe, is alive and well in **Dublin. Ma Hawkins Cafe** (478–275–1713), near the Laurens County Courthouse at 124 West Jackson Street, Dublin, has been a citadel of Southern home cooking since 1931. Now operated by a grandson of the foundress, the cheerful cafe specializes in Southern-style breakfast—if you've been timid about sampling grits, Ma Hawkins is the place—and lunch and dinner plates highlighted by corn bread, chicken and dumplings, fried chicken, slowly simmered turnip greens and other fresh vegetables, and homemade desserts. The cafe is open for breakfast, lunch, and dinner Monday through Saturday. No credit cards are accepted, but it's hard to spend more than $10.

Dublin's nineteenth-century Irish heritage is reflected in its annual **St. Patrick's Day Festival,** a lively round of parades, beauty pageants, arts and crafts, square dancing, softball, and golf tournaments. Along the emerald-green lawns of the city's **Bellevue Avenue,** many photogenic Greek Revival and Victorian showplaces parade year-round. Less genteel, but a lot of good-natured fun, **East Dublin's Redneck Games,** in early July, pits competitors in such feats as armpit serenade, bobbing for pigs' feet in plastic buckets, the hubcap hurl, watermelon seed spitting, and pond diving—judged on your form as you belly flop into a gooey pit of wet Georgia red clay. Dublin radio station WQZY-FM came up with the games to spoof Atlanta's 1996 Summer Olympics. For information call (478) 272–4422.

George L. Smith State Park, off Highway 23, 4 miles southeast of Twin City, is a quiet retreat with twenty-one fully equipped camping sites, furnished cottages, picnic areas, and a fishing lake with rental boats. An 1880s covered bridge with a working gristmill is the park's scenic landmark. Cornmeal from the mill is sold in the park office. Write P.O. Box 57, Twin City 30471, or call (478) 763–2759 or (800) 864–PARK for camping reservations. Two very nice bed-and-breakfasts are in the Emanuel County seat of Swainsboro: **Coleman House** (478–237–9100, www.colemanhouseinn.com), 323 North Main Street and **Edenfield House Inn** (478–237–3007, www.bbonline.com/ga/edenfield), 426 West Church Street. Both are inexpensive.

Michael Guido Gardens is a lush little oasis 2 miles from I–16 exit 104 at Metter. Adjoining Sower Studios, where TV evangelist Michael Guido, D.D., produces his national "Seed from the Sower" broadcasts, "God's Three Acres" is planted with shade trees, flowers, Biblical topiaries, and a topiary of Guido himself. Fountains and waterfalls splash, birds sing, and a brook winds past gazebos, benches, and a 24-7 chapel. In December the gardens are illuminated with Christmas lights and Nativity scenes. Visitors can tour the broadcast studios Monday through Friday and meet the Sower in person. The gardens are open daily, free of charge, 600 Lewis Street, Metter, (912) 685–2222, www.guidogardens.org. As you exit I–16, stop at the Metter Welcome Center, in a former lumber company commissary, for information on Guido Gardens and other area attractions. Phone (912) 685–6988, (888) 704–3431, www.metter-candler.com.

Magnolia Springs State Park, Highway 25, 5 miles north of Millen, is one of the prettiest and quietest in the whole park system. Huge old trees bend

---

TOP ANNUAL EVENTS

St. Patrick's Day Festival,
March 17, Dublin,
(912) 272–5546

Old South Farm Days,
mid-March, Tea Grove Plantation,
Walthourville,
(912) 368–7412

Harness Racing Festival,
first weekend in April, Hawkinsville,
(912) 783–1717

Baxley Tree Festival,
early April, Tri-County Fairgrounds,
Baxley,
(912) 367–7731

Sweet Onion Century Bike Ride,
early April, Vidalia,
(912) 538–5892

Mossy Creek Barnyard Festival,
mid-April, I–75 near Perry,
(912) 922–8265

Okefenokee Art Festival & Earth Day Celebration,
mid-April, Okefenokee National Wildlife Refuge, Folkston,
(912) 897–1184

Vidalia Onion Festival,
late April–early May,
(912) 538–8687

Georgia National Fair,
early October, Georgia National Fairgrounds & Agricenter, Perry,
(912) 988–6483

Big Pig Jig,
second weekend in October, Vienna,
(912) 268–4500

Dublin Antique Fair Show and Sale,
mid-November, National Guard Armory, Dublin,
(912) 272–5546

Buzzard Day,
first Saturday of December, Reed Bingham State Park, Adel,
(912) 896–3551

Hazlehurst Holiday Tours,
mid-December, Hazlehurst,
(912) 375–4543

their limbs over clear springs flowing at an estimated nine million gallons a day. It's a lovely spot to spread a picnic. You can also swim, dabble your bait for fish, and walk along nature trails. You may even want to camp out overnight or stay in a furnished cottage. There is a $2.00 per visit parking fee. Contact Magnolia Springs State Park, Route 5, Box 488, Millen 30442, (478) 982–1660 or (800) 864–PARK, www.gastateparks.org, for camping and cottage reservations.

Adjoining the park, the **Bo Ginn Aquarium and Aquatic Education Center** has twenty-six tanks showing off many species of Georgia fish. Call (478) 982–4168, www.gastateparks.org.

Tree-shaded **Statesboro** (population 21,000) is the Bulloch County seat and home of 14,000 Georgia Southern University students. The **University Museum,** (912) 681–5444, http://welcome.georgiasouthern.edu/museum news/, has a fascinating collection of dinosaur fossils, do-touch exhibits, and revolving scientific and technological displays. The "star" attraction is the **Plant Vogtle Whale,** a 45-million-year-old leviathan that scientists believe walked on sturdy legs. It was discovered at Georgia Power Company's Plant Vogtle in neighboring Burke County.

The **Center for Wildlife Education and Lamar Q. Ball Jr. Raptor Center,** Georgia Southern University, Statesboro, (800) 568–3301 and (912) 681–0831, www.welcomegeorgiasouthern.edu/wildlife, is Georgia Southern's most popular attraction. Visitors follow a self-guided nature walk through six natural habitats that house fourteen birds of prey native to Georgia. They include bald eagles, falcons, ospreys, hawks, and several types of owls. They were rescued after being injured and can't return to the wild. Look up and you'll see a bald eagle camped in a hot tub–size aerie in the forks of a live oak tree, an osprey perched on a limb overlooking a cypress swamp, and a barred owl roosting in the rafters of an old barn strung with sheaves of drying tobacco. The center was designed by naturalist Jim Fowler, former host of Mutual of Omaha's *Wild Kingdom* TV series. Fowler also designed Albany's Chehaw Wild Animal Park. The center is open Monday through Friday from 9:00 A.M. to 5:00 P.M. and Saturday and Sunday from 1:00 to 5:00 P.M. Free admission.

Near the campus, the ten-acre **Botanical Gardens** grow around a restored nineteenth-century farmhouse and outbuildings. The gardens are open dawn to dusk daily; free admission. After trekking around the gardens, bring your best boardinghouse reach to the **Beaver House Inn & Restaurant,** 121 South Main Street, Statesboro, (912) 764–2821. The dining room table groans under a delicious family-style buffet that includes fried chicken, fish, baked ham, roast beef, and numerous vegetables, relishes, and desserts. It's open for lunch daily, dinner daily except Sunday. **Vandy's Barbecue,** downtown at 22 Vine Street, Statesboro, (912) 764–2444, is another culinary landmark.

The Victorian/Federal-style **Statesboro Inn and Restaurant,** built in 1872, is a lovely bed-and-breakfast near downtown Statesboro and the Georgia Southern campus. It's located at 106 South Main Street, Statesboro, (912) 489–8628 or (800) 846–9466, fax (912) 489–4785, www.Statesboroinn.com. Architectural features include a spacious veranda, Palladian windows, and numerous brass and wood treatments. Guests stay in the main house or the adjacent Craftsman-style Brannen House. All nineteen rooms have private baths, antiques, phones, and cable TV. The dining room's upscale fare features duck, chicken, seafood, beef, and elegant desserts. Dinner Monday through Saturday. Moderate.

Statesboro is a short drive north of I–16 exit 116, 60 miles west of Savannah. Contact Convention and Visitors Bureau, 332 South Main Street, Statesboro 30458, (800) 568–3301, or log on to www.visit-statesboro.com.

Vidalia Sweet Onions, Fruitcakes, Rattlesnakes

The sandy soil of Toombs, Treutlen, and neighboring southeastern Georgia counties yields a favorite gourmet delicacy. The well-known **Vidalia sweet onion** takes its name from the Toombs County town of Vidalia. During the summer, you can buy 'em by the sackful or carload at roadside stands in and around the town of 10,000. For information on farm tours, phone (912) 538–8687, www.vidaliaga.com.

Claxton, seat of Evans County, a short drive south of I–16 exit 116, is famous for fruitcakes and rattlesnakes. As you drive into the small town, you're very nearly intoxicated by the sweet aroma of baking fruitcakes. More than six million pounds of the holiday treats are produced annually in Claxton's modern bakeries. You can get information on **fruitcake plant tours** and other area attractions at the Claxton Welcome Center, 4 North Duval Street, Claxton 30417, (912) 739–1391, www.claxtonevanschamber.com.

If you're here in mid-March, you can take part in the festivities surrounding the annual **Rattlesnake Roundup.** Begun, simply, in 1968 as an effort to reduce the venomous reptile's threat to man and beast, the roundup has grown into a major happening, with a parade, hundreds of arts and crafts booths, home cooking, and such rattler-related events as awards for the most snakes brought in, the longest, the fattest, and so on. A reptile expert "milks" the snakes of their deadly venom, which is used in antivenom serums and other medicines.

Ever wonder what twenty-five million crickets sound like? The answer is at **Armstrong's Cricket Farm** in Glennville. Purportedly the world's largest

Sweet, Sweet Vidalia Onions

Vidalia onions are so sweet that many people eat 'em like apples or dressed up like this:

HONEY BAKED ONIONS

Preheat oven to 325°.

Peel and trim 4 large, white, Vidalia sweet onions. Cut in half and place in a buttered baking dish, flat sides up.

In a separate bowl mix:

1½ cups tomato juice

1½ cups water

6 teaspoons melted butter

6 teaspoons honey

Pour sauce over onions. Bake for one hour, or until soft.

VIDALIA ONION TART

This dish takes a little time, but it's worth it.

Tart dough:

2 cups plus l tablespoon flour

Pinch of salt

5¼ ounces butter, chilled and cut into small pieces

¼ cup ice water

Filling for tart:

3 Vidalia onions, chopped

2 tablespoons butter

1 cup heavy cream

1 whole egg, plus one additional egg yolk

Salt, pepper, nutmeg, and cumin seeds

1 tablespoon bacon, finely minced and sautéed

For the tart, place flour and salt in a mixing bowl. Add butter and work into the flour. Add water and form into dough (don't work dough too much). Chill at least two hours. Roll out dough to ⅛-inch thickness and fit into pie pan. Prick the dough all over with a fork. Set aside.

Sauté onions in butter just until tender. Add heavy cream and reduce until it thickens. Remove from the heat and mix in the beaten egg and additional egg yolk. Season to taste with salt, pepper, and nutmeg (freshly ground if possible). Pour filling into prepared tart shell and sprinkle finely minced bacon and cumin seeds on top. Bake on the bottom rack of a preheated 425° oven 20 to 25 minutes, or until done. Serves 6.

cricket farm, Armstrong's sells buckets full of the chirping insects to anglers and reptile farms, where they're fed to snakes, frogs, and lizards. Owner Jeff Armstrong says, "One cricket in a room will drive you crazy, but twenty-five million sounds like a big humming engine." Find out for yourself at the cricket farm, which is open Monday through Saturday, 306 Gordon Street, Glennville, 15 miles south of I–16 exit 116/Georgia Highway 301/25, (912) 654–3408.

In neighboring Tattnall County, **Gordonia-Altamaha State Park,** P.O. Box 1047, Reidsville 30453, (912) 557–7744, has twenty-five tent and trailer sites with water and electricity, hot showers, and restrooms, as well as a swimming pool, a boat dock, and plenty of good fishing places. There's also a new nine-hole golf course. Call (800) 864–PARK or log on to www.gastateparks.org for camping reservations.

If you're a fishing family, you may come close to nirvana in Wayne County. One county removed from the Atlantic Coast, Wayne includes 60 miles of the **Altamaha River,** a waterway rich with several varieties of bass, bream, perch, and catfish. **Altamaha River Campground,** 249 Joe Naia Road, Jesup, (912) 586–6300, has three big fishing lakes, a spring-fed swimming lake, campsites, and nature trails.

Lake Grace, on Highway 301 near the Wayne County seat of Jesup, is a local favorite. The 250 acres include plenty of secluded fishing spots, as well as opportunities for boating, swimming, waterskiing, picnics, and camping. Contact the park superintendent at (912) 579–6475.

Pine Lake Campground (912–427–3664), Highway 341 near the small community of Gardi, features a stocked twenty-acre lake tailored for bank fishing. You can also enjoy a swimming pool, shaded picnic areas, and forty campsites with electricity, water, and restrooms.

Jaycee Landing (912–427–7987), on Highway 301 north, Jesup, has a number of boat ramps in the Altamaha, as well as a general store with food and all your favorite kinds of fishing bait. Campsites have water, electricity, restrooms, and showers.

For more information on recreational lakes and rivers, working farm tours, golf courses, fairs, and festivals, contact the Jesup-Wayne County Chamber of Commerce, 124 Northwest Broad Street, Jesup 31545, (912) 427–2028, (888) 224–5983, www.waynechamber.org.

When you've bagged your limit, enjoy a large sample of Southeast Georgia cooking at **Jones' Kitchen,** on Main Street in Jesup, (912) 427–4100. The all-you-can-eat daily luncheon spread includes fresh local fish, chicken, meat loaf, vegetables, several kinds of salads, and a peach or apple cobbler for less than you'd pay for lunch at a fast-food outlet.

Jesup, an industrious town of 10,000, has a number of beautifully main-tained Victorian homes, which you can drive past with a brochure provided by the chamber of commerce.

The **Edwin L. Hatch Nuclear Plant Visitors Center,** on U.S. Highway 1 (11036 Hatch Parkway, Baxley), 14 miles north of the center of Baxley, will tell you all you ever wanted to know about this controversial source of energy. The story is told with films, hands-on exhibits, and animated displays. Open Monday through Friday from 8:30 A.M. to 5:00 P.M. Phone (912) 367–3668 or (800) 722–7774, www.baxley.org. Admission is free.

You can unwind at 170-acre **Lake Mayers,** a locally popular resort with fishing, boating, swimming, waterskiing, and picnic areas. Lake Mayers is off U.S. Highway 341, 8 miles west of Baxley, (912) 367–8190, www.baxley.org.

Nonmembers may play the **Appling Country Club's** 9-hole golf course, 4628 Hatch Parkway, Baxley, (912) 367–3582. Contact Baxley-Appling County Tourism Board, 305 West Parker Street, Baxley 31513, (912) 367–7731, www.baxley.org.

Land of Trembling Earth

Okefenokee Swamp Park, off Highway 1, 8 miles south of Waycross, is the most popular of three entrances to the vast, mysterious "Land of Trembling Earth." Although most of the park is actually outside the boundaries of the 700-square-mile, 412,000-acre Okefenokee Swamp National Wildlife Refuge, guided boat tours and cypress boardwalks lead you well into this fascinating world.

The Swamp Park is the most casual visitor-oriented of the three entrances—the others are in neighboring Charlton County—with numerous exhibits, inter-pretive centers, wildlife shows, and other visual displays.

Stop first at the cedar-roofed welcome center adjacent to the paved park-ing areas. Mounted wildlife exhibits and the real thing viewed through one-way windows, along with a twenty-minute film, are an excellent orientation. From there, climb the 90-foot observation tower, peer into the dark tannic waters from the boardwalk, and see some of the Okefenokee's three dozen varieties of reptiles at the Serpentarium.

Gate admission—$12 for adults, $11 for children 5 to 11; free for children under 5—includes all exhibits and shows. A half-hour, one-hour, or two-hour boat tour ($16, $20, $30) includes an even more extensive look at the hundreds of species of birds, otter, armadillo, black bear, deer, and other critters that inhabit the swamp. You'll also see some of the 15,000 gators as they cruise among the reeds and cypresses like ironclad gunboats.

If this two-hour sojourn was too brief, you can arrange with park officials for a guide who'll boat you back into really deep waters, where you can see what songwriter Stephen Foster only fantasized: the headwaters of the Suwannee River, which rise in the swamp and flow into Florida.

Okefenokee Swamp Park, U.S. Highway 1 South, Waycross, (912) 283–0583, www.okeswamp.com, is open daily in spring and summer from 9:00 A.M. to 6:30 P.M., fall and winter from 9:00 A.M. to 5:30 P.M.

Two other attractions also mirror the swamp's colorful heritage. *Obediah's Okefenok* (5115 Swamp Road, Waycross, 912–287–0090, www.okefenokee swamp.com), on a small island at the swamp's southwestern edge, was the early 1800s home of the Obediah Barber family. Their restored cabin and outbuildings are filled with authentic tools and household necessities. Open daily. Admission is $4.50 for adults, $3.50 for seniors 55 and older, and $3.00 for children 6 to 17.

The *Okefenokee Heritage Center,* 1460 North Augusta Avenue near downtown Waycross, is an indoor/outdoor museum with historical displays, artwork, a 1912 locomotive and depot, an 1840s farmhouse, a print shop, and antique vehicles. Open daily. Admission is $3.00 for adults, $2.00 for children. Phone (912) 285–4260, www.okeheritage.org.

Nearby *Laura S. Walker State Park and Golf Course,* Waycross, (912) 287–4900, has campsites with water, electricity, showers, and restrooms ($10 a night); a swimming pool; a playground; a golf course; fishing; and picnic tables. There is a $2.00 parking fee. For reservations call (800) 864–PARK, www.gastate parks.org or contact Waycross and Okefenokee Tourism Bureau, 315-A Plant Avenue, Waycross 31503, (912) 283–3744, www.okefenokeetourism.com.

Three gateways lead you into the primeval mysteries of the 412,000-acre *Okefenokee Swamp National Wildlife Refuge.* Suwannee Canal Recreation Area and Stephen C. Foster State Park are in Charlton County, while the Okefenokee Swamp Park is near Waycross, in Ware County.

Administered by the U.S. Fish and Wildlife Service, *Suwannee Canal Recreation Area* is what remains of one man's frustrated efforts to drain the Okefenokee back in the 1880s. He left behind an 11-mile-long waterway that now provides an easy avenue for boaters, anglers, and sightseers. *Okefeno-kee Adventures,* Route 2, Box 3325, Folkston 31537, (912) 496–7156, (866) THESWAMP, www.okefenokeeadventures.com, is the U.S. Fish and Wildlife Service's concessionaire. It offers one- and two-hour nighttime and overnight guided boat tours through the swamp, where you'll see many of the swamp's thousands of gators, turtles, fish, egrets, heron and other bird species, and learn a great deal about this primordial environment. The tour boats are covered with a canopy, but be sure to bring sunscreen, insect repellent, and bottled water. You can also rent motor boats, canoes, kayaks, and bicycles. But be aware that getting lost in the swamp's many tributaries is very easy. The Concession Building stocks groceries, cold drinks, fishing gear, bug spray, and other necessities. The Camp Cornelia Cafe prepares sandwiches and salads.

The nearby **Robert S. Bolt Visitors Center** has a fifteen-minute orientation film and interpretive exhibits on the swamp's plant and animal life, some of which you can see from nature trails, a boardwalk, and an observation tower.

A short drive from the concession building and museum, **Chesser Island Homestead** is the pine and cypress cabin once home to several generations of the Chesser family.

Okefenokee Swamp Park

Suwannee Canal Recreation Area, Route 2, Box 336, Folkston 31537, (912) 496–7836, is open daily sunrise to sunset. A $4.00 gate fee is charged at the Folkston entrance by the Okefenokee Swamp National Wildlife Refuge. Drive on Highway 121/23 for 8 miles south of Folkston, then turn right (west) at the Okefenokee Refuge sign and continue 3 miles.

Stephen C. Foster State Park, (912) 637–5274, is so far off Georgia's beaten path that to get there from Suwannee Canal you'll have to detour through northeastern Florida. From Suwannee Canal, drive 15 miles south on Highway 23 to St. George, 37 miles west on Highway 94 and Highway 2 in Florida, and back into Georgia at Fargo. From Fargo, go right on Highway 177 and for 18 miles cross a domain of sentinel pines and palmetto thickets, swampy canals, egrets, great blue heron, deer, gators, armadillos, opossum, raccoons, reptiles, and amphibians. Beyond a sign warning that the gates close between sundown and sunup, you arrive at Stephen Foster's compound.

The state park is an eighty-acre island entirely within the Okefenokee Swamp National Wildlife Refuge. Rangers conduct boat tours, replete with swamp legends and lore, practical lessons in fauna and flora, and lots of hilarious tall tales. You're bound to see plenty of gators, exotic birds and plants, turtles, and trees. You may also rent boats and canoes and venture forth on your own. There are also a ¼-mile hiking trail, picnic shelters, a playground, and a small museum.

Staying overnight, serenaded by the symphony of the swamp, is an unforgettable experience. Campsites with electricity, water, hot showers, and restrooms are available, as are two-bedroom cottages completely furnished with full kitchens and fireplaces, heat, and air-conditioning. There is a $2.00 per visit parking fee. The park's small grocery has minimal supplies, so be sure to stock up before leaving Fargo.

It is open from 7:00 A.M. to 7:00 P.M. from mid-September to the end of February and from 6:30 A.M. to 8:30 P.M. from March 1 to mid-September. For cottage and camping reservations call (800) 864–PARK or log on to www.ga stateparks.org. When the gates are locked at night, only a dire emergency will open them before sunrise. This is done to protect you from roaming critters and the critters from roaming poachers. Also, bear in mind that a swamp is full of mosquitoes, other biting pests, and uncomfortable summer heat and humidity. Bring insect repellent and dress comfortably. In addition to the Folkston route, you may get to the park on Highway 441 to Fargo.

If you're wondering where everybody in **Folkston** is most any time of day, check out the covered platform that overlooks the *"Folkston Funnel,"* twin sets of tracks that carry more than 70 trains a day through the town of 2,300. Day and night, hundreds of Folkston folks and out-of-towners gather on the 32-foot-long, 15-foot-wide platform 2 blocks west of Highway 301. Train-spotting passion was sparked by Marvin "Cookie" Williams, an avid model-train collector whose enthusiasm for the real thing attracted others to the sport and led to a tourism development grant that funded the platform. While they're spotting passenger trains, coal trains, refrigerator cars, orange juice trains from Florida, military transports, and trains carrying chemicals and timber, the "spotters" enjoy the platform's camaraderie, picnic tables, grill, ceiling fans, and floodlights that illuminate trains that pass in the night. For information phone Folkston City Hall, (912) 496–2563, www.folkston.com.

Valdosta and the Great Southeast

Depending on your perspective, **Lowndes County** is either the jumping-off place for Florida or your reentry point to Georgia. With 95,000 residents, Lowndes is Georgia's sixteenth most populous county. Valdosta, the county seat, with close to 50,000 residents, is the state's tenth largest city. With so much traffic flowing back and forth from Florida on I–75, much of the city is devoted to chain motels, fast-food strips, and factory outlet malls. Behind these contemporary distractions, under canopies of live oaks and palm trees and banks of azaleas and camellias, the city has many historic homes, churches, and public buildings.

Stop for free information and the Historic Tours self-guided map at the Valdosta-Lowndes County Convention and Visitors Bureau's Tourism Information Center off I–75 exit 16, One Meeting Place, Valdosta 31601, (229) 245–0513 and (800) 569–8687, www.valdostatourism.com. Among the twenty-six landmarks, the most outstanding is *The Crescent.* Built in 1898 at a cost of $12,000 by Valdosta educator William S. West, the grand twenty-three-room neoclassical mansion is graced by thirteen Doric columns supporting a crescent-shaped portico. In 1913 President Woodrow Wilson attended a gala dinner in the ballroom. Now maintained by the Valdosta Garden Center, the mansion has been restored to its original grandeur and appointed with many original furnishings and period antiques. Guided tours Monday through Friday, 2:00 to 5:00 P.M. Donations accepted. The gardens are always in bloom. It's at 904 North Patterson Street, Valdosta, (229) 244–6747.

You're driving through south Georgia on a hot summer day. The kids are cranky, and you can't wait to see Orlando. Outside of Valdosta, a billboard advertises *Wild Adventures Theme Park,* "Over 100 Rides & Attractions." Stop for the day or a couple of days—you might forget all about Florida. True to its billing, Wild Adventures, I–75 exit 13, Valdosta, (229) 559–1330, (800) 808–0872, www.wildadventures.net, has one hundred things to see and do, without the crowds and lines at the Florida theme parks. Seven roller coasters and five water rides range from wild to mild. A tram puts you up close and personal with elephants, antelopes, zebra, lions, tigers, kangaroos, wallabies, birds, monkeys, and reptiles. You can pet small animals and hand-feed giraffe. A yearly concert calendar, included in gate admission, features top-name celebrities like Travis Tritt, Trisha Yearwood, Alabama, Wynonna, and Lynyrd Skynyrd. Admission, good for two days, is $39.95, plus tax, for adults, and $34.95 for ages 3 to 9 and those age 55 and over.

Before heading on, relax a while at Valdosta's parks, boating and fishing lakes, and public golf courses and tennis courts.

The small Lowndes County town of *Hahira,* north of Valdosta at I–75 exit 84, is a center of Georgia's tobacco industry. From July to October you can witness the age old ritual of tobacco auctioning at the town's warehouses. If you're here the first week of October, drop by the *Hahira Honeybee Festival.* To get the buzz on what's happening in town, and enjoy good home cooking, take a seat for breakfast or lunch at *The City Cafe* on Main Street. The Hahira Chamber of Commerce, Hahira 31632, (229) 794–2567, www.hahira.ga.us, offers tobacco and honey tours.

At *Reed Bingham State Park,* off Highway 37, Adel, 6 miles west of Adel, the Cook County seat, you can go boating, fishing, waterskiing, and swimming on a 375-acre lake. The park also has a nature trail, campsites, and

Mummified Dog

Pity poor "Stuckie," the hound that chased a rabbit up a hollow tree and ended up as mummified as Old King Tut. Displayed at the Southern Forest World Museum, 1440 North Augusta Avenue, Waycross, (912) 285–4056, the unfortunate 4-year-old brown and white doggie was discovered, years after his demise, by loggers who were cutting his "tomb" into pulpwood. A chimney effect in the hollow tree created upward drafts of air that kept his scent from insects and predators. The tree also provided a relatively dry environment, and its tannic acid leatherized Stuckie's skin and even preserved his last, terrified howl for help. While you're here, you can walk through a giant loblolly pine, listen to a talking tree, and view exhibits on forest management by the timber companies that support the museum. Open Tuesday through Saturday 9:00 A.M. to 5:00 P.M. Adults $2.00, children $1.00.

picnic grounds—and one rather unusual event. ***Buzzard Day,*** the first Saturday of December, hails the thousands of buzzards that roost in the park each winter. Enjoy arts and crafts and musical entertainment while you watch the skies. Phone (229) 896–3551. For campsite reservations call (800) 864–PARK, www.gastateparks.org.

The ***Jefferson Davis Memorial State Historic Site,*** Highway 32, in the small community of Irwinville, commemorates the site where the Confederate president was captured by Union troops on May 10, 1865. The museum has Civil War artifacts and part of the tree where Davis was standing when captured. A park around the museum has nature trails and picnic areas. Open Tuesday through Saturday from 9:00 A.M. to 5:00 P.M. and Sunday from 2:00 to 5:30 P.M. Admission is $1.00 for adults, 50 cents for children. Phone (229) 831–2335.

In ***Douglas,*** stop first at the Douglas Area Welcome Center in the historic ***Ashley-Slater House,*** 211 South Gaskin Street, (912) 384–1873 and (888) 426–3334, www.douglasga.org. The neoclassical 1914 mansion is furnished with original antiques, a 70-foot pastoral mural in the dining room, and (some say) ghosts of the original owners, who can't bear to depart their lovely home.

Railroad buffs will enjoy the ***Heritage Station Museum's*** exhibits in the old Georgia & Florida train depot in downtown Douglas, (912) 389–3461. Other exhibits highlight Coffee County's abundant agriculture. Open Monday through Saturday. Admission $1.00. Several antiques and gift shops are in the Main Street City's vibrant downtown.

Broxton Rocks Preserve, 778 pristine acres north of Douglas, contains some of the most dramatic outcrops of ancient sandstone in the southeastern United States. Formations sculpted by rivers millions of years ago, and dense woodlands and swampy bogs, are home to more than 500 species of plants, birds, and animals, many of them threatened and endangered. Entrance to the Rocks is by appointment with The Nature Conservancy of Georgia, which owns the property, (404) 873–6946.

General Coffee State Park, 46 John Coffee Road, Nicholls, 6 miles east of the center of Douglas, offers a wealth of recreational opportunities. You can fish the lake and streams for catfish, gar, and bream, and swim in the outdoor pool. A nature trail winding through the wooded 1,490-acre park puts you in photo range of many species of birds, reptiles, deer, and other critters. There are also playgrounds and picnic shelters. Heritage Farm has nature trails, wildlife habitats, antique farm equipment, a cane mill, and barnyard animals. You can stay overnight in full-service campsites and in a group cabin sleeping thirty-six. Phone (912) 384–7082. For camping and cabin reservations call (800) 864–PARK or log on to www.gastateparks.org.

In Douglas, which is home to South Georgia College and is a pretty college town of 15,000 folks, you can play the 18-hole *Beaver Kreek Golf Club* course (485 Beaver Creek Road, Douglas, 912–384–8230), or you might want to try your swing at the 9-hole *Douglas Community Golf Course* (SGC Tiger Road, Douglas, 912–384–7353). Rental clubs are available at both. After your round, drive into Douglas's revived downtown area—it's one of Georgia's Main Street Program cities—and enjoy dinner Tuesday through Saturday at *Fern Bank Bar and Grill* (235 Peterson Avenue South, Douglas, 912–384–4385), a historic brick-walled building with good steaks, seafood, and Southern dishes and many relics from the city's past.

The small town of *Fitzgerald* (population 8,600) is a living memorial to the nation's post–Civil War reunification. In the 1890s Indiana newspaper publisher P. H. Fitzgerald envisioned a place where he and other Union veterans could live in peace with their former Southern foes. When Ben Hill County farmers sent trainloads of food in response to a Midwestern drought, it became the chosen place. The town was laid out on a grid, with streets on the west side named for Confederate generals, those on the east side for Union generals. Other streets were named for Northern and Southern trees and flowers.

The *Blue and Gray Museum,* in the former train depot at 116 North Johnston Street, Fitzgerald, displays thousands of Civil War artifacts, including uniforms, weapons, newspaper articles about Lincoln's assassination, and the history of this unique town. It's open April 1 to October 1, Monday through Friday, from 2:00 to 5:00 P.M. Adults $3.00, students $1.00. Phone (229) 426–5069, (800) 386–4642, www.fitzgeraldga.org.

You usually need to commit a crime to merit "time." Seventeen miles west of Fitzgerald is Ashburn's *Crime and Punishment Museum,* where you just pay your "dime." The museum is located in a former jail that housed inmates upstairs and the jailers and their families downstairs. The fortress was built in 1906 at a cost of $10,000, and was known to inmates and Turner Countians as "Castle Turner" for its ornate Romanesque architecture. Jailers and their families kept the grounds so attractively landscaped, travelers sometimes mistook it for a hotel.

Today visitors can experience the original draconian cells, the death cell, the hanging hook, and the trap door, where, in the interest of time and economy, two felons could be dispatched at a time.

After the grim tour, visitors are ushered into the cheerful Last Meal Cafe, where Southern-style comfort meals "to die for" are served in the jailers' former living quarters.

The Crime and Punishment Museum and Last Meal Cafe, 241 East College Avenue, Ashburn, (800) 471–9696, (229) 567–9696, www.jailmuseum.com, are open Tuesday through Saturday from 8:00 A.M. to 5:00 P.M. Adults $6.00, seniors $4.00, students $2.00.

Before leaving Ashburn, take a gander at "The World's Largest Peanut," standing a majestic 20 feet tall, along I–75. Take exit 82/GA 107 into Ashburn and follow the signs to the Peanut and a gazebo, where you can have a tree-shaded picnic.

If you're around here in late March, join the fun of the annual *Fire Ant Festival.* One of the highlights is the Fire Ant Calling Contest. "You can call 'em any way you want," festival sponsors say, "but if they answer, you're in a whole heap o' trouble."

Until July 4, 1986, most motorists passed through the little Telfair County seat of *McRae,* 25 miles north of Fitzgerald, without a second thought. Nowadays, they have a reason to stop, get out of their cars, and take a picture. Right in the middle of town, where Highways 341, 441, 280, 23, and 319 come together, there's a replica of the Statue of Liberty, a Liberty Bell, and copies of the Declaration of Independence, the Constitution, and other documents. "Miss Liberty" stands 32 feet tall—a ½-scale reproduction of the original in New York Harbor. And she's entirely homemade: Her head is carved from a black gum tree, her torch from cypress, and her fiberglass coating was created by a McRae boat manufacturer. Contact the Telfair County Chamber of Commerce, 120 East Oak Street, McRae 31055, (229) 868–6365, www.telfair.com.

Little Ocmulgee State Park, with *Pete Phillips Lodge and Convention Center,* off Highway 441, 2 miles north of McRae, is a resort park with lots of things to keep you happily occupied. You can challenge the park's well-maintained 18-hole, par-72 golf course and rent carts and clubs at the pro shop. You can also swim, play tennis, and hike nature trails. Pete Phillips Lodge and

Conference Center has thirty modern motel-type guest rooms, an outdoor pool, a full-service restaurant, and meeting rooms. You can also pitch your tent or park your RV in full-service campsites and stay in furnished cottages. For camping, cottage, and lodge reservations, phone (800) 864–PARK or log on to www.gastateparks.org. For general information, contact the Park Superintendent, P.O. Box 149, McRae 31055, (229) 868–7474.

Places to Stay in Southeast Georgia

EASTMAN

Dodge Hill Inn,
5021 Ninth Avenue,
(478) 374–2644,
www.dodgehillinn.com
Ann and Don Dobbs are gracious hosts at this 1912 home, filled with antiques and original art. Five guest rooms have private baths, TV, refrigerators, and phones. Make yourselves at home in the parlor, read, and play the grand piano. Breakfast, included in the rate, is one of the best

reasons for staying here. The huge spread includes fresh fruit, hot baked breads, ham, biscuits, pancakes, cheese grits, and eggs. Inexpensive.

FOLKSTON

Folkston House,
802 Kingsland Drive,
(912) 496–3445,
www.folkstonhouse.com
Innkeeper Jeanne Scott has seven antiques-furnished guest rooms, with private baths, near downtown Folkston, convenient for visits to the Okefenokee Swamp National Wildlife Refuge and "trainspotting" at the "Folkston Funnel." Full breakfast at moderate rates.

The Inn at Folkston,
509 West Main Street,
(888) 509–6246,
fax (912) 496–6256,
www.innatfolkston.com
After a big day exploring the Okefenokee Swamp National Wildlife Refuge or the Cumberland Island National Seashore, Roger and Genna Wangness's restored 1920s heart-pine bungalow is only a few minutes away. Four spacious guest rooms have feather beds, private baths, and plenty of AC. You can recount your day's adventures in wicker chairs and rockers on the front veranda. Rates include full breakfast. Inexpensive.

HELPFUL WEB SITES

Baxley-Appling County Tourism Board,
www.baxley.org

Dublin-Laurens County Welcome Center,
www.dublin-georgia.com

Folkston/Okefenokee Chamber of Commerce,
www.folkston.com

Statesboro Tourism Office,
www.visit-statesboro.com

Waycross/Ware County Tourism Bureau,
www.waycrossga.com

Valdosta-Lowndes Convention & Visitors Bureau,
www.valdostatourism.com

HOMERVILLE

The Helmstead,
One Fargo Road,
(912) 487–2222,
(888) 224–3567,
fax (912) 487–6197,
(800) 502–6303.
Jane Helms's four guest rooms welcome business travelers and visitors to the neighboring Okefenokee Swamp National Wildlife Refuge. Rooms have private baths, and continental breakfast is included in the inexpensive rates.

PERRY

Sugar Hill Bed & Breakfast,
2450 Sugar Hill Road,
Unadilla,
(478) 627–3557.
Four guest rooms with private baths in a mid-1800s farm house 4 miles from I–75 exit 122. Also a swimming pool. Inexpensive rate includes full breakfast.

Places to Eat in Southeast Georgia

FOLKSTON

Vickery House,
108 South First Street,
(912) 496–7942.
Cozy downtown dining room is a good choice for weekday lunch. Specialties include quiche, crepes, soups, fresh vegetables, salads, baked desserts, and daily blue-plate specials. Lunch is served Wednesday through Friday.

McRAE

Southern Star Grill,
752 Oak Street,
(229) 868–2507.
This is where hungry folks in McRae and neighboring towns come for country fried steak, herbed roast chicken, sesame fried catfish, great desserts, and other treats. Lunch Monday through Saturday, dinner Tuesday through Saturday. Inexpensive.

METTER

Jomax Barbecue,
Highway 121,
(912) 685–3636.
Traveling the long, lonely stretches of I–16 between Macon and Savannah, with only a few scattered fast-food outlets to sate your hunger, Jomax is a pleasant and tasty surprise. Tuck into the chopped barbecued pork or ribs, draped with a piquant house-secret sauce (available in bottles to take home), with slabs of starchy white bread and cole slaw and you'll be ready to hit the highway high on the hog. Lunch and dinner Monday through Saturday. Inexpensive.

Northwest Georgia

Cloudland Canyon to Georgia's Rome

Cloudland Canyon State Park, in far northwest Georgia's remote and rugged Dade County, contains one of the Southeast's most awesome natural sights. The park's namesake and centerpiece is a steep canyon cut into the western flank of Lookout Mountain by ***Sitton Creek Gulch.*** You can stand by the rim and peer into misty reaches 1,800 feet deep. Better still, lace up your hiking boots, follow woodland trails down to three waterfalls on the canyon floor, and get really off the beaten path on 6 miles of backcountry trails.

After you hike, unwind with a swim in the park pool or a few quick sets of tennis. Also in the heavily forested 2,120-acre park are sixteen completely furnished cottages and seventy-five tent and trailer sites, with electrical and water connections, showers, and restrooms. For camping and cottage reservations call (800) 864–PARK. Contact Park Superintendent, Route 2, Box 150, Rising Fawn 30738, (706) 657–4050, www.gastateparks.org.

According to tradition, Cherokee Indians named their children for symbolic signs that caught their eye after birth. So the Cloudland community of ***Rising Fawn*** owes its poetic name

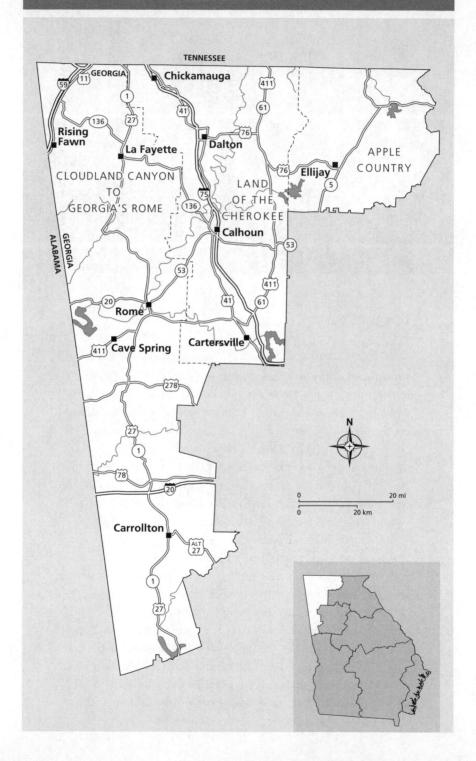

TENNESSEE

GEORGIA

Chickamauga

Rising Fawn

La Fayette

Dalton

CLOUDLAND CANYON
TO
GEORGIA'S ROME

Ellijay

APPLE
COUNTRY

LAND
OF THE
CHEROKEE

Calhoun

Rome

Cave Spring

Cartersville

GEORGIA

ALABAMA

Carrollton

N

0   20 mi

0   20 km

to a chief who legend says looked out of his lodge on the happy morning his son was born and saw a newborn fawn wobble to its feet by its mother's side.

After a vigorous day in the park, make tracks for **Geneva Wooten's Restaurant,** (706) 398–1749. Across Highway 136 from the Cloudland entrance, the homey cafe is the eating-meeting-greeting destination for folks from miles around. At breakfast, lunch, and dinner, country cooking just doesn't get any better.

Hidden Hollow Country Inn, 5 miles down the mountain from Cloudland Canyon, is one of those discoveries you can hardly wait to tell your best friends about. Tommy and Bonnie Jean Thomas preside over a gaggle of rustic but very comfortable family-size cabins around a small lake full of Canada geese. Cabins are filled with well-worn furniture, cards, board games, dog-eared magazines, and coffee, but there are no TVs or phones to ruffle your peaceful ruminations. For entertainment snag a fish in the lake, hike in the woods, and watch the sun come up and go down. Inexpensive. No meals are served, but Geneva Wooten's and other restaurants are close by. The inn is at 463 Hidden Hollow Lane, Chickamauga, (706) 539–2372, www.hiddenhollowresort.com.

NORTHWEST GEORGIA'S TOP HITS

Cloudland Canyon State Park	Gordon-Lee Mansion
Booth Western Art Museum	Dalton carpet outlets
James H. Floyd State Park	Prater's Mill Country Fair
Howard Finster's "Paradise Garden"	Vann House
Capitoline Wolf	Fort Mountain State Park
Clock Tower Museum	Cohutta National Wilderness
Chieftains Museum	New Echota State Historic Site
Lock and Dam Park	Etowah Native American Mounds State Historic Site
Funk Heritage Center	
Berry College	Red Top Mountain State Park and Lodge
Martha Berry Museum and Art Gallery	William Weinman Mineral Center & Museum
John Tanner State Park	
Chattanooga and Chickamauga National Military Park	Ellijay's Georgia Apple Festival
	Col. Oscar Poole's Pig Hill of Fame

Be sure to bring your fishing gear when you head for **James H. Floyd State Park.** Off Highway 27, 3 miles southeast of the Chattooga County seat of Summerville, the 270-acre park is renowned as one of the state's finest fishing places. Two stocked lakes—thirty and thirty-five acres—offer excellent bass-fishing opportunities from the banks. Only boats with trolling motors are allowed.

Area anglers say you can expect to reel in impressive largemouth bass, as well as big catches of catfish and bream. Youngsters can learn some of the fine art of fishing during the park's annual fishing rodeo in mid-May. Admission is free, and prizes are awarded for the first, largest, and most fish caught.

johnwisdom's "midnightride"

Boston has its Paul Revere, and Romans remember their own courageous rider who saved the day (and their necks). Learning that Union troops were approaching the city, mail carrier John Wisdom rode off in a desperate attempt to mobilize defenders. He abandoned his mail buggy after 20 miles, begged and borrowed horses, which he changed six times, and galloped 65 miles in less than nine hours.

The approaching Union troops saw Rome's defenders armed with shotguns, squirrel guns, and muzzle-loading rifles and retreated into captivity by Confederate General Nathan Bedford Forrest. Rome's grateful citizens gave Wisdom $400 and a silver service.

Floyd State Park's twenty-five tent and trailer sites have water and electrical hookups and convenient showers and restrooms. You'll also find a playground, picnic areas, and hiking trails in the neighboring Chattahoochee National Forest. Contact Park Superintendent, Route 1, Summerville 30747, (706) 857–0826. Call (800) 864–PARK or log on to www.gastateparks.org for camping reservations.

Three miles north of Summerville, turn right off U.S. Highway 27 onto Rena Street and prepare for an otherworldly visit to **Howard Finster's "Paradise Garden,"** (706) 857–5791, (800) FINSTER, www.finster.com. One of America's premier folk artists, the late Reverend Finster, who died in 2001, made his garden a jumble of gaudily painted angels, birds, animals, 14-foot Coke bottles, heaven-bound buses, surreal images of Elvis and Marilyn Monroe—and everywhere you look, biblical passages and admonitions. Paintings and wooden figures by Finster, his son, and grandson sell from $20 to $2,500. The garden is open Saturday 10:00 A.M. to 5:00 P.M. and by appointment. Adults $5.00, seniors $3.00, children $3.00.

Like its Italian counterpart, Georgia's **Rome** spreads over seven green hills, in the foothills of the state's northwestern Appalachian Mountains. In the rivers department, the Georgia city of 30,000 has the edge. Instead of one mere Tiber, the Floyd County seat has three: the Etowah and Oostanaula, which join up downtown and form the Coosa. It may not have personages to match the Caesars, but a *dramatis personae* of Cherokee Indian chieftains, Southern aristocrats, cotton traders, Civil War soldiers, and riverboat paddle wheelers have made a rich and colorful cast, all the same. The city got its name quite by chance. In 1834 two traveling salesmen and a cotton planter put their choice of names in a hat. "Rome" was the fortuitous choice; otherwise, the city might be known today as Warsaw or Hamburg. A revitalized downtown, focusing on the three rivers, ensures Rome of a future as exciting as its past.

Begin your Roman holiday at the Greater Rome Visitors Center (706–295–5576 or 800–444–1834, fax 706–236–5029, or www.romegeorgia.com), a rejuvenated Southern Railway passenger depot, circa 1900, and a retired caboose at 402 Civic Center Drive, off Highway 20 and Highway 27 near downtown. Information is available Monday through Friday 9:00 A.M. to 5:00 P.M., Saturday 10:00 A.M. to 3:00 P.M., and Sunday noon to 3:00 P.M.

"The Between the Rivers Walking Tour"—it can also be driven, of course—leads you past thirty-eight historic downtown landmarks. If you've

TOP ANNUAL EVENTS

Atlanta Steeplechase,
mid-April, Kingston Downs, Kingston,
(404) 237–7436

Historic House & Garden Pilgrimage,
late April, Rome,
(706) 291–7181

Kingston Confederate Memorial Day,
late april, Kingston,
(770) 387–1357

Cedar Valley Arts Festival,
early May, Cedartown,
(770) 748–0397

Prater's Mill Country Fair,
Mother's Day Weekend, Dalton,
(706) 275–6455

Cherokee County Indian Festival,
early May, Canton,
(770) 735–6275

CHVA Car Show & Southeastern National Meet,
mid-June, Cartersville High School, Cartersville,
(770) 386–2964

Georgia Apple Festival,
mid-October, Ellijay,
(706) 635–7400

Candles & Carols of Christmases Past,
early December, Martha Berry Museum, Rome,
(800) 220–5504

Coosa River Christmas Lighted Boat Parade,
early December, Rome,
(800) 444–1834

been to the Italian Rome, you'll probably recognize the statue in front of City Hall here on Broad Street, downtown. The *Capitoline Wolf,* a replica of the Etruscan sculpture on ancient Rome's Capitoline Hill, depicts the city's mythical founders, Romulus and Remus, being nurtured by a she-wolf. It was a 1929 good-will gift from Benito Mussolini, a gift that was a tad embarrassing to the towns-people. In smalltown Georgia, 1929, people were unaccustomed to seeing babies suckling their mother's bare breast in public, even if the mother was a wolf.

The *Town Clock,* on Clock Tower Hill, is the city's symbol and one of its most beloved landmarks. Built in Waltham, Massachusetts, in 1871, the four 9-foot-diameter clock faces rest upon a handsome brick and cypress water tower. So many people wanted to climb the 104-foot tower that the city opened it as the *Clock Tower Museum.* You can walk up the spiral staircase and take in panoramic views of the city's hills and rivers. Also admire the handsomely restored clock works and murals depicting chapters in the city's history. It's open Saturday from 10:00 A.M. to 4:00 P.M. and Sunday from 1:00 to 5:00 P.M. from April to November and other times by appointment. Free admission. Phone (706) 236–4430.

Myrtle Hill Cemetery, on another of the city's seven hills, is a beautiful tree-shaded sanctuary where the first Mrs. Woodrow Wilson, 377 Confederate soldiers, and other notables are buried. You're welcome to stroll and admire the panoramic views of Rome's rivers and green hills. Phone (706) 295–5576.

Until recently the Etowah, Oostanaula, and Coosa had to flood before Romans would pay them any attention. Nowadays the 2½-mile *Heritage Trail* walking, biking, and hiking route, shaded by big trees, takes inhabitants and visitors along the Oostanaula from the *Rome–Floyd County Public Library* downtown to the Chieftains Museum. If you'd like to get out on the water, the visitors bureau can direct you to a canoe rental.

You can also unwind at *Lock and Dam Park,* a publicly owned camp-ing/RV/fishing/boating park in a mountain setting beside a 1910 lock on the Coosa River. Facilities include twenty-five fully equipped RV campsites, a fishing pier, canoe rentals, boat ramp and docks, a bait shop, and a snack bar. Call (706) 234–5001 for information.

Rocky Mountain Recreation and Public Fishing Area is a joint venture of the Georgia Department of Natural Resources and Oglethorpe Power Corporation. The 5,000-acre retreat in northern Floyd County has two recreational lakes (357 and 202 acres) for swimming, fishing, and boating. You can also enjoy picnic pavilions, hiking trails, and other outdoor activities and camp out at thirty-nine RV sites and nine wooded tent sites. For information, call the Greater Rome Visitors Bureau at (800) 444–1834.

Rome Area History Museum, 305 Broad Street, Rome, (706) 235–8051, www.romehistorymuseum.com, covers nearly two centuries of northwest Georgia's past. Exhibits focus on the Civil War, the Cherokees, cotton, and commerce. A *Gone With the Wind* exhibit has photos, collectibles, and costumes from the book and movie. Open Tuesday through Saturday from 10:00 A.M. to 5:00 P.M. and Sunday from noon to 5:00 P.M. Admission is $3.00.

If golf's your game, check out the *Stonebridge Golf Club,* (706) 236–5046 and (800) 336–5046, www.romestonebridge.com. Owned by the city of Rome, the 18-hole, par-72, 6,971-yard layout is at the base of Lavendar Mountain, on the Berry College grounds. Rolling fairways, water, and big stands of hardwoods and pines are scenic to look at and challenging to play. The course is named for an old stone bridge over a lake on the ninth fairway. Greens fees won't handicap your budget.

The *Chieftains Museum* is Rome's oldest historical landmark. Built as a frontier log cabin in 1794, Chieftains was the home of Major Ridge, the Cherokee leader who signed a treaty with the U.S. government that partially contributed to the expulsion of the Cherokees from Georgia and the tragic "Trail of Tears." Along with Cherokee history, the museum's artifacts tell the story of Rome as a river town and its role in the antebellum South and the Civil War. An open archaeological dig and a nineteenth-century riverboat are on the grounds. It's at 501 Riverside Parkway, Rome, off Highway 27, (706) 291–9494, www.chieftains museum.org. Hours are Tuesday through Friday from 9:00 A.M. to 3:00 P.M. and Saturday from 10:00 A.M. to 4:00 P.M. Adults $3.00, seniors $2.00, students $1.50.

rometrivia

Early one morning, while I was standing in front of Rome's City Hall photographing the statue of the Capitoline she-wolf nursing Ancient Rome's mythical founders, Romulus and Remus, a bedraggled citizen of the streets shuffled up. He watched silently for a few moments, then finally said: "I ain't believing none of it."

"How's that?" I replied.

"I ain't believing no dog ever nursed no human kids," he said firmly. "No, sir; it ain't happened." Having set the truth straight, he cocked his head and marched proudly away.

When in Rome, shoppers from across northwestern Georgia, neighboring Alabama, Chattanooga, Tennessee, and Atlanta (65 miles north and south, respectively) do as savvy Romans do: They pass up the shopping center same-old-same-olds and hunt for unique treasures on downtown Rome's Broad Street and the Berry College campus, ten minutes from downtown. Downtown's most popular shop is *The White Rabbit* (nationally known lines of gifts and collectibles), 538 Broad Street, (706) 235–2162. At ***Old Havana Cigar Company,*** 327 Broad Street, (706) 295–0546, enjoy a glass of wine or a cup of coffee while you choose among 230 types of cigars from Honduras, Dominican Republic, Nicaragua, and Puerto Rico.

Born to privilege, the remarkable and very determined Miss Martha Berry founded the Berry School in 1902. Her original small school is now ***Berry College,*** a four-year liberal arts college set among 28,000 acres of woodlands, forests, and fields. Automobile magnate Henry Ford funded the English Gothic–style Ford Buildings complex in 1924. As you're driving around the campus, watch out for deer impulsively crossing the roads—there are said to be 8.4 white-tails for each of the college's 2,000 students. About 90 percent of the students still work for part of their tuition.

The "Miracle of the Mountains," as the school's story is called, is chronicled at the ***Martha Berry Museum and Art Gallery,*** across from the campus on Highway 27. Exhibits, photos, and a twenty-eight-minute film trace Miss Berry's life and her numerous honors. Nearby ***Oak Hill,*** a classic, white-columned Old South Greek Revival mansion built in 1847, was the Berry family's home. Students lead tours through rooms filled with antiques, art, and family memorabilia. An easygoing nature trail loops through gardens and woodlands. The Martha Berry Museum and Art Gallery and Oak Hill are open Monday through Saturday from 10:00 A.M. to 5:00 P.M., Sunday from 1:00 to 5:00 P.M.

On the campus of Berry College

Admission $5.00. Phone (800) 220–5504 and (706) 291–1883, www.berry .edu/oakhill.

You're also invited to visit the scenic campuses of **Shorter College** and **Darlington Lower School,** neighbors on Shorter Avenue west of downtown.

If you'd like to get a little lost in the woods, make an appointment to visit **Marshall Forest,** on Horseleg Creek Road, Rome, off Highway 20, 4 miles west of downtown. The lush 170-acre preserve, administered by the Georgia Conservancy, includes ninety acres of fields and eighty acres of forests, where northern red and chestnut oaks mingle with long-leaf southern pines. About 300 species of wildflowers and other plants grow on the Flower Glen Trail. The Big Pine Braille Trail offers blind visitors the opportunity to stop at twenty stations describing fifty-three plant species, thirty-one species of trees, and nineteen species of vines and shrubs. Call the Rome Visitor Center for information, (800) 444–1834, or the Nature Conservancy, (404) 873–6946, www.nature .org/georgia.

Cave Spring, a village of 950 residents and one traffic light 16 miles south of Rome (via Highway 411), is pure Norman Rockwell. The **Hearn House B&B,** a comfy community-owned inn in an 1840s schoolhouse, features five guest rooms with private bath and breakfast for $50 to $60 per night. When you're well rested, lace up your walking shoes and head across **Rolater Park** to the limestone cave that gave the town its name. The spring water flows out of the cave into a tree-shaded pond. Around the pond and the park are picnic tables and pavilions, restrooms, and a spring-fed 1.5-acre swimming pool shaped like the state of Georgia. The pool has bathhouses, snack bars, and plenty of room to spread your towels.

Around the square more than a dozen antiques stores and flea markets are a collector's dream. More than a hundred artists and craftspeople come for the **Cave Spring Arts Festival** the second weekend of June. For information and bed-and-breakfast reservations, contact City of Cave Spring, P.O. Box 365, Cave Spring 30124, (706) 777–8439 and (800) 444–1834.

John Tanner State Park, off Highway 16, 6 miles west of Carrollton, is a popular getaway for west Georgians and east Alabamians. Six furnished one-bedroom cottages and thirty-six full-service campsites surround a lake with a sandy swimming beach, rental fishing boats, and tree-shaded picnic shelters. There is a $2.00 parking fee. Contact Park Superintendent, 354 Tanners Beach Road, Carrollton 30117, (770) 830–2222. For campsite and cottage reservations, call (800) 864–PARK, www.gastateparks.org.

Fans of Oscar-winning actress **Susan Hayward** (*I Want to Live*, 1959) can visit her gravesite at Our Lady of Perpetual Help Catholic Church, 210 Centerpoint Road, Georgia Highway 113, Carrollton. In 1957 Hayward married businessman Eaton Chalkley and moved with him to Carrollton, where they raised horses and cattle. When Chalkley died in 1966, Hayward moved back to California. When she died of brain cancer in 1972, she was buried beside him in the church cemetery across from their former home. Open daily, no admission fee. For information contact Carrollton Area Convention and Visitors Bureau, 102 North Lake Shore Drive, Carrollton 30117, (770) 214–9746, www.visitcarrollton.com.

Land of the Cherokee

In the hellish heat of September 19 and 20, 1863, nearly 130,000 Americans engaged in one of the bloodiest battles of the entire Civil War. When it was over, Confederate forces under the command of General Braxton Bragg had a costly and dubious victory. They had repulsed the outnumbered Union armies under General William Rosecrans but were too weakened to pursue the Federals as they fled to safety around Chattanooga, Tennessee. Subsequent Union victories at Chattanooga's Lookout Mountain and Missionary Ridge and the capture of the city's vital railway hub opened General William T. Sherman's route to Atlanta and the sea.

The 5,500-acre Chickamauga battlefield is now part of the ***Chattanooga and Chickamauga National Military Park.*** The major sites are adjacent to Highway 27, near Chattanooga and Chickamauga. Stop first at the National Park Service Visitors Center for the audiovisual orientation and the many exhibits. The Fuller Collection of Military Arms has more than 400 weapons from the French and Indian Wars through present-day conflicts.

Park rangers in Civil War uniforms demonstrate cannon and rifles. The Chattanooga Symphony Orchestra has free outdoor concerts here on summer Sunday evenings. Bring a blanket and a picnic supper and join the festivities!

From the visitor center, follow Highway 27 for 3 miles through the park. Battle sites are marked by earthworks, cannon batteries, and farm buildings. Impressive monuments have been placed by states whose sons in blue and gray died here more than 125 years ago. The park is open all the time. The visitor center is open daily from 8:00 A.M. to 5:45 P.M. Contact Park Superintendent, P.O. Box 2128, Fort Oglethorpe 30742, (706) 866–9241, www.nps .gov/chch.

The ***Gordon-Lee Mansion,*** on the edge of the battlefield park, invites you to spend the night in antebellum luxury. Built in 1847, the white-columned Greek Revival residence on seven acres of gardens and grounds served as Union headquarters and a hospital during the battle. Six guest rooms, an adjoining log house, and public areas are furnished with Civil War–era

Carpet Shopping Tips

If you're planning to do serious carpet shopping, do your homework ahead of time. Have a good idea of what you're looking for, how much you'll need, the color and style, and what you can afford to pay. Do comparison shopping in your local stores— the more than one hundred outlet stores in Dalton and neighboring towns like Calhoun and Chatsworth offer prices up to 70 percent less than you'll pay in a retail store. You can get a list of the Carpet & Rug Outlet Council stores from the Dalton-Whitfield Chamber of Commerce, (706) 278–7373, and the Dalton Convention and Visitors Bureau, (800) 331–3258. Most outlets deal in "seconds," that is, those with some problems that exclude them from the "A list." It's often just a small tear or a color that doesn't match the mill's specifications. Be sure to examine it thoroughly. Having your carpet shipped will be much easier than trying to take it home yourself.

antiques. Rates ($75 to $125) include evening wine and cheese on the veranda and a continental-plus breakfast. Contact Gordon-Lee Mansion, 217 Cove Road, Chickamauga, (706) 375–4728 or (800) 487–4728, fax (706) 375–4586, www .gordonlee mansion.com.

Before leaving the area, see **Lookout Mountain, Missionary Ridge,** and other major parts of the Chattanooga and Chickamauga National Military Park.

If you've been planning to recarpet your home or cover your pool deck or patio with Astroturf, put off that major purchase until you've been to **Dalton.** Seat of northwest Georgia's green and hilly Whitfield County, industrious Dalton, with a population of 25,000, is the long-reigning "Carpet Capital of the World."

About 66 percent of all the tufted carpeting manufactured in the United States rolls off the giant looms of Dalton's more than seventy-five modern plants. If you're in a buying frame of mind or would just enjoy browsing the latest styles and colors, dozens of **Dalton carpet outlets** offer a full range of floor coverings at greatly reduced prices. The Dalton Convention and Visitors Bureau, 2211 Dug Gap Battle Road, Dalton 30722, (706) 270–9960, (800) 331–3258, www.dalton cvb.com, open Monday through Saturday, can provide you with an up-to-date outlets directory. You can also find out about guided tours of area mills, Civil War and Native American sites, restaurants, and lodgings.

Dalton's $5 billion carpeting industry was born around 1900, when a Whitfield County farm girl named Catherine Evans produced a hand-tufted chenille bedspread, copied from a family heirloom, and promptly sold it for the handsome price of $2.50. Encouraged by her success, she made more of the brightly colored cotton bedspreads, and these, too, were eagerly snapped up by tourists and local homemakers. Other homebound women began following her lead, and by the early 1920s, tufted bedspreads had grown into a major "cottage industry."

The bedspreads usually featured flowers and other patterns, but the brilliantly plumed male peacock was such a runaway favorite that Highway 41, the major highway leading into Dalton, became popularly known as "Peacock Alley."

In the 1920s, a machine invented in Dalton was able to mass-produce the cotton bedspreads. Another wizard soon realized that by tufting more densely and adding a sturdy backing the same machinery could be adapted to the manufacture of carpeting. Dalton—and households the world over—were never again the same.

The original "cottage craft" of chenille bedspreads is still alive. You can find a practical souvenir with a peacock, Elvis Presley, Jesus Christ, the Confederate battle flag, and other designs at stores around Dalton and along Highway 41—the original "Peacock Alley"—between Dalton and the Tennessee border. Figure on paying a bit more than $2.50, however!

Some of the early chenille bedspreads are among the exhibits at *Crown Gardens and Archives,* in the original Crown Cotton Mill at 715 Chattanooga Avenue, Dalton, (706) 278–0217. The museum also has historical displays, a Black Heritage room, an outdoor spring, and picnic areas. It's open Tuesday through Friday. Admission is free.

With its influx of executives and workers from across the nation and several countries, this surprisingly cosmopolitan little city is very active in the fine arts. The *Creative Arts Guild,* 520 West Waugh Street, Dalton, (706) 278–0168, www.creativeartsguild.org, is a tastefully contemporary complex with two art galleries and a forum for live theater, dance, and other cultural programs. It's open daily. Admission is free.

Dalton is also a festive city. The *Red Carpet Festival,* the first weekend of May, celebrates Dalton's famous industry with parades, pagentry, square dancing, bluegrass and gospel music, and plenty of barbecue and other hearty Southern cooking.

On the second weekends of May and October, the *Prater's Mill Country Fair* centers on Benjamin Franklin Prater's circa 1859 gristmill. While the huge millstones turn out silky cornmeal, 185 artists and craftspeople sell their wares to the tune of bluegrass fiddlers, clog dancers, and gospel singers. There are pony rides and other special treats just for the youngsters.

Dalton Depot Restaurant & Trackside Cafe, 110 Depot Street, five minutes from I–75, (706) 226–3160, is the carpet city's liveliest eating and drinking address. The cleverly regeared old wooden train depot has a something-for-everyone menu: stuffed jalapeños and quesadillas, filet mignon, baby back ribs, prime rib, ribeye and sirloin steak, chicken several different ways, fish and shrimp, sandwiches and salads, and bar drinks and 130 brands of beer. Lunch and dinner are served Monday through Saturday.

When Daltonites are in the mood for a dress-up dinner, they head for the **Cellar Restaurant and Lounge** in the Dalton Shopping Center, 1331 West Walnut Avenue, (706) 226–6029. Veal, seafood, steaks, soups, salads, cocktails, and wines are served at lunch, Monday through Friday, and dinner, Monday through Saturday, at moderate prices.

Vann House was a showplace of nineteenth-century Cherokee accomplishment. At the junction of Highways 52-A and 225, 3 miles west of modern-day Chatsworth, the sturdy three-story house, with brick walls 2 feet thick, was built in modified Georgian style in 1804–1805. Owner James Vann was a half-Cherokee, half-Scot who helped create a Moravian mission for the education of young Cherokees. When Vann died in 1809, his son Joseph inherited the house and surrounding farmlands. He prospered until 1830, when the state of Georgia confiscated his lands for violating a law forbidding White men to work for Indians.

The Georgia Department of Natural Resources has restored the house and refurnished and redecorated the rooms in early nineteenth-century style. An intricately carved "floating staircase" is one of Georgia's earliest surviving examples of cantilevered construction. Elsewhere are Bibles, dinnerware, and dining room and bedroom furnishings. Vann House, at the intersection of Highways 52-A and 225, Chatsworth, (706) 695–2598, (800) 864–PARK, www.gastateparks .org, is open Tuesday through Saturday from 9:00 A.M. to 5:00 P.M., Sunday from 2:00 to 5:30 P.M. Admission is $2.00 for adults, $1.00 for children 6 to 18; free for children under 6.

On Highway 52, 7 miles east of Chatsworth, **Fort Mountain State Park** is a superscenic park on a forested, 2,800-foot peak of the Blue Ridge Mountains' Cohutta Range. The park's namesake is a puzzling rock wall, or foundation, that winds nearly 900 feet around the mountainside. Whether it was an ancient Indian fortress, a bastion built by twelfth-century Welsh explorers, or part of some other inscrutable mission is a matter of speculation. The stone observation tower nearby is no mystery. It's a legacy of the Depression-era Civilian Conservation Corps.

History lessons aside, you can relax in Fort Mountain's lake, hike nature trails, play miniature golf, and set the kids loose on the playground. The 115 campsites have water, electricity, hot showers, and restrooms. Fifteen two- and three-bedroom cottages come with kitchen appliances, towels, sheets, and logs for the fireplace. Contact Park Superintendent, Fort Mountain Park Road,

Chatsworth 30705, (706) 695–2621. For reservations, call (800) 864–PARK or log on to www.gastateparks.org.

The 38,000-acre **Cohutta National Wilderness** in northwestern Georgia is a favorite of backpackers who really like to get away from it all. The parking area at Dally Gap, near McCaysville, is near the trailhead for Jack's River Trail, which winds through the eastern side of the wilderness. At 17 miles, Jack's River is longer than many trails in the wilderness and is one of the most scenic, with big stands of trees, ferns, and wildflowers. You'll probably see white-tailed deer, beaver, and many species of birds. Be alert for black bears. For information contact Cohutta Wildlife Management Area, (707) 635–7400.

The Cherokee assimilated themselves into the way of life established by the White settlers, then were ruthlessly crushed at **New Echota State Historic Site,** near modern-day Calhoun. In the 1820s New Echota was laid out as the capital of the Cherokee Nation that included parts of Georgia, the Carolinas, Tennessee, and Alabama. Here, the Cherokee legislature formulated laws, enforced by a series of district courts and a supreme court. The Indians wore European-style dress, used the farming methods of the White settlers, and lived in stone and frame houses with the most modern conveniences of the day. The more affluent owned black slaves. The first North American tribe to formulate its own written alphabet, the Cherokee published a bilingual newspaper, circulated as far as Europe.

Gold discovered on Cherokee lands in the late 1820s brought it all to an end. Supported by President Andrew Jackson, the state of Georgia confiscated all Cherokee lands and in 1838 forced the Indians into exile in what is now Oklahoma. Thousands perished along this "Trail of Tears."

New Echota has been meticulously reconstructed as a state historic site. Stop first to see the orientation slide show and exhibits in the reception center. Then take a self-guided walking tour that includes the supreme court building, the printing presses of the *Cherokee Phoenix* newspaper, a tavern/general store, and the home of the Reverend Samuel Worcester, a Massachusetts minister who established a mission for the Cherokee. Park rangers frequently demonstrate arrowhead making and hunting techniques. Books about the Cherokee civilization are on sale at the reception center. In late October the **Cherokee Fall Festival** is a weekend of Native American crafts, cooking, and storytelling.

New Echota State Historic Site, I–75 exit 317, Calhoun, (706) 624–1321, (800) 864–PARK, www.gastatepark.org, is open Tuesday through Saturday from 9:00 A.M. to 5:00 P.M. and Sunday from 2:00 to 5:30 P.M. Admission is $3.00 for adults, $2.00 for children 6 to 18; free for children under 6.

Barnsley Gardens Resort, off I–75 exit 306, 10 miles west of Adairsville, dates to 1841, when English cotton broker Godfrey Barnsley brought his wife,

New Echota

Julia, from Savannah and built an Italianate villa and formal gardens on 10,000 acres of former Cherokee land. Some 160 years later, Hubertus Fugger, a Bavarian prince, has complemented Barnsley's gardens with plush lodgings, a European spa, a stem-winding golf course, and other resort amenities. Thirty-three English-style guest cottages, with one to four bedrooms, have plush furnishings, private baths, wood-burning fireplaces, heart-pine floors, front porch rockers, TVs, CD players, and other luxuries. Along with the 18-hole championship golf course and multifaceted spa, guests can enjoy the outdoor pool, bratwurst and German brews in a Bavarian beer garden, fine cuisine in the formal dining room, and Godfrey Barnsley's restored gardens and the romantic ruins of his villa, where Godfrey and Julia reportedly still appear from time to time. Julia's image is on the tiered fountain in the formal gardens. The golf course, gardens, spa, and dining room are available to nonguests. Double occupancy: $275 to $400. Golf, tennis, romantic getaway, and other package plans are available. Barnsley Gardens Resort, 597 Barnsley Gardens Road, Adairsville, (770) 773–7480, (877) 773–2447, www.barnsleyresort.com, fax (770) 773–1779.

While you're in the area, browse the antiques shops around Adairsville's downtown square.

Between A.D. 1000 and 1500, the Etowah tribe migrated into the fertile Etowah River Valley, near today's Cartersville, and created a remarkably sophisticated culture. Beans, squash, corn, and fruit that the women cultivated complemented game trapped by the men in surrounding forests and the abundant fish in the Etowah. As part of a vast trading network, the Etowahs made tools, arrowheads, axes, and household implements from Great Lakes copper and Mississippi and Ohio Valley flint. Gulf Coast seashells were fashioned into ceremonial jewelry.

Surrounded by a deep moat and log stockade, a compact city of clay and wooden houses sheltered as many as 4,000 members of the tribe. The heart of the city was a half dozen rectangular earthen mounds. The *Etowah Mounds State Historic Site* was the forum for religious rites conducted by chiefs and priests and the final resting place of these dignitaries.

Stop first at the excellent small museum and reception center, where dioramas and artifacts from the mounds tell the story of this mysteriously vanished tribe. The exhibits are highlighted by a priest's burial chamber and beautifully carved busts of a woman and a warrior. A film traces the history of the Etowahs. With a diagrammed map, cross the moat and explore the grass-covered mounds. Ninety-two steps take you up 63 feet to the top of Mound "A," from which the priest conducted rituals for the townspeople assembled below in the plaza. Mound "C," one of the smallest, was a principal burial site and the source of most of the artifacts in the museum. Park rangers periodically lead moonlight walks around the site.

About a fifteen-minute drive west of I–75 exit 288, via Highway 113/61, Etowah Mounds State Historic Site, Route 1, Cartersville, (770) 387–3747, (800) 864–PARK, www.gastateparks.org, is open Tuesday through Saturday from 9:00 A.M. to 5:00 P.M. and Sunday from 2:00 to 5:30 P.M. Admission is $3.00 for adults, $2.00 for children; free for children under 6.

For more insights into ancient Native American cultures, visit the new *Funk Heritage Center* at Reinhardt College, in Waleska, on Highway 140 northeast of Cartersville. You'll enter the Funk's John and Ethel Bennett History Museum through a 50-foot-long structure that resembles an Iroquois longhouse, where several families would have lived communally. Historians believe the northeastern Iroquois traded with Cherokees and other southeastern tribes. The left and right wings of the museum were inspired by temple mounds built at Etowah, at Cartersville, and elsewhere in the Southeast during the Mississippian period, A.D. 1000–1500. The Rogers Gallery of Contemporary Indian Art exhibits some 400 paintings, sculptures, and other creativity. A majority were created by descendants of southeastern Cherokees, Creeks, and other tribes that were removed west of the Mississippi during the 1830s "Trail of Tears." Also on permanent exhibit, the Sellars Collection of Ancient Hand Tools includes thousands of tools and implements dating back as far as the seventeenth century. Funk Heritage Center, 7300 Reinhardt College Parkway, Waleska, (770) 720–5971, www.reinhardt.edu/funk.htm, is open Monday through Friday 9:00 A.M. to 4:00

BILL'S FAVORITES

Cloudland Canyon State Park

Geneva Wooten's Restaurant

Hidden Hollow Country Inn

Howard Finster's "Paradise Garden"

Martha Berry Museum and Art Gallery

Cave Spring Antiques Shops

Chattanooga and Chickamauga National Military Park

Fort Mountain State Park

Cohutta National Wilderness

New Echota State Historic Site

Col. Oscar Poole's Pig Hill of Fame

P.M., Saturday 10:00 A.M. to 5:00 P.M., and Sunday 1:00 to 5:00 P.M. Adults 18 and older, $6.00; seniors 65 and older, $5.50; age 18 and under, $4.00.

The ***Booth Western Art Museum,*** in downtown Cartersville (population 20,000), draws us into the once-upon-a-time America of cowboys and Indians, cowgirls and gunslingers, buffalo hunters and rodeo "bulldoggers," stagecoaches and iron horses, big skies and endless horizons, movie icons and pulp fiction heroes. Opened in August 2003, the 80,000-square-foot museum is one of the newest and largest Western art museums anywhere in the United States. The permanent collection's more than 250 paintings and sculptures are by some of America's leading contemporary Western artists. The Civil War Gallery's twenty-five paintings dramatize the conflict from the first shots at Manassas to surrender at Appomattox. The Reel West Gallery's vintage movie posters and illustrations bring back those thrilling days at the Saturday matinee, when Roy Rogers and Gene Autry quelled the bad guys and rode victoriously into the sunset just before the final credits. In the Presidential Gallery, all forty-three U.S. presidents are represented by a portrait or photograph and an original signed document. At Sagebrush Ranch, kids have a great time riding the make-believe range in a lifelike bouncing stagecoach, dressing up as cowboys and cowgirls and creating their own Western masterpieces. Booth Western Art Museum, I–75 exit 288/Cartersville Main Street, 501 Museum Drive, Cartersville, (770) 387–1300, www.boothmuseum.org. The museum has a gift shop, cafe, and 140-seat theater with an orientation film about the collections. Open Tuesday, Wednesday, Friday, and Saturday 10:00 A.M. to 5:00 P.M., Thursday 10:00 A.M. to 8:00 P.M., Sunday 1:00 to 5:00 P.M. Adults $6.00, seniors $5.00, students $4.00, age 12 and under free.

4-Way Lunch, Main Street, downtown Cartersville, no phone, has been a landmark of swift (not "fast") food and service for more than seventy years.

THIS IS NOT BURGER KING, a sign over the coffeepot advises, YOU DON'T GET IT YOUR WAY, YOU GET IT OUR WAY, OR YOU DON'T GET IT. Another caution about the service: I CAN ONLY PLEASE ONE PERSON A DAY—AND TODAY AIN'T YOUR DAY. Crowds line up every weekday morning for bacon, eggs, grits, and biscuits, and many come back at lunch for first-class burgers, hot dogs, chopped steak, and stew. With only eleven seats at the red Formica counter, there's no lollygagging— when you're done, it's time to move on and let other hungry patrons have their 4-Way fix.

Red Top Mountain State Park and Lodge, on exit 285 off I–75 south of Cartersville, is one of the nicest and prettiest in the whole system. A wealth of recreational opportunities, campsites, and cottages are spread over the wooded hillsides around 12,000-acre Lake Allatoona. During warm weather, you can sun on a sandy beach, swim, and waterski. The rest of the year, bring tennis racquets, fishing gear, picnic supplies, and hiking shoes. Boaters may bring their own or rent houseboats and pontoon boats at the park marina. A small grocery is at the reception center.

Red Top's twenty two-bedroom cottages are completely furnished and include fireplaces. The 286 camping sites have electricity, water, hot showers, and restrooms. The park's Red Top Mountain Lodge has thirty-three modern guest rooms in a quiet cove with a full-service restaurant. The park office is open daily from 8:00 A.M. to 5:00 P.M. Contact Superintendent, 50 Lodge Road, Cartersville 30120, (770) 975–0055. Call (800) 864–PARK for camping, cottage, and lodge reservations, or log on to www.gastateparks.org for more information.

North of Cartersville, less than a mile from I–75 exit 290, the attractive, well-planned *William Weinman Mineral Center & Museum* is an intriguing stopover for rockhounds and other nature lovers. Gemstones, minerals, fossils, crystals, arrowheads, geodes, and other specimens are displayed in brightly lighted glass cases. Some of the specimens are from right here in northwestern Georgia's own mineral-mining regions; others are imports from South America, Africa, Australia, Mexico, and the Western United States.

In a simulated limestone cave, with authentic stalactites and stalagmites, you can trace the eons-long formation of caves with easy-to-follow diagrams and explanations. The cave's treasures also include a mastodon's sixty-pound molar and a fossilized box turtle. Other exhibits include a huge array of arrowheads and flint weapons, fluorescent minerals, petrified wood, brilliantly polished geodes, rock crystal, and colorful birthstones. Books, jewelry, and mineral samples are for sale in the gift shop.

The museum, 51 Mineral Museum Drive, White (I-75 Exit 293), (770) 386–0576, www.weinmanmuseum.org, is open Monday through Saturday from 10:00 A.M. to 5:00 P.M. Admission is $4.00 for adults, $3.50 for seniors, $3.00 for children 6 to 12; free for children 5 and under.

Apple Country

Gilmer County, in the Blue Ridge Mountains about ninety minutes due north of Metro Atlanta, is "Georgia's Apple Capital." Dozens of orchards dotting the county's green mountainsides annually produce more than 300,000 bushels of Granny Smiths, Red and Golden Delicious, Yates, Jonathans, Stayman Winesaps, Rome Beauties, and exotic Asian newcomers such as Fujis and Mutsus. In the fall, when the trees are loaded with fruit, visitors by the thousands are invited into the orchards to pick their own basketsful. Those who'd just as soon leave the labor to somebody else can buy all they can haul home at farm stores that line the highways leading to **Ellijay,** the Gilmer County seat. They also can take away freshly squeezed apple cider, apple pies and cakes, and recipe books to prepare just about everything with apples.

To celebrate the harvest, **Ellijay's Georgia Apple Festival,** two weekends in mid-October, puts on parades, apple pie–eating and apple-cooking contests, arts and crafts, mountain music and dancing, and a host of other festivities. Ellijay is a delightful small town with 1,700 amiable inhabitants. It may remind you of Sheriff Andy Taylor's bucolic hometown of Mayberry.

When your appetite's worked up again, get ready for some serious barbecue. As you drive into town on the four-lane Zell Miller Mountain Parkway (Highway 515), you can't help but notice **Col. Oscar Poole's Pig Hill of Fame.** For $5.00 you, too, can have your name painted on one of thousands

Root, Root, Root for the Rome Team

If you've forgotten how much fun a night at the ballpark can be, a night of minor league baseball with the Rome Braves will bring it all back. So, buy some peanuts and Cracker Jacks, hot dogs, nachos, and ice cream and find a seat in the R-Braves' sparkling new, $15-million State Mutual Stadium. While the Atlanta Braves Class-A farm hands take their first steps toward the big show, the 5,200 seats in the retro-style ballpark will put you so close you can practically reach out and pat them on the back. And all for ticket and hot dog prices that won't require you to take out a second mortgage on your homestead. For tickets, phone (706) 368–9388, www.romebraves.com.

of little plywood piggies that graze on the hillside beside Col. Poole's yolk-yellow **Real Pit Bar-B-Q** establishment, (706) 635–4100. (Col. Poole is also a Methodist minister, and your $5.00 goes to church missions.) Inside, the barbecue is seriously delicious.

Whitewater rafters, canoeists, and kayakers flock to the Ellijay and Cartecay Rivers that flow out of the mountains, right into Ellijay. Contact the Gilmer County Chamber of Commerce, 368 Craig Street, Ellijay 30539, (706) 635–7400, www.gilmerchamber.com.

At **Sugar Creek Farm and Inn,** 1050 Cox Road, Blue Ridge, (888) 662–8253, (706) 258–4494, www.sugarcreekfarmandinn.com, you can kick back in Glenn and Nancy Berns' hospitable country home and get face to face with their herd of Suri alpacas and their Great Pyrenees watchdog, Moses. Five large guest rooms (four with private bath) have sitting rooms overlooking the alpaca pastures and woodlands. Moderate overnight rates include Nancy's full breakfast and the opportunity to help Glenn feed and tend his friendly llama-kin alpacas. The animals earn their keep by giving up their thick, silky coats for luxurious sweaters, caps, capes, gloves, and other items produced and sold at **Georgia Mountain Fiber,** the Berns' shop in **Hampton Square,** 11 Mountain Street, in downtown Blue Ridge, (706) 632–6767, www.georgiamountainfiber.com. A restyled old manufacturing plant, Hampton Square shines with studio shops that create museum-quality jewelry, stained and blown glass, pottery, paintings, wood, and fiber pieces eagerly sought by tourists and residents of this booming second-home mountain community. As you go from shop to shop, stop for a lunch-and-dinner pickme-up at **Blue Jeans Pizza and Pasta Factory,** (706) 632–6503. The Ladies

Col. Oscar Poole's Pig Hill of Fame

Dulcimer Society and other groups play for your enjoyment. You can satisfy your hunger for antiques and collectibles in scads of shops on downtown Blue Ridge's Main Street.

The *Blue Ridge Scenic Railroad* takes train enthusiasts in enclosed and open-air cars on a 26-mile round-trip through the mountains and along the Toccoa River between the Fannin County towns of Blue Ridge and McCaysville. The excursion operates between March and December and is especially popular in September and October when the high country's fall foliage is at its colorful peak. The Christmas Express and Halloween Haunted Express are other popular special events. Adults, $22 to $28, senior citizens, $18 to $28, ages 3 to 12, $11 to $15. 241 Depot Street, Blue Ridge, (706) 632–9833, (800) 934–1898, www.brscenic.com.

Places to Stay in Northwest Georgia

CAVE SPRING

Cedar Creek Park,
6770 Highway 411 between Rome and Cave Spring, (706) 777–3030.
Fifty RV sites with full hookups, $13.50 daily, $80.00 weekly, and twenty-four tent sites with water, restrooms, and showers, $9.00 daily. Guests can enjoy a driving range and canoeing, tubing, and fishing on Cedar Creek.

Hearn House Inn Bed and Breakfast,
Rolater Park,
10 Georgia Avenue, (706) 777–3382.
Five guest rooms in a two-story Federal-style house that once housed 1840s Baptist seminary students. Rooms are attractively furnished in period style, with private and shared baths. TV in common area. Full breakfast with nightly rate. Inexpensive.

The Tumlin House Bed & Breakfast,
38 Alabama Street, (706) 777–0066 and (800) 939–3880, fax (706) 777–9267.
Three queen-size bedrooms and one twin bedroom in an 1842 Victorian country house built by the great-aunt of current innkeepers J.C. and Nancy Boehm. All rooms are furnished in comfortable Victorian style, with TV and VCR. Rooms with private bath or shared baths, including full breakfast. On Saturday night, the Boehms prepare a

HELPFUL WEB SITES

Dalton Convention & Visitors Bureau,
www.daltoncvb.com

Northwest Georgia Travel Association,
www.ngeorgia.com

Rome Convention & Visitors Bureau,
www.romegeorgia.com

Cartersville-Bartow County Convention & Visitors Bureau,
www.notatlanta.org

six-course gourmet dinner, open to guests and nonguests for $25 a person. The house is a short walk to antiques and gift shops and eateries around Cave Spring's picturesque downtown park. Inexpensive.

FORT OGLETHORPE

Captain's Quarters Bed & Breakfast Inn,

13 Barnhardt Circle, (706) 858–0624, www.cqinn.com
With American military history on all sides, Captain's Quarters is a handsomely restored Renaissance Revival house, originally built to house members of Fort Oglethorpe's elite Sixth Cavalry. Dwight D. Eisenhower was stationed at the post before joining WWI. The post was closed in 1946, and much of it is now part of the Sixth Cavalry Museum. The front of the house faces the post's former parade ground; the back of the house overlooks Chickamauga National Battlefield, scene of a crucial Civil War battle. Accommodations include two large suites and six other rooms with private baths. Four rooms have original fireplaces. Moderate rates include full breakfast.

ROME

Claremont House Bed & Breakfast,

906 East Second Avenue, (706) 291–0900 and (800) 254–4797, www.theclaremonthouse.net
This is a showplace Victorian Gothic mansion built in 1882. Innkeepers Chris and Holly McHagge have lavished their public spaces and guest rooms with antiques, woodburning fireplaces, and elaborately carved woodwork. Champagne in the parlor, rocking chairs on the verandas, and full gourmet breakfast served in the dining room are part of the experience of this historic downtown home. Inexpensive to moderate.

Places to Eat in Northwest Georgia

CARTERSVILLE

Appalachian Grill,

14 East Church Street, (770) 607–5357, wwww.ngeorgia.com/food/Appalachian-grill.html
Fitted out like an Appalachian Mountain lodge, with stone and brick walls and aged wood, this cozy downtown Cartersville favorite features a hearty menu of prime rib, seafood, chicken, steaks, sandwiches, and salads. Crab cakes, Cajun popcorn shrimp, and french dip sandwiches are among regulars' favorites. Full bar. Lunch and dinner Monday through Saturday. Inexpensive to moderate.

D Morgan's,

28 West Main Street, (770) 383–3535.
Executive Chef Derek Morgan has brought sophisticated global cuisine to a renovated former storefront in Cartersville's increasingly urbane downtown area. Pork tenderloin served with traditional Southern blackeyed peas and garlicky spinach is among the standouts. Grilled scallops are given the haute cuisine treatment with caramelized fennel, caper spatzle, and almond brown butter. Desserts like tart Key lime pie are all made in-house. The wine list is strong and there's a full bar. Dinner Tuesday through Saturday. Expensive.

M'Vorneen's Irish Pub,

110 South Museum Drive, (770) 386-1033.
Now this quiet town of 20,000 has some place to go after dark. Pub fare, 100 flavors of beer, and easy camaraderie are served up in a casual new watering hole in an old downtown Cartersville basement. Monday through Saturday. Inexpensive.

ROME

La Scala Restaurant & Bar,
465 Broad Street,
downtown,
(706) 238–9000.
This attractively done Italian dining room does a *bella* job with pasta, seafood, chicken, and veal dishes and offers many innovative surprises. Signature dishes include chicken Margherita, "dedicated to a beloved young woman," grilled sliced chicken with spinach, red roasted bell peppers, black olives, and ziti pasta; salmon Florentine on a bed of fresh spinach; and cioppino posillipo, a hearty stew of calamari, mussels, shrimp, and bay scallops in a tomato-based sauce, served over angel hair pasta. Dinner Monday through Saturday. Moderate to expensive.

Longhorn Steaks,
Midtown Crossing
Shopping Center,
144 Shorter Avenue,
(706) 235–4232.
Grilled steaks and salmon, with bodacious baked potatoes and other trimmings, in a kicked back faux-Western saloon setting. Lunch and dinner daily. Inexpensive to moderate.

Partridge Cafe,
360 Broad Street,
(706) 291–4048.
Good ol' Southern home-cooking has made this downtown eatery a landmark for more than sixty years. Lunch and dinner daily. Inexpensive.

Schroeder's Deli,
406 Broad Street,
(706) 234–4613.
A favorite downtown Rome destination for pizza, calzones, soups, and sandwiches. Lunch and dinner Monday through Saturday. Inexpensive.

DALTON

The Oakwood Cafe,
201 West Cuyler Street,
(706) 278–4421.
Legions of Daltonians wouldn't think about starting their day without Oakwood omelets, hot cakes, and ham and sausage biscuits. They're back at lunch and dinner for steaks, chicken, chops, and seafood. Breakfast, lunch, and dinner are served Monday through Saturday. Inexpensive to moderate.

Middle Georgia

Cherry Blossoms and Fried Green Tomatoes

For travelers caught in the relentless grind of interstate traffic, Macon can be a quick and refreshing retreat to a slower, easier era. Only a few minutes from the major highways, ***Downtown Macon Historic District*** offers a glimpse at beautifully restored Greek Revival and Victorian homes, churches, and public buildings on quiet, tree-shaded streets. Three landmark houses are open year-round. Others invite guests during the late March Cherry Blossom Festival and September Jubilee.

Your first stop should be the ***Macon-Bibb County Convention and Visitors Bureau,*** in Terminal Station, downtown at 200 Cherry Street, Macon 31201, (800) 768–3401 and (478) 743–3401. You can pick up free maps, brochures, information, and self-guided tours.

Whether with a guide or on your own, the ***Hay House*** (478–742–8155, www.hayhouse.org) will be a highlight. Five years abuilding, the opulent Italian Renaissance palazzo was finished in April 1861 just as Macon and Georgia were marching off to the War Between the States. Behind the stately red-brick facade, the twenty-four rooms are a treasure trove of

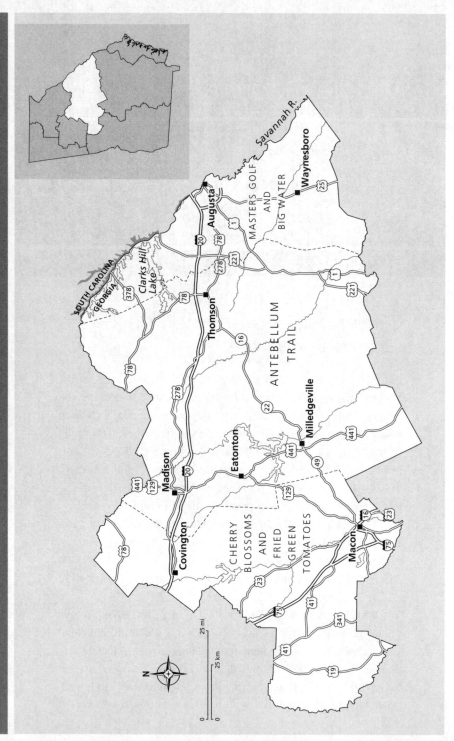

stained glass, statuary, European and American furnishings, silver and crystal, paintings, and silk and damask draperies and wall coverings. Long before air-conditioning, a cleverly concealed ventilation system kept the high-ceilinged rooms surprisingly cool even on the most torrid summer days. Located at 924 Georgia Avenue, Macon, Hay House is open Monday through Saturday from 10:00 A.M. to 4:30 P.M., Sunday 1:00 to 4:30 P.M. Admission is $8.00 for adults, $7.00 for senior citizens, $4.00 for students; free for children 6 and under.

MIDDLE GEORGIA'S TOP HITS

Downtown Macon Historic District

Hay House

Cannonball House

The Tubman African American Museum

Ocmulgee National Monument

Georgia Music Hall of Fame

Jarrell Plantation

Piedmont National Wildlife Refuge

Whistle Stop Cafe

Indian Springs State Park

High Falls State Park

Social Circle

Blue Willow Inn Restaurant

Old Governors Mansion

Flannery O'Connor Room

Milledgeville Trolley Tour

Milledgeville Ghost Walk

The Uncle Remus Museum

Rock Eagle

Madison–Morgan County Cultural Center

Morgan County African-American Museum

Hard Labor Creek State Park

Rutledge antiques and craft stores

Burnt Pine Plantation

A. H. Stephens State Historic Park

Confederate Museum

Washington Historical Museum

Callaway Plantation

Kettle Creek Battleground

McDuffie County Upcountry Plantation Tour

Old Market House

Riverwalk Augusta

National Science Center's Fort Discovery

Morris Museum of Art

Masters Golf Tournament

Mistletoe State Park

Elijah Clark State Park

Boll Weevil Plantation

Just around the corner at 856 Mulberry Street, Macon, a white-columned Greek Revival achieved lasting notoriety when a Union shell crashed through the facade and landed in the front hallway. Walk through the **Cannonball House** and adjoining **Macon Confederate Museum** (478–745–5982, www.cannonballhouse.org) for a look at the stray missile, Civil War photos, artifacts, china, crystal, weapons, uniforms, and such rare treasures as Mrs. Robert E. Lee's rolling pin. It's open Monday through Saturday from 10:00 A.M. to 4:00 P.M. Admission is $5.00 for adults, $4.00 for senior citizens, $1.00 for students, and 50 cents for children 12 and under.

Every Georgia schoolchild learns, at least for the moment, Sidney Lanier's romantic poems "The Marshes of Glynn" and "The Song of the Chattahoochee." Poet, lawyer, linguist, and musician, Lanier was born in 1842 in the tidy Victorian cottage at 935 High Street, Macon. His desk, furnishings, and personal effects are displayed at **Lanier Cottage** (478–743–3851, www.historicmacon.org) Monday through Friday from 9:00 A.M. to 4:00 P.M., Saturday from 9:30 A.M. to 12:30 P.M. Admission is $3.00 for adults, $2.50 for seniors, and $2.00 for students.

Macon's modern musical heritage includes Rock 'n' Roll Hall of Famer "Little Richard" Penniman, soul singer Otis Redding (a bridge over the Ocmulgee River is named for him), and the Allman Brothers Band. Duane Allman and fellow band member Berry Oakley—both killed in 1970s motorcycle accidents—are buried in much-visited graves at **Rose Hill Cemetery.** Maconites from all the way back to the 1830s and 600 Confederate and Union soldiers are also in the historic cemetery at 1091 Riverside Drive, Macon. Call (478) 743–3401, (800) 768–3401, www.maconga.org, for information.

The **Tubman African American Museum,** downtown at 340 Walnut Street, Macon, (478) 743–8544, www.tubmanmuseum.com, displays paintings, sculpture, and other creative endeavors by Black American, African, and Caribbean artists and craftspeople. The **Resources Room** has available reference materials and books on Black Americans. The museum's shop sells handcrafted jewelry, paintings, posters, recordings, and books. A mural depicting contemporary Black characters features Colin Powell as a military hero. Open Monday through Saturday from 10:00 A.M. to 5:00 P.M., Sunday from 2:00 to 5:00 P.M. Admission is $5.00 for adults, $3.00 for children 6 to 12; free for children under 6.

Ocmulgee National Monument, a short drive from downtown, is a mustsee for anyone fascinated by ancient Native American civilization. A dozen ceremonial and burial mounds, the highest nearly 45 feet, were built by Mississippian Indians between about A.D. 900 and 1100. They were succeeded at the site by Creeks, who remained here until their expulsion to Oklahoma in the 1830s.

Stop first at the National Park Service Visitors Center and see a short film, artifacts unearthed from the mounds, and dioramas on the cultures that flourished here. You can climb steep wooden stairs to the flat top of the 45-foot-high **Great Temple Mound** and to the crest of the surrounding smaller mounds. You may also see them from the comfort of your car. A sound-and-light presentation brings the circular **Earthlodge** back to life, as tribal elders discuss plans for a war, the effects of a drought, and other important issues. The monument is at 1207 Emery Highway, Macon, (478) 752–8257, www .nps.gov/ocmu. Hours are (daily) 9:00 A.M. to 5:00 P.M. Free admission.

The **Georgia Music Hall of Fame,** 200 Martin Luther King Jr. Boulevard, Macon, (478) 750–8555, (888) 427–6257, www.gamusichall.com, takes you on a delightful tune-filled stroll through the Peach State's incredibly rich musical heritage.

The $6 million, 43,000-square-foot downtown Macon "musical village" showcases such varied homegrown talents as Ray Charles, Lena Horne, Travis Tritt, Trisha Yearwood, Savannah songwriter Johnny Mercer, Augusta-born opera diva Jessye Norman, the Allman Brothers Band, Capricorn Records,

TOP ANNUAL EVENTS

Macon Cherry Blossom Festival,
mid- to late March,
(800) 768–3401

Madison's Spring Tour of Homes,
mid-April,
(706) 342–4743

Washington-Wilkes Tour of Homes,
early April, Washington,
(706) 678–2013

Masters Golf Tournament,
early April, Augusta,
(800) 726–4067

Riverwalk Bluegrass Festival,
early May, Augusta,
(706) 592–0054

Oliver Hardy Festival,
early October, Harlem,
(706) 556–3448

Blind Willie McTell Blues Festival,
early October, Thomson,
(706) 595–5584

Ocmulgee Indian Celebration,
late September, Ocmulgee
National Monument, Macon,
(800) 768–3401

Twelve Days of Christmas,
mid-November to end of December,
Milledgeville,
(800) 653–1804

Christmas at Callaway Plantation,
early December, Washington,
(706) 678–7060

bandleader Harry James, and Macon's own Otis Redding and "Little Richard" Penniman. You can sit in theaters and watch music videos of gospel, pop, and rock performers and listen to dozens of your favorites on headphones placed around the museum. The indoor "musical village" also has a 1950s soda fountain and a gift shop with recordings by 115 Georgia artists. Open Monday through Saturday 9:00 A.M. to 5:00 P.M., Sunday 1:00 to 5:00 P.M. Admission is $8.00 for adults, $6.00 for senior citizens 60 and older and students 17 and older with ID, $3.50 for children 4 to 16; free for children under 4.

The *Georgia Sports Hall of Fame,* a 43,000-square-foot museum across from the Music Hall of Fame, 301 Cherry Street, Macon, (478) 752–1585, www.georgiasportshalloffame.com, showcases heroes of golf, football, baseball, basketball, and other endeavors. You'll be able to test your skills on interactive and virtual reality games. Open Monday through Saturday 9:00 A.M. to 5:00 P.M., Sunday 1:00 to 5:00 P.M. Admission is $8.00 for adults, $6.00 for military personnel, college students with ID, and senior citizens 60 and older, $3.50 for children 6 to 16; free for children 5 and under.

Douglass Theatre, 335 Martin Luther King Jr. Boulevard, Macon, (478) 742–2000, www.douglastheatre.org, was built in 1921 by African-American businessman Charles Douglass. The downtown Macon theater hosted many of the country's most acclaimed performers. Among the talents that delighted audiences for more than three decades were Duke Ellington, Bessie Smith, Cab Calloway, Nat King Cole, Billie Holliday, James Brown, "Ma" Rainey, and Macon's own Otis Redding and "Little Richard" Penniman. Restored and reopened in 1996, the Douglass now has state-of-the-art facilities for movies

Harlem's Oliver Hardy

One of the silver screen's most popular and recognizable comedians was born in 1892 in the small eastern Georgia town of Harlem. Rotund fussbudget Oliver Hardy left home when he was eight years old and joined a traveling show as a boy soprano. Weary of the road, he attended Georgia Military Academy and studied law at the University of Georgia.

But greasepaint was apparently in his blood. He opened Milledgeville's first movie house and was so intrigued by the films, he became a comic villain in a theater company. In the mid-1920s, he went to Hollywood and teamed up with his sidekick and foil, Stan Laurel. It was a match made in the stars. They appeared together in more than one hundred pictures and performed on radio, stage, and TV. Hardy died in 1957, and his memory lives on at Harlem's *Laurel and Hardy Festival* in early October. Visitors enjoy a Laurel and Hardy filmfest and a look-alike contest.

and live performances and an archive of Black history in music, film, and drama. Open for tours Monday through Saturday from 9:00 A.M. to 5:00 P.M., Sunday from noon to 5:00 P.M. Donations accepted.

To get in the proper antebellum spirit, make reservations at the **1842 Inn,** 353 College Street, Macon, (478) 741–1842 or (800) 336–1842. The twenty-two guest rooms in the circa-1842 Greek Revival showplace and an adjacent cottage are decorated with antiques, fresh flowers, fireplaces, and all the contemporary comforts. Some rooms have whirlpool baths. Double rates (expensive) include continental breakfast and afternoon wine and hors d'oeuvres.

During the last ten days of March, more than 250,000 Japanese cherry trees set the stage for the city's annual **Cherry Blossom Festival** highlighted by concerts, home and garden tours, parades, and other activities. You won't be in town very long before proud Maconites tell you that in sheer numbers of blossoming trees, if nothing else, their festival is bigger than Washington, D.C.'s.

Cherry blossom season or not, you'll still enjoy a drive by the stately homes on north Macon's **"Cherry Blossom Trail,"** several miles of streets marked by pink and white signs.

Twila Faye's Tea Room & Soda Fountain, Highway 41, off I–75/ Bolingbroke, (478) 994–0031, is a sweet old-fashioned retreat from the crass commercialism and junk food of I–75. The soda fountain and lunchroom is a delightful place to sip sodas; sundaes; phosphates; cherry, vanilla, and lemon Cokes; a big choice of teas (served English style with finger sandwiches, scones, and shortbread tea cakes); and lunch on salads, house-made soups, and a variety of nutritious sandwiches. It's open from 11:00 A.M. to 5:00 P.M. Monday through Saturday.

Jarrell Plantation State Historic Site is a homespun juxtaposition to the romanticized Old South of Tara and Twelve Oaks, dashing beaux and ladies fair. At the end of a tree-shaded graveled road off Highway 18 between Forsyth and Gray, you enter a world where unrelenting hard work—not flirtation and idle mint juleps—was the rule of society. From the early 1840s, when John Fitz Jarrell built the first dwelling, until 1958, when the last direct heir died, the plantation was worked by three generations of Jarrells. They planted cotton, ran gins and gristmills, and battled boll weevils, depressions, and General William Tecumseh Sherman himself. Nowadays, the dwellings, work buildings, barnyards, and fields are maintained by the Georgia Department of Natural Resources as a living memorial to the state's agricultural heritage.

You'll enter the plantation through the scuppernong arbor, whose juicy fruit Jarrell women turned into pies and jellies. A flock of guinea fowl, squawking like so many feathered burglar alarms, alerted the family that visitors were approaching. These days, the guinea fowl still sound off, and an assortment of barnyard animals—a goat, a horse, a brown milk cow, a burro, a couple of sheep—press against the fence for the hay held out by children.

At the modern visitor center, you can watch a film on the plantation's history and pick up a self-guided walking-tour map.

At the 1847 plantation's plain first dwelling, you can visualize the womenfolk sitting in a circle, busily making quilts and clothes while hearty stews bubbled on the wood-burning stove. At the mill complex down the hill from the house, workmen get the steam engine ready to grind the sugarcane into syrup.

Jarrell Plantation—Route 1, Box 40, Juliette 31046, (478) 986–5172, (800) 864–PARK, www.gastateparks.org—is open Tuesday through Saturday from 9:00 A.M. to 5:00 P.M., Sunday from 2:00 to 5:00 P.M. Admission is $4.00 for adults, $2.50 for children 6 to 18; free for children 5 and under. It's 18 miles south of I–75 exit 185 at Forsyth, 18 miles north of I–75 exit 171 at Macon.

The *Piedmont National Wildlife Refuge,* a 35,000-acre preserve 10 miles down the graveled road from the plantation, has a visitor center and hiking trails. You can bring your fishing gear and try your luck in the Ocmulgee River. Phone (478) 986–5441.

If you saw the movie *Fried Green Tomatoes* or read the Fannie Flagg novel it was based on, you'll be glad to know it wasn't pure fiction. After the movie's highly successful 1991 run, enterprising folks in the almost-ghost town of *Juliette* bought up the store that served as the movie's cafe and reopened the "new" *Whistle Stop Cafe,* (478) 992–8886, (888) 642–4628, www.thewhistle stopcafe.com. Fried green tomatoes are served, along with barbecue, fried chicken, meat loaf, pork chops, and other home-cooked favorites. Southern-style breakfast is also served. The block of stores and the white frame depot around the cafe have also been revived as antiques and gift shops. Adding to the atmosphere, local kids dive off the dam near the textile mill, just as they did in the film. The Whistle Stop Cafe is open Tuesday through Sunday 11:00 A.M. to 6:00 P.M. It's in downtown Juliette, 10 miles off I–75 north and south exit 186. Inexpensive.

A quiet and peaceful recreation place now, *Indian Springs State Park,* near Jackson, has a long, colorful, and tragic history. For many centuries Creeks and other tribes gathered at a sulfur spring whose waters were believed to have magical powers to cure ailments and restore vitality. In the spring of 1825, Creek Chief William McIntosh signed an illegal treaty ceding all tribal lands to the state of Georgia. The fraudulent treaty so enraged the dispossessed natives that they murdered McIntosh and several of his followers. A valid treaty in 1828 finally ended Creek dominion, and the town of Indian Springs was founded, along with what's believed to be the oldest state park anywhere in the United States.

Nowadays people still flock to the sulfur springs and take home jugs of the strong-smelling water. They swear by its ability to restore health and vitality and offer this advice to those who quail at the rotten-egg smell: Just let it sit for two to three days, and the aroma will vanish, but not the curative strength of the minerals.

The handsome fieldstone buildings in the park were built during the Great Depression by the Civilian Conservation Corps. Along with the mineral waters, artifacts and historical displays are on view at the *Indian Museum.* Around a 105-acre lake are a swimming beach, fishing, rental boats, nature trails, and picnic areas. Campsites with electrical and water hookups are $10 a night. Completely furnished two-bedroom cottages, with log-burning fireplaces, are available. There is a $2.00 per visit parking fee. Contact Park Superintendent, 678 Lake Clark Road, Flovilla 30216, (770) 504–2277. For reservations, call (800) 864–PARK or log on to www.gastateparks.org.

Fresh Air Bar-B-Que (770–775–3182), on Highway 42 between Jackson and Indian Springs State Park, is one of the holy grails of this savory Georgia art form. Except for wooden planking that covered the old sawdust floor a few years ago, and one change of ownership more than fifty years ago, this rambling, wooden barbecue shack has changed only marginally since it served its first platter in 1929.

The pine board tables have been in place for more than forty years. Pork is slowly cooked over hickory and oak coals right behind the ordering counter. It's sweet and succulent, with a tangy pièce de résistance provided by a secret sauce prepared by the family that has operated the place since the early 1940s. Along with barbecued pork, the simple menu includes only Brunswick stew,

BILL'S FAVORITES

Cherry Blossom Festival	Antebellum Madison
Hay House	Antebellum Washington
Indian Springs State Park	Riverwalk Augusta
The buffet tables at the Blue Willow Inn Restaurant	National Science Center's Fort Discovery
Old Governors Mansion	Morris Museum of Art
Antebellum Milledgeville	

cole slaw, slabs of starchy white bread, soft drinks, and iced tea. It's open Monday through Thursday from 7:00 A.M. to 7:30 P.M., Friday and Saturday until 9:30 P.M., and Sunday until 8:30 P.M. During the summer, it usually remains open a half hour to an hour later.

High Falls State Park, off Highway 36 (I–75 exit 198), about 12 miles south of Indian Springs, is another rustic off-the-beaten-path retreat. The centerpiece is a series of scenic whitewater cataracts of the *Towaliga River* rushing over mossy rocks. According to legend, Creek Indians "cured" their victims' scalps around the Towaliga—hence the name, which means "roasted scalp."

Two hiking trails offer views of the falls, the river, and adjacent woodlands. You can wade into the river, but be extremely careful of the slick, mossy rocks. Also in the 995-acre park, you'll find a 650-acre lake for fishing and boating, a swimming pool, and 142 tent and trailer sites, with water and electrical hookups. There is a $2.00 per visit parking fee. Contact Park Superintendent, Route 5, Box 108, Jackson 30233, (478) 993–3053, (800) 864–PARK, www.gastate parks.org. For reservations call (800) 864–PARK. It's 1.8 miles east of I–75 exit 198/High Falls Road.

The little Walton County town of *Social Circle,* about 8 miles west of Hard Labor Creek on Highway 11, is a delightful place to stroll and browse. The nineteenth-century storefronts have been brightly repainted, and three are antiques shops. The wooden shelves in Claude Wiley's Store are stacked to the ceiling with canned goods, overalls, farm products, and household necessities. The town allegedly got its name when a stranger happened onto a cluster of idling locals and found them so friendly he proclaimed, "Why, this is sure some social circle."

The *Blue Willow Inn Restaurant,* 294 North Cherokee Road, Georgia Highway 11, Social Circle, 770–464–2131, www.bluewillowinn.com, is like a nostalgic Sunday dinner at Grandma's. The dining room of the 1890s Victorian house is filled with a bountiful buffet that includes fried chicken, pork chops, chicken and dumplings, baked ham, an array of vegetables (including state-of-the-art fried green tomatoes), congealed salads, cake, and fruit cobbler—all at astonishingly modest prices. After your feast, sit on front porch rockers, walk in Billie and Lewis Van Dykes's gardens, and stroll down Social Circle's Main Street. Open Tuesday through Friday from 11:00 A.M. to 2:30 P.M. and 5:00 to 8:00 P.M., Saturday from 11:00 A.M. to 3:30 P.M. and 4:30 to 9:00 P.M., and Sunday from 11:00 A.M. to 9:00 P.M. Willow on Fifth, with the same yards-long buffet, is now open in downtown Macon. See "Places to Eat in Middle Georgia," page 146.

Lake Oconee, a mammoth Georgia Power Company impoundment of the Oconee River, is a major destination for outdoor recreation. The 19,000-acre lake, with a 375-mile shoreline, has numerous marinas, campsites, picnicking areas, and swimming beaches. The Georgia Power Company office at the lake (800–886–LAKE, www.visitlakeoconee.com) can supply further information about recreational facilities. The lake is easily accessible from I–20.

The ***Ritz-Carlton Lodge at Reynolds Plantation,*** One Oconee Lake Trail, Greensboro, (800) 241–3333, (706) 467–0600, www.ritzcarlton.com/resorts/reynoldsplantation, brings high luxury to Lake Oconee's shores. The Adirondacks-style Lodge's 251 guest rooms and suites have all the deluxe bells and whistles. Guests enjoy fine wining and dining, play water sports, tennis, and four superb golf courses, and pamper themselves in the wellness center. Expensive.

The Ritz-Carlton and other upscale developments around the lake have been a boon to nearby Greensboro. Antiques shops around the courthouse square attract browsers and buyers, who can also visit a couple of historic curiosities. The ***Old Rock Gaol,*** a fortresslike jail built in 1807 and in use until 1895, bears a grim resemblance to Paris' notorious Bastille, on which it was allegedly modeled. Granite walls 2 feet thick, with small barred windows and a rooftop gallows, warned citizens to stick to the straight and narrow. Or else. It can be toured by appointment with the Greene County Chamber of Commerce, 111 North Main Street, Greensboro 30642, (706) 453–7592, (866) 341–4466, (800) 886–5253, www.greeneccoc.org.

The Iron Horse, visible in a pasture on Highway 15 at the Oconee River Bridge, was originally a public sculpture placed on the University of Georgia campus in 1954. But after students looked the gift horse in the mouth, then shamefully vandalized it, the 2,000-pound scrap-iron sculpture was relocated in a cornfield where he safely grazes in sight but out of harm's way.

Antebellum Trail

Milledgeville was Georgia's capital city from early after the American Revolution until after the War Between the States. Laid out in 1803–1804 on a precise grid of broad streets and public squares, it was the only American city other than Washington, D.C., specifically planned as a capital. In its own way, it was to post-Revolutionary Georgia what Brasilia was to mid-twentieth-century Brazil: a magnet intended to lure settlers away from the comforts of the Atlantic coast.

Statesmen and public officials eased the burdens of the wilderness by building palatial Greek Revival mansions filled with the finest American and European furnishings, books, and art. Halcyon days ended in the fall of 1864, when General William T. Sherman's Union army, marching from Atlanta to Savannah, captured the city.

According to which legend you choose to believe, Milledgeville was spared Sherman's torch because (a) he was met at the outskirts by fellow brothers of the local Masonic lodge, who pleaded for leniency; (b) he didn't want to burn a town he'd chosen as temporary headquarters; or (c) he had a local lady friend and did not wish to break her heart.

Whatever the reasons, Milledgeville had no military significance. Union troops burned the military arsenal and stoked molasses down the pipes of the Episcopal church, which was used as a horse stable. When the "March to the Sea" resumed, the Governor's Mansion and everything of nonmilitary importance was left unharmed. The Reconstruction government moved the capital to Atlanta, an action ratified by the state's voters in 1868.

The Old State Capitol and Old Governor's Mansion are the most tangible landmarks of Milledgeville's tenure as Georgia's capital city from 1838 to 1868. When Union troops occupied the city in 1864, they held a mock session of the state legislature in the Gothic-style capitol and "revoked" the Ordinance of

The Ghost and Miss Katherine

My only encounter with a ghost was one dark and stormy night in Milledgeville. A photographer and I were guests of Miss Katherine Scott, who'd lived in her antebellum home on North Jefferson Street since the early 1900s. Wise and witty, she'd been an English professor at Georgia College for Women for many years and wasn't pleased with the way her teachings had influenced her most famous student, Flannery O'Connor. "I read one of her books," she bristled, "and Flannery could have done the world a big favor by killing off that odious main character on the first page instead of the last."

Her home's original owner was an unsavory character named Sam Walker, who'd reputedly buried several slaves and a few wives in his backyard. When his son came home from boarding school with typhus, skinflint Sam refused him a doctor. The boy eventually died in the four-poster bed at the top of the stairs. Sam saw a vision of his deceased son, condemning him to walk the staircase to the bedroom (where I was to spend a sleepless night) as long as the house stood.

In the wee hours of that night, with rain, thunder, and lightning crashing, and a grandfather clock bonging every quarter hour, I heard a heavy tread on the staircase, then another, and another. Something crashed onto the floor downstairs. I didn't come out from under the covers until first light. "Well, I guess you heard Sam doing his mischief last night," Miss Katherine smiled. "See, he even threw that picture on the floor. The hook's still in the wall."

The photographer was staying in the room next to Miss Katherine's and swore she didn't get up and do the ghostly walk herself. When he processed his pictures, a vaporous image was clearly visible, lurking over the top of the stairs.

Secession that took Georgia out of the Union in 1861. Recently restored, the building, at 301 East Greene Street, Milledgeville, (478) 453–1803, www.old capitolmuseum.com, is now a classroom building for Georgia Military College. Cadets lead tours Monday through Friday that include a historical museum and the antebellum House Chamber. Adults $2.00, students $1.00.

The Old Governor's Mansion, built in 1838 in Palladian Greek Revival style, underwent a $10 million restoration, completed in 2005, that returned it to its 1850s grandeur. One of Georgia's most beautiful public buildings, the rose-hued mansion with four Ionic columns and a wealth of antiques, art, and unique architectural features, is at 120 South Clark Street, Milledgeville, (478) 445–4545, www.gcsu.edu/mansion. Open Tuesday through Saturday from 10:00 A.M. to 4:00 P.M., Sunday 2:00 to 4:00 P.M. Adults $10.00, seniors $6.00, students $2.00.

American literature fans should also visit the **Flannery O'Connor Room** (478–445–4047, www.library.gcsu.edu) in the library of Georgia College and State University. The late author wrote her two novels (*The Violent Bear It Away* and *Wise Blood*) and short story collections while living here. She died in 1964 and is buried in Memory Hill Cemetery. The Flannery O'Connor Room at her alma mater displays first editions, manuscripts, gifts from admirers, memorabilia, and drawings she did as a hobby. It's in the Ina D. Russell Library, Georgia College, Milledgeville. Open by appointment.

O'Connor's fans shouldn't miss **Andalusia,** the author's 544-acre farm on Highway 441, four miles northwest of Milledgeville, where she wrote many of her stories. A self-guided tour includes the gently rolling farmland that inspired so much of her fiction, the main house, barns, equipment and milk-processing sheds, horse stable, and three tenant houses. On your tour, you'll probably encounter some of the "residents": white-tailed deer, wild turkeys, red-tailed hawks, beavers, raccoons, opossums, birds, reptiles, and amphibians. In the main house, rooms open to the public include O'Connor's bedroom, the dining room, and the kitchen. Guests are invited to view the video production of O'Connor's story, *The Displaced Person,* which was filmed on location at Andalusia in 1976. Andalusia is open for tours on Monday, Tuesday, and Saturday from 10:00 A.M. to 4:00 P.M. Admission $5.00. For information, contact the Milledgeville Convention & Visitors Bureau, 200 West Hancock Street, Milledgeville 31061, (800) 653–1804, www.andalusiafarm.org.

The best way to enjoy the town's heritage is on a two-hour motorized **Milledgeville Trolley Tour,** which covers the major landmarks and includes a visit to the Governor's Mansion. Guides weave a wealth of humor and anecdotes into their historical narrative. Tours leave the Milledgeville Convention and Visitors Bureau, 200 West Hancock Street, Milledgeville 31061, Tuesday and Friday at 10:00 A.M. Adults are $10.00, children 6 to 12, $5.00. The tourism office (478–452–4687 and 800–653–1804; www.milledgevillecvb.com) also has free maps and information for self-guided walking tours. It's directly across the street from the handsome *Baldwin County Courthouse.*

Milledgeville is a "high-spirited" town. If you'd like to hear about some of its specters, join the *Milledgeville Ghost Walk.* The hour-and-a-half stroll through the historic district begins at dusk Wednesday through Saturday, and you never know who (or what) you'll encounter along the way. Adults are $6.50, children 6 to 12, $4.50. Phone (478) 485–0741 for reservations.

For dinner Tuesday through Sunday, try the crisply fried catfish and hush-puppies, shrimp, and other fresh seafood at *Chobys Landing* (478–453–9744), 3090 Highway 441 north. It's on *Lake Sinclair,* north of town, with docking facilities near the door. *Cafe South,* 2465 North Columbia Street, downtown Milledgeville, 478–452–3164, is where ravenous students and other townsfolk satisfy their craving for perfectly prepared fried chicken, fish, sweet potato casserole, turnip and collard greens, squash soufflé, pecan pie, and other Southern comfort food. Lunch every day except Saturday. Inexpensive.

Antebellum Inn, in Milledgeville's downtown historic district, 200 North Columbia Street, Milledgeville, phone and fax (478) 454–5400, www.antebellum inn.com, has five guest rooms and suites, with private bath, cable TV, phone, pool, and wraparound verandas, all in an 1890s Victorian home. Moderate rates include full breakfast.

After Milledgeville's history lesson, you'll probably be ready for some quiet relaxation. Lake Sinclair, a 15,330-acre, 420-mile shoreline impoundment of the Oconee River, has plenty of stretching room. Marinas, fishing docks, and camp-grounds are off U.S. Highway 441 north of Milledgeville.

Milledgeville's literary lioness was Flannery O'Connor. Eatonton, about 15 miles north on U.S. 441, was the birthplace in 1848 of Joel Chandler Harris, who turned the slave legends he heard as a youngster on a Putnam County plantation into the *Uncle Remus: Tales.*

The *Uncle Remus Museum* (706–485–6856, www.eatonton.com), on Highway 441, Eatonton, south of the town of 4,800, has Harris's personal mementos and illustrations of the tales of the devilish Br'er Rabbit, sly-but-perpetually-outwitted Br'er Fox, dumb ole Br'er Bear, and, of course, the Tar Baby. Also in the log cabin, which was created from two original slave cabins, you'll see first editions, a diorama of an antebellum plantation, and other his-torical artifacts. The museum is open daily during the summer from 9:00 A.M. to 5:00 P.M. and closed on Tuesday the rest of the year. Adults are $1.00; children, 50 cents. Eatonton also is the home of Alice Walker, Pulitzer Prize–winning author of *The Color Purple.*

As you drive past the Putnam County Courthouse in the center of Eatonton, look for the little likeness of Br'er Rabbit on the lawn facing Highway 441. Many well-kept antebellum homes are on the shady streets leading off the courthouse square. Putnam County is also the center of Georgia's dairy industry, so you'll spot several contented herds as you drive out of town.

Rock Eagle, 4 miles north of Eatonton, is a relic of Indian civilizations that flourished here more than 6,000 years ago. A creamy white quartz effigy—about 10 feet high, 103 feet from its head to its tail, 32 feet from wingtip to wingtip—the great bird seems poised for flight. Archaeologists believe Rock Eagle was a focus for Indian tribal rituals. The best views are from an observation tower. It's located in a 4-H Club Center, on Highway 74, off Highway 441, (706) 484–2800, www.rockeagle4h.org.

Morgan County, between Augusta and Atlanta, claims **Madison,** (I–20 exit 114/Highway 441), one of Georgia's prettiest antebellum towns. In 2000, *Travel Holiday* magazine named Madison "The Best Small Town in America." Before leaving, you can relax at a state park with an 18-hole golf course, fish and swim at a 19,000-acre lake, and hunt quail on a private preserve.

Strolling along the tree-shaded streets and picturesque town square, admiring Madison's treasury of glorious antebellum architecture, we should say "thank you" to a United States senator who put himself between the town and General William T. Sherman's torch. In late 1864, Atlanta in ruins 60 miles away and the cruel "March to the Sea" in full stride, Sherman's Union army approached Madison's outskirts. They were met by former Senator Joshua Hill, a foe of secession who'd been acquainted with Sherman in Washington. He peacefully surrendered the town, which was miraculously spared war's ravages.

Your first stop should be the **Madison–Morgan County Chamber of Commerce Welcome Center,** 115 East Jefferson Street, Madison, (706) 342–4454, (800) 709–7406, www.madisonga.org. In this former 1880s fire station on the courthouse square, you can load up on walking-tour maps and brochures and get any information you may need on festivals, bed-and-breakfasts, and restaurants. Stop next at the **Madison–Morgan County Cultural Center,** 434 South Main Street, Madison, (706) 342–4743, www.morgan.public.lib.ga.us. The Romanesque-style redbrick schoolhouse, circa 1895, is now the hub for regional arts, theater performances, and the source of walking-tour maps of the fetching little town of 3,000. The former schoolrooms now show pottery, weaving, paintings by Georgia artists and traveling exhibitions, nineteenth-century furniture, farm implements, clothing, and Civil War artifacts. You can also see a log cabin from the early 1800s and an 1890s schoolroom, complete with pot-bellied stove and hickory switch. The center's August theater festival features everything from Shakespeare to Tennessee Williams. The center is open

Tuesday through Saturday from 10:00 A.M. to 4:30 P.M., Sunday from 2:00 to 5:00 P.M. Admission is $3.00 for adults, $2.50 for seniors, $2.00 for students; 6 and under free. No charge on Wednesday.

With a self-guided tour map, walk through the *Madison National Historic District* and admire more than three dozen gorgeous Greek Revival, Neoclassical, Victorian, Federal, and Romanesque homes, many of them graced by gardens and stately trees. A number of these old beauties are open to the public during Madison's May and December festivals.

The *Morgan County African-American Museum,* 156 Academy Street, Madison, (706) 342–9191, documents the contributions Blacks have made to the area's cultural and social life. Located in the 1895 Horace Moore House, the museum has rooms with period furnishings, a reference library, paintings, books, and exhibits. Open Tuesday through Friday from 10:00 A.M. to 4:00 P.M. and Saturday from noon to 4:00 P.M. Admission is $3.00 for adults, $2.00 for children.

You can take a guided tour of *Heritage Hall,* 277 South Main Street, Madison, (706) 342–9627, www.friendsofheritagehall.com, a white-columned 1830s Greek Revival showplace near the courthouse square. Look for romantic messages etched on the windows, and be mindful of a mysterious presence that sometimes evidences itself in an upstairs bedroom. Open daily from 10:00 A.M. to 5:00 P.M. Adults are $5.00; students, $2.00.

Madison's town square is one of Georgia's most delightful, and the *Morgan County Courthouse* one of the grandest in the 159 counties. Several antiques and handicraft stores will draw your attention as you stroll around the square. When hunger strikes, head for the cafeteria line at *Ye Old Colonial* (Courthouse Square, Madison, 706–342–2211), a unique dining landmark on the square. Once upon a time the building was a bank, which accounts for the high ceilings, tiled floors, and a small dining room in the one-time vault. These days you can cash in on excellent fried chicken, barbecue, fish, Southern-style vegetables, and hearty breakfasts with biscuits and buttery grits. Service is continuous from breakfast through lunch and dinner Monday through Saturday (11:00 A.M. to 8:00 P.M.).

Three of Madison's loveliest homes welcome bed-and-breakfast guests: *Brady Inn,* 250 North Second Street, (706) 342–4400; *Southern Cross Guest Ranch/B&B,* 1670 Bethany Church Road, (706) 342–8027, (800) 342–8027, www.southcross.com; and *The Farmhouse Inn,* 1051 Meadow Lane, (706) 342–7933, www.thefarmhouseinn.com.

The *Steffen Thomas Museum and Archives,* near the rural Morgan County community of Buckhead, houses hundreds of oil and watercolor paintings, mosaics, and sculptures by late German-born expressionist artist Steffen

Thomas, who did most of his work in Atlanta. Like many artists, Thomas was his own model: "The Goat of Mentelle" is the self-portrait sculpture of the artist as a billy goat. (He lived on Mentelle Street in Atlanta.) The museum is at 4200 Bethany Road, 3 miles from I–20 exit 121. Open Tuesday through Saturday 1:00 P.M. to 4:00 P.M. Phone (706) 342–7557, www.steffenthomas.org.

Hard Labor Creek State Park, 12 miles west of Madison, near the small community of Rutledge, is a nice place to relax for a day, or several days. The recreational possibilities include a very good 18-hole golf course and a lake for swimming, boating, and fishing. Plenty of picnic tables are spread among the pines, and there's a playground for the youngsters. If you're planning to play the 6,682-yard, par-72 course, bring your own clubs. You may rent an electric cart in the clubhouse, which has showers and a snack bar. The park's fifty campsites have water, electricity, restrooms, and showers; twenty two-bedroom cottages are completely furnished, including towels, sheets, and kitchen utensils. There is a $2.00 per visit parking fee. The park office is open daily from 8:00 A.M. to 5:00 P.M. Contact Superintendent, 1400 Knox Chapel Road, Rutledge 30663, (706) 557–3001. For reservations call (800) 864–PARK, or log on to www.gastateparks.org.

Until recently **Rutledge** (I–20 exit 105, www.smallbutspecial.com) was a couple of blinks as you passed through on the way to Hard Labor Creek. During the past few years, a group of citizens has bought up much of the town of 650 and attracted a cadre of artists and craftspeople from as far away as New England. **Rutledge antiques and craft stores** on the main street sell handmade quilts, handcrafted furniture, original artwork, pottery, and antiques. At **Red Door Studio** (706– 557–9020) Molly Lesnikowski crafts birdhouses from Victorian textile spindles, and also sells watercolor paintings and painted furniture. **Kudzu & Grits Folk Arts** (706–557–8694) sells work by area artists. At **Rutledge Hardware** (706–557–1770), changed only marginally the past half century, Paul Jones fills orders for galvanized tubs, cast-iron cookware, tools, seed, farm implements, and chamber pots "like my great-grandpa used." The **Barn Raising's Shelves** (706–557–2956) are filled with gifts and collectibles, bath products and lotions. When it's time for a break, many shoppers enjoy ice cream and colorful shaved ices at **The Caboose** (706–557–9020), a revamped 1910 railroad car. The entire delightful town is now on the National Register of Historic Places.

For breakfast, lunch, and dinner, locals and visitors take tables and booths at **Yesterdays Cafe** (706–557–9337). Teri and Alan Bragg's delicious repertoire includes Southern breakfast, highlighted by blueberry pancakes, omelets, and Teri's biscuits; lunchtime burgers, sandwiches, soups, and blue-plate specials; and dinner entrees like catfish filet in herb crust, ribeye steak, chicken Dijon,

Where, Oh Where, Can Jim Williams Be?

Finding Jim Williams wasn't easy. I'd heard that the *Midnight in the Garden of Good and Evil* protagonist was at rest in the old cemetery in Gordon, the little Wilkinson County town from which he escaped to become the rich, famous arbiter of Savannah's party-loving society and the star in the most glorious scandal in the port city's history. But after prowling through the weedy burial ground in downtown Gordon (population 2,400), I knew this clearly wasn't a place the fastidious Mr. Jim would literally be caught dead. I finally found him, instead, outside of town, in a vast garden of stone a few yards from the prim, white frame Ramah Primitive Baptist Church. His black granite marker, inscribed JAMES ARTHUR WILLIAMS, DEC. 11, 1930, JAN. 14, 1990, is well-kept and weedless. But I can't believe he's happy out here in the quiet country churchyard, 200 miles from his old compadres. And I'm sure he'd love to get his manicured hands on whoever keeps putting pots of plastic flowers on his stone. But in case he's tempted to break out and have another fling at his glamorous old life, his mama is right there to rein him in. If you'd like to drop by, he's on the left side of the cemetery, on Highway 57 at Highway 18, between Macon and Irwinton.

and linguine Alfredo, topped off with house specialty buttermilk pie. Wine and beer are available. Open for breakfast, lunch, and dinner Tuesday through Sunday. Inexpensive to moderate.

A. H. Stephens State Historic Park, on Highway 22, Crawfordville, outside the small town of Crawfordville, includes the home and gravesite of Alexander Hamilton Stephens, governor of Georgia and vice-president of the Confederacy. *Liberty Hall,* the two-story frame house Stephens built around 1830, is filled with his furnishings, personal effects, and the wheelchairs to which he was bound much of his life.

The adjoining *Confederate Museum* (706–456–2602, 800–864–PARK, www.gastateparks.org) is highlighted by a bronze statue of Stephens by Gutzon Borglum, sculptor of the U.S. presidents on Mount Rushmore, South Dakota. This fine collection of memorabilia also includes dioramas of soldiers in the heat of battle and the quiet of the campfire; rifles and shot; field gear; battle flags; and touching personal belongings—Bibles, prayer books, and blood-stained photos of wives and sweethearts.

As in all wars, Civil War soldiers used sharp-edged humor to help blunt the insidious enemies of fear and homesickness. "In this army," a Confederate foot soldier wrote, "one hole in the seat of the breeches indicates a captain, two holes is for a lieutenant, and the seat of the pants all out is for us privates." Liberty Hall and the Confederate Museum are open Monday and Wednesday through Saturday from 9:00 A.M. to 5:00 P.M., Sunday from 2:00 to 5:30 P.M. Closed Tuesday. Admission is $2.00 for adults, $1.00 for children 5 to 18; free for children under 5.

After your history lesson, relax at the park's recreation area. A ¼ mile from Liberty Hall, you'll find a swimming pool, two fishing lakes, picnic shelters, and thirty-six tent and trailer sites, with water and electrical hookups, showers, and restrooms. The museum and park are 2 miles from I–20 exit 148. There is a $2.00 per visit parking fee. On a more modern note, the 2002 Reese Witherspoon film *Sweet Home Alabama* was filmed in Crawfordville.

Incorporated in 1780, the picture-book little town of **Washington** was the first American community named in honor of the father of our country. Skirted by General William T. Sherman's rampaging "March to the Sea" and treated kindly by progress and time, the town of about 5,000 is today like a living Williamsburg. More than thirty Greek Revival homes, churches, and public buildings predate 1850. Most of them are still well-maintained residences. Three antebellum landmarks are open to visitors year-round.

The ***Robert Toombs House State Historic Site***, 216 East Robert Toombs Avenue, Washington, (706) 678–2226, www.gastateparks.org, was the home of Georgia's "Unreconstructed Rebel," U.S. senator, and Confederate secretary of state. At odds with the Confederacy—he was resentful of Jefferson Davis's presidency—as well as the Union, he fled to the Caribbean and Europe after the war. Returning in 1880, he scorned political pardon. "I am not loyal to the government of the United States," he declared, "and do not wish to be suspected of loyalty." The guided tours of his Greek Revival house include a documentary film, anecdotes, historical exhibits, and several rooms with period furnish-

Robert Toombs House

ings. Open Tuesday through Saturday from 9:00 A.M. to 5:00 P.M., Sunday from 2:00 to 5:30 P.M. Admission is $3.00 for adults, $1.75 for children 6 to 18; free for children under 5.

The **Washington Historical Museum,** 308 East Robert Toombs Avenue, Washington, (706) 678–2105, www.washingtonwilkes.com/attractions.html, houses an outstanding collection of Civil War artifacts, including Jefferson Davis's camp chest (given to him by English sympathizers), weapons, uniforms, signed documents, photographs, and furnishings. The main floor of the circa 1835–1836 two-story frame house is furnished as a typical nineteenth-century double parlor, dining room, and bedroom. The ground floor has been restored as a period kitchen. The grounds are noted for beautiful landscaping and one of Georgia's largest camellia gardens. Hours are Tuesday through Saturday from 10:00 A.M. to 5:00 P.M., Sunday from 2:00 to 5:00 P.M. Admission is $3.00 for adults, $2.00 for children ages 5 to 12, under age 5 free.

Callaway Plantation, 5 miles west of Washington on Highway 78, Washington, (706) 678–7060, is a living heritage museum rich in lessons about Southern antebellum life. Three restored homes and the adjoining farm are like a walk back in time. The redbrick, white-columned manor house was the heart of a 3,000-acre cotton plantation. Rooms are furnished with period antiques and many unique architectural features. The outbuildings include a hewn log cabin, circa 1785, with early domestic and agricultural tools and primitive furniture and a smokehouse, barn, pigeon house, and cemetery. Surrounding fields are planted with cotton, corn, cane, and vegetables, just as they were in the mid-nineteenth century. The plantation has been owned by the same family since the late eighteenth century, and it's open Tuesday through Saturday from 10:00 A.M. to 5:00 P.M., Sunday from 2:00 to 5:00 P.M. Admission is $4.00 for adults, $1.50 for children 12 to 18, $1.00 for children 6 to 11.

The **Mary Willis Library,** 204 East Liberty Street, Washington, (706) 678–7736, is an architectural gem, with a place in history and a mystery in its foyer. Georgia's first free public library, the redbrick high-Victorian landmark with its stately round tower was founded in 1888 by Dr. Francis T. Willis in honor of his daughter, Mary, whose likeness is the centerpiece of a priceless Tiffany Studios stained-glass window. The mystery revolves around an old iron trunk in the foyer. Did it once hold part of a shipment of "Lost Confederate Gold" that still attracts fortune hunters to Wilkes County? It's keeping a tight lid on the secret.

Washington also figured in the Revolutionary War. A marker at **Kettle Creek Battleground,** 8 miles south of town on Highway 44, Washington, commemorates the patriots' 1779 rout of the British and the Redcoats' subsequent withdrawal from this area of Georgia. Picnic tables are at the site. Call (706) 678–2013.

When hunger overwhelms your hunt through history, head for **Washington Jockey Club** (706–678–1672), an attractive cafe on the courthouse square. Midday fare includes sandwiches, soups, salads, plate lunches, and homemade desserts Monday through Saturday. Dinner is served Tuesday through Saturday. Inexpensive to moderate.

Many of Washington's most magnificent homes are open during the early April **Washington-Wilkes Tour of Homes.** Contact Washington-Wilkes Chamber of Commerce, P.O. Box 661, Washington 30673, (706) 678–2013, www .washingtonwilkes.com.

If your group numbers at least ten, you can take a trip through history on the **McDuffie County Upcountry Plantation Tour.** You'll set out from the Thomson–McDuffie County Tourism Bureau in the restored train depot and stop at the **Rock House,** a 1785 fieldstone farmhouse; **Alexandria,** a stately Virginia-influenced brick plantation house and boxwood gardens from 1805; and the site of November's **Belle Meade Fox Hunt.** A number of gracious antebellum homes line Thomson's tree-shaded streets. Contact Thomson–McDuffie County Tourism Bureau, 111 Railroad Street, Thomson 30824, (706) 597–1000, www.thomson-mcduffie.org. You can stay overnight at the **1810 Country Inn & Winery,** built sometime around that year. Ten guest rooms have antiques and private baths. The house has original heart-pine walls, antiques, eight fireplaces, and a restored smokehouse. Inexpensive rates include an elaborate Southern breakfast. Contact 1810 Country Inn, 254 North Seymour Drive, Thomson, (706) 595–3156, or (800) 515–1810, www.countryinnandwinery.com.

The **Old Market House** is a souvenir of the period from 1796 to 1805 when little Louisville ("Lewis-ville") was Georgia's capital. Built in the 1790s, the Market's weathered timbers are held together by 1-inch-diameter wooden pegs. The Market's bell was cast in France in 1722 and was on its way to a New Orleans convent when it was hijacked by pirates and somehow ended up in Louisville. Louisville's tenure as state capital was immortalized by the Great Yazoo Land Fraud of 1795, which cost Georgia the territory that later became the states of Alabama and Mississippi. Contact the Jefferson County Chamber of Commerce, 302 East Broad Street, Louisville 30434, (478) 625–8134, www .jeffersoncounty.org.

Masters Golf and Big Water

Augusta, a metro area of 250,000, traces its heritage to 1736, when General James Edward Oglethorpe, founder of the Georgia Crown colony, laid it out as the state's second city, after Savannah. Fought for during the Revolutionary War and skirted by General William T. Sherman's "March to the Sea," Augusta has mild winters and a genteel Old Southern lifestyle that caught the attention of post–Civil War Northern aristocrats, who found the right formula for golf—a pastime that symbolizes this city to people around the world.

For many years Augusta almost forgot that the Savannah River ran by its doorstep. All that is changing rapidly as **Riverwalk Augusta** becomes a new center of downtown activity. The main entrance to Riverwalk is at Eighth and Reynolds Streets, a block off Broad Street. The top of the old river levee has been turned into an inviting brick esplanade with seating clusters overlooking the river, historical displays, and playground and picnic areas. Major hotels, shops, and dining are along the Riverwalk. Stop first at the Augusta Visitor Information Center, inside the Augusta Museum of History, 560 Reynolds Street, Augusta 30901, (706) 724–4067, (800) 726–0243, www.augustaga.com, for information and historic exhibits on Augusta's once-lucrative trade in "white gold." It's open Monday through Saturday from 10:00 A.M. to 5:00 P.M., Sunday from 1:00 to 5:00 P.M. Self-guided walking and driving tours as well as group tours are available at the welcome center.

The **Augusta Museum of History** is now part of Riverwalk's excitement. Early in 1996 the sixty-year-old "municipal attic" moved into a new 48,000-square-foot home at Sixth and Reynolds Streets. The twenty-three permanent galleries are filled with Revolutionary and Civil War weapons and uniforms, Native American culture, natural history (including a major dinosaur exhibit), space exploration, communications, vintage photographs, and a tribute to the city's and Georgia's founder, General James Edward Oglethorpe. Savannah River marine life inhabits a small aquarium. Train buffs shouldn't miss "Old No. 302," the Georgia Railroad's last steam engine. Contemporary times are represented by exhibits on the 1960s Civil Rights movement and stage costumes worn by James Brown, Augusta's flamboyant "Godfather of Soul." The museum is at 560 Reynolds Street, Augusta. Open Tuesday through Saturday from 10:00 A.M. to 6:00 P.M., Sunday from 2:00 to 5:00 P.M. Adults are $4.00; children and seniors, $3.00. Phone (706) 722–8454, www.augustamuseum.org.

National Science Center's Fort Discovery, One Seventh Street at Riverwalk, Augusta, (800) 325–5445, (706) 821–0200, www.nationalsciencecenter .org, one of Riverwalk's most popular attractions, is a world of fun and educational experiences for people of all ages. The 275 hands-on, interactive exhibits range from simple games for young children to more complicated lessons to tax the brain power of serious science students. You're invited to ride a bike on a high wire, walk on the moon, maneuver robots, and play the newest multimedia games. Special shows are held in the 250-seat Paul Simon Theater, and there's a snack bar when all this fun works up your appetite. The two-story, 128,000-square-foot museum is open Monday through Saturday from 10:00 A.M.

to 5:00 P.M., Sunday from noon to 6:00 P.M. Admission is $8.00 for adults, $6.00 for senior citizens and ages 4 to 17.

Morris Museum of Art is at Riverfront Center, 1 Tenth Street at Riverwalk, Augusta, (706) 724–7501, www.themorris.org. Two centuries of Southern art are represented in this museum designed like a private home. The permanent collection includes works by Augusta native Jasper Johns and mixed media artist Robert Rauschenberg. Special exhibits are held throughout the year. Open Tuesday through Saturday from 10:00 A.M. to 5:30 P.M., Sunday from 12:30 to 5:30 P.M. Admission is $5.00 for adults, $3.00 for students and senior citizens.

Woodrow Wilson's Boyhood Home is one of Augusta's newest attractions. In 1858, when the future twenty-eighth president was one year old, his father became pastor of Augusta's First Presbyterian Church. The family lived thirteen years in the church-owned manse in downtown Augusta. Wilson's earliest memory was hearing of Abraham Lincoln's 1861 election. In 1865 he saw Federal troops escorting captive Confederate President Jefferson Davis through the streets. In 1871 he met Robert E. Lee, a guest of the city. He scratched his name, "Tom," (his first name was Thomas)—which is still visible—on a parlor window and left scuff marks from his shoes on the dining room table, one of thirteen church-owned pieces in the house when the Wilsons lived there. The only item that belonged to the Wilsons and that is still in the house is a butter dish, part of a silver service given to the family their first Christmas in Augusta. In 1991 historic Augusta, Inc., purchased the house from owners who'd used it as a flower shop and beauty shop. Following a $2 million restoration, the two-story redbrick house is open for guided tours Tuesday through Saturday, 10:00 A.M. to 4:00 P.M. Adults $5.00, seniors $4.00, students $3.00. 419 East Seventh Street. Phone (706) 722–9828, www.wilsonboyhoodhome.org.

Golf in the Garden

Augusta Golf and Gardens will eventually be home to the Georgia Golf Hall of Fame. Until then, visitors are welcome to walk through beautifully tended theme gardens, cooled by mini-waterfalls, fountains, and ponds. Rest a spell on the benches, and please don't pick the daisies! Life-size bronzes of Arnold Palmer, Jack Nicklaus, Ben Hogan, and other champions of Augusta's Masters Tournament are watching you. Near the Riverwalk, One Eleventh Street, Augusta, (706) 724–4443, (888) 874–4443, www.gghf.org. Open seasonal hours; guided tours by appointment. Adults $7.00, seniors and military $6.00, children $5.00.

New York has its Erie Canal; Georgia has the **Augusta Canal National Heritage Area.** Built in 1845 to harness water power of the Savannah River, it's the nation's only industrial canal still used for its original purposes. It's also one of Augusta's newest visitor attractions, offering history, recreation, and unique experiences at its Interpretive Center and boat tours on 8.5 miles of waterway and towpath. Located inside Enterprise Mill, a colossal nineteenth-century redbrick textile mill once powered by the harnessed waters of the Savannah River, the Interpretive Center's film and exhibits explain the canal's construction by African-American, Irish, Chinese, and Italian laborers and also the mechanics and physics of turning water into industrial power. Large windows reveal the working 1920-era electrical turbines that are once again generating hydroelectric power. Artifacts and audiotape interviews with former mill workers enhance the experience that's culminated with hour-long tours in shallow-draft, nineteenth-century, Petersburg-style canal boats. The Interpretive Center, at Enterprise Mill, 1450 Greene Street, Augusta, (888) 659–8926, (706) 823–0440, is open Monday through Saturday 10:00 A.M. to 6:00 P.M., Sunday 1:00 to 6:00 P.M. Boat tours are Tuesday and Thursday 11:00 A.M. and 1:30 P.M., and Saturday 11:00 A.M., 1:30 and 3:00 P.M. Tickets to the Interpretive Center and boat tour can be purchased separately or in combination: Adults, $5.00 interpretive center, $6.00 boat, $10.00 combo; seniors 55 and over and military, $4.00 center, $5.00 boat, $8.00 combo; ages 6 to 18, $3.00 center, $4.00 boat, $6.00 combo; 5 and under, center free, $4.00 boat.

Ezekiel Harris House, 1840 Broad Street, Augusta, (706) 724–0436, is Augusta's second-oldest structure. In 1797 Harris came to the area from South Carolina with plans to build a town to rival Augusta as a tobacco market. On a hill overlooking Augusta, the house is an outstanding example of post-Revolutionary architecture. The gambrel roof and vaulted hallway are reminiscent of New England. Tiered piazzas are supported by artistically beveled wooden posts. Rooms are furnished with period antiques. It's open Monday through Friday from 1:00 to 4:00 P.M., Saturday from 10:00 A.M. to 4:00 P.M. Adults are $2.00; students, 50 cents.

Meadow Garden, Independence Drive near the intersection of Walton Way and Thirteenth Street, Augusta, (706) 724–4174, was the home of George Walton, one of Georgia's signers of the Declaration of Independence. Built around 1791, it's the city's oldest documented structure and has been restored and refurnished by the Georgia Society, Daughters of the American Revolution. Hours are Monday through Friday from 9:00 A.M. to 4:00 P.M., Saturday and Sunday by appointment. Admission is $2.00 for adults, $1.00 for children and seniors.

Gertrude Herbert Institute of Art, 506 Telfair Street, Augusta, (706) 722–5495, www.ghia.org, is an architecturally unique early nineteenth-century residence that showcases regional and Southeastern contemporary art. Built in 1818 by Augusta Mayor Nicholas Ware, the elliptical three-story staircase, Adam-style mantels, and other rich ornamentation earned it the name "Ware's Folly." Hours are Tuesday through Friday from 10:00 A.M. to 5:00 P.M., Saturday from 10:00 A.M. to 2:00 P.M. Admission is $2.00 for adults, $1.00 for children and seniors.

The *Lucy Craft Laney Museum of Black History,* 1116 Phillips Street, Augusta, (706) 724–3576, www.lucycraftlaneymuseum.com, honors the beloved late educator, born in slavery, who established Augusta's first Black secondary schools and a nurses' training school. Her former home has exhibits and photos on her remarkable life and many contributions to African-American culture. Open Tuesday through Friday 9:00 A.M. to 5:00 P.M., Saturday 10:00 A.M. to 4:00 P.M., Sunday 2:00 to 5:00 P.M. Adults $3.00, children $1.00.

Until the 1960s, Broad Street, America's second widest main street after New Orleans' Canal Street, was downtown Augusta's hub. When suburban malls suffocated its retail trade, Broad nearly died of neglect. Happily, it's coming back to life as the *Broad Street Artist Row.* More than a dozen art galleries, antiques and gift shops, and fun little restaurants have taken over deserted mercantile stores. Have lunch or dinner at *Nacho Mama's,* 976 Broad Street, (706) 724–0501, for killer burritos, tacos, and margaritas. Or stop at *Luigi's,* 590 Broad Street, (706) 722–4056, which has seen Broad Street through good and bad times since 1946. Spin your favorite Bing Crosby, Andrews Sisters, and Glenn Miller platters on your personal booth jukebox while you tuck into good old Italian-American spaghetti and meatballs, lasagna, and ravioli.

Kids and kids at heart shouldn't miss *Fat Man's Forest* (706–722–0796). A rambling array of added-on buildings at 1545 Laney-Walker Boulevard, Fat Man's is locally renowned for its holiday paraphernalia. At Halloween people come from miles around to rent costumes, purchase pumpkins and made-to-order jack-o'-lanterns, and send their youngsters through the haunted house. At Christmas the kids ride a festive train while grown-ups browse for trees, gifts, and decorations. Whatever the season, it's a fun place to wander and marvel at the Fat Man's ingenuity. After your adventure in the "forest," step next door for tasty adventures in Southern homecooking at Fat Man's Cafe. Lunch Monday through Saturday from 11:00 A.M. to 3:00 P.M. Phone (706) 733–1740.

Kids and adults who love wild things will have a wonderful time exploring *Phinizy Swamp Nature Park,* Lock-and-Dam Road, Augusta, (706) 828–2109, www.phinizyswamp.org. The park's 1,150 acres of uncorrupted wetlands, swamps, nature trails, boardwalks, and observation decks put you in sight of herons, egrets, red-shouldered hawks, otters, alligators, amphibians, and other free-ranging creatures. Open daily. Free.

For golfers around the globe, Augusta is Christmas, the World Series, the rainbow's end. In late March and early April, fortunate faithful congregate along the dogwood- and azalea-rimmed fairways of storied *Augusta National Golf Club* to hail the game's elite as they pursue the Green Jacket, symbolic of the *Masters Golf Tournament* championship. Unless you know a player or a club member, tickets to the championship rounds will be impossible to find. But don't despair. You can see all the greats up close—even take their pictures—during the practice rounds preceding the tournament. The bad news is the *Masters Practice Rounds* have become so popular that tickets must now be purchased in advance. To receive an application form, write to Masters Tournament Practice Rounds, P.O. Box 2047, Augusta 30903-2047.

If you'd like to play, the *Jones Creek Course,* an 18-hole public layout at 777 Jones Creek Drive, Evans, (706) 860–4228, is considered the "poor man's" Augusta National. Designed by renowned golf architect Rees Jones, it has an excellent practice facility and professional instructors. Rental clubs and carts are available.

Bass anglers and those seeking more off-the-beaten-path relaxation should look into a minivacation at *Mistletoe State Park.* About 35 miles north of Augusta, on 76,000-acre Clarks Hill Reservoir, this very tranquil park reputedly commands some of America's finest bass fishing waters. You may also swim and boat in the lake, hike 5 miles of woodland trails, and ride rental bikes around the 1,920 acres. Two-bedroom furnished cottages and camping sites with water, electricity, showers, and restrooms are available. There is a $2.00 per visit parking fee. Contact Park Superintendent, 3723 Mistletoe Road, Appling 30802, (706) 541–0321. For camping and cottage reservations, call (800) 864–PARK or log on to www.gastateparks.org.

Elijah Clark State Park, north of Mistletoe, is another wooded retreat on the western shores of Clarks Hill Lake. Twenty furnished cottages and 165 tent and trailer sites are a few steps from the water. You'll also find marinas, docks, boat ramps, a swimming beach, nature trails, and plenty of picnic areas. The park was named for Revolutionary War hero Elijah Clark. A Colonial museum displays relics from the period. The park is on Highway 378, 7 miles east of Lincolnton. Phone (706) 359–3458 for information. For reservations, call (800) 864–PARK or log on to www.gastateparks.org.

Burke County, between Augusta and Savannah, hails itself as "The Bird Dog Capital of the World." You can test its veracity with an organized bird and game hunt at *Boll Weevil Plantation,* Route 2, Box 356A, Waynesboro 30830, (706) 554–6227. You can stay overnight at *Steadman House Bed & Breakfast,* 828 Liberty Street, Waynesboro, (706) 437–1228, (877) 835–9439, www.steadman house.com. Contact the Burke County Chamber of Commerce, 828 Liberty Street, Waynesboro, (706) 554–5451. Inexpensive.

Places to Stay in Middle Georgia

MACON

The Crowne Plaza Macon,
108 First Street,
(912) 746–1461,
fax (912) 746–7420.
This is downtown Macon's only full-service first-class hotel. The 177 guest rooms and public areas were a $10 million redo in 1997–1998. The Bourbon Street Cafe serves New Orleans and Cajun cuisine in a faux-Bourbon Street setting. Bogart's Martini and Cigar Extravaganza and the Big Easy Lounge are popular gathering places for downtown workers, residents, and visitors. The hotel also has an outdoor pool and a fitness center. Doubles are inexpensive to moderate.

JULIETTE

The Jarrell 1920 House,
715 Jarrell Plantation Road,
(888) 574–5434 and
(478) 986–3972,
www.jarrellhouse.com
Philip and Amelia Haynes's 1850s-style plantation house, built in 1920, was originally part of what's now Jarrell Plantation State Historic Site. There are two large guest rooms with private baths. Rate includes full breakfast. The Friday and Saturday weekend package includes Saturday breakfast at the Whistle Stop Cafe in nearby Juliette. Guests are also given a tour of the neighboring Jarrell Plantation State Historic Site. The house is 18 miles east of I–75 exit 185. Inexpensive.

WASHINGTON

Blackmon-Wingfield House,
512 North Alexander Avenue,
(706) 678–2278.
Inexpensive.

Hill and Hollow Farm,
2090 Thomson Road,
(706) 678–4439.
Inexpensive.

Holly Ridge Country Inn,
2221 Sandtown Road,
(706) 285–2594.
Inexpensive.

Hunter Finnell House,
217 Lexington Avenue,
(706) 678–7593.
Inexpensive.

Wisteria Hall,
225 East Robert Toombs Avenue,
(706) 678–7779.
Inexpensive.

You'll sleep in the bower of history at any of these Washington inns.

HELPFUL WEB SITES

Macon Convention & Visitors Bureau,
www.maconga.org

Milledgeville Visitors Center,
www.milledgevillecvb.com

Augusta Convention & Visitors Bureau,
www.augustaga.org

National Science Center,
www.nationalsciencecenter.org

Washington-Wilkes Chamber of Commerce,
www.washingtonwilkes.com

AUGUSTA

Azalea Inn,
312–316 Greene Street,
(706) 724–3454,
(877) 292–5324,
www.theazaleainn.com
Twenty-one large suites in a redone Victorian home have queen or king beds and private baths with whirlpool tubs; some have kitchenettes. Rates include continental breakfast. Moderate.

Partridge Inn,
2110 Walton Way,
(706) 737–8888 and
(800) 476–6888,
fax (706) 731–0826,
www.partridgeinn.com
This full-service inn has 155 executive, studio, and deluxe suites. Many have kitchens and balconies. Dining room serves upscale American and continental lunch and dinner; there's also a full bar. Rates include Southern buffet breakfast. Moderate to expensive.

Places to Eat in Middle Georgia

MACON

Nathalia's,
2720 Riverside Drive,
(912) 741–1380.
Nathalia's has satisfied Macon's hunger for classical Italian cooking since 1984. Grilled veal chops, risotto, osso buco, seafood, pasta, and chicken dishes are complemented by light, delicate sauces. (No heavy red sauces.) French, Italian, and American wines are available by the glass. Dinner is served Monday through Saturday. Moderate to expensive.

Tic Toc Room,
408 Martin Luther King Jr. Boulevard, downtown Macon,
(478) 744–0123.
New Southern, Italian, and American cuisines are showcased in a stylishly revamped former downtown Macon music club, where Macon native "Little Richard" Penniman got his start. Before and after dinner, enjoy live music and a full bar in the upstairs lounge. Dinner Monday through Saturday. Moderate to expensive.

Willow on Fifth,
Fifth and Cherry Streets, downtown Macon,
(478) 745–9007.
Social Circle's Blue Willow Inn has brought its award-winning Southern buffet to downtown Macon. Fried chicken, roast beef, baked ham, an array of vegetables, salads, soups, and desserts are presented at lunch and dinner daily. Seafood smorgasbord is the Friday and Saturday night feature. Inexpensive.

AUGUSTA

French Market Grille,
Surrey Center,
425 Highland Avenue,
(706) 737–4865.
Chuck and Gail Baldwins' spicy Louisiana Cajun cooking has kept Augustans coming back for more than fifteen years. They can't seem to get enough of the Baldwins' delectable gumbo, Cajun crawfish étouffée, jambalaya, and pecan praline pie. Lunch and dinner are served daily. Moderate to expensive.

La Maison,
in a restored mansion in the Old Town Historic District at 404 Telfair Street,
(706) 722–4805.
La Maison prepares the city's most sophisticated cuisine. Former Atlanta chef Heinz Sowinski's repertoire includes a wide range of French, German, Swiss, and other specialties. For adventurous tastes, the "Game Sampler" is a platter of three or four exotic, richly sauced meat dishes such as pheasant, smoked venison, quail, and wild boar. Magnificent desserts reflect Sowinski's European culinary heritage. Cocktails and a large selection of American, Australian, and European wines round out the menu. Dinner is served Monday through Saturday. Moderate to expensive.

Le Cafe de Teau,
1855 Central Avenue,
(706) 733–3505.
First-rate lamb, steaks, grilled duck, and seafood are accompanied by dinnertime jazz at this upbeat cafe. Dinner is served daily except Monday. Moderate to expensive.

Luigi's,
590 Broad Street, downtown Augusta,
(706) 724–0501.
Enjoy spaghetti and meatballs, lasagna, ravioli, and other hearty Italian-American dishes while you play your favorite 1940s and '50s tunes on your booth jukebox. Dinner Monday through Saturday. Inexpensive.

Coastal Georgia

Historic Savannah

Founded in 1733, **Savannah** is one of America's truly special cities. Not long after founding father General James Edward Oglethorpe came ashore on Yamacraw Bluff and dispersed his 144 settlers, he set about planning Savannah in a style befitting the capital of a Crown colony named for King George II. He hunkered down in his damask tent on the bluffs and with military precision laid out a grid of straight, broad streets, braided at 2-block intervals by spacious public squares. Initially, the twenty-four squares were mustering places for troops and convenient locales for citizens to draw water and exchange news.

In 1793 Eli Whitney, a visiting New Englander given to tinkering with gadgets, devised a mechanized way to separate cotton seeds from the fluffy white bolls. His cotton gin revolutionized Southern planting. On the tragic downside, it also perpetuated the waning practice of slavery and indirectly led to the Civil War. Soon, real gold earned from "white gold" enabled planters, merchants, and shipbuilders to embellish Oglethorpe's squares with English Regency, Georgian, Federal, and Gothic Revival showplaces, filled with fine furniture and art objects

COASTAL GEORGIA

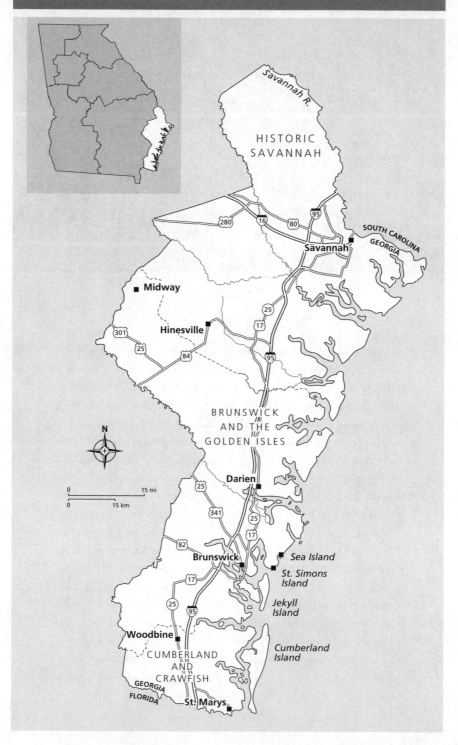

HISTORIC
SAVANNAH

Savannah R.

280 16 80 95

Savannah

SOUTH CAROLINA
GEORGIA

■ Midway

25

301 17

■ Hinesville

25

25 84 95

BRUNSWICK
AND THE
GOLDEN ISLES

N

0   15 mi
0   15 km

Darien

25

341 25

17

82

Brunswick ■ Sea Island
17   ■ St. Simons
Island

25

Jekyll
Island

95

■ Woodbine

CUMBERLAND
AND
CRAWFISH

Cumberland
Island

GEORGIA
FLORIDA St. Marys

shipped from Europe. As "front yards" for the affluent, the squares were dressed up with trees, flowering plants, benches, fountains, and memorials to Revolutionary heroes and other notables.

In the 1950s, much of the city's heritage teetered on the brink of extinction. Scores of venerable landmarks, even a couple of Oglethorpe's squares, were crunched in the jaws of progress before the Historic Savannah Foundation rode in like the cavalry and saved the day. To date, more than 1,500 historic structures have been restored in the 2.2-square-mile **Savannah National Historic District,** the nation's largest.

Before you leave home, phone the Savannah Convention & Visitors Bureau, (877) 728–2662, for advance information. When you arrive, stop first at the Savannah Visitors Center, 303 Martin Luther King Jr. Boulevard, Savannah 31401, (912) 238–1779, www.savannahvisit.com. Inside the former 1860s Central of Georgia Railway depot, you'll find everything you need: free brochures, tour and restaurant information, lodging reservations, and an orientation film. The center adjoins the **Savannah History Museum,** with displays, multimedia presentations, a steam locomotive, and homage to famous citizens like songwriter Johnny Mercer ("Moon River," "Moonlight in Vermont," and countless other standards). You can also see the movie prop bus stop bench where Tom Hanks told his tale in the Oscar-winning film *Forrest Gump.* Outside the Visitors Center, take one of the many guided orientation tours in an open-air tram or air-conditioned van or minibus.

COASTAL GEORGIA'S TOP HITS

Savannah National Historic District	Sapelo Island Tours
Midnight in the Garden of Good and Evil tours	Hofwyl-Broadfield Plantation State Historic Site
Mighty Eighth Air Force Museum	Brunswick
Fort Jackson/Oatland Island Education Center	"Folkston Funnel"
Tybee Lighthouse and Museum	Jekyll Island Historic District
Skidaway Island State Park	Fort Frederica National Monument
Wormsloe State Historic Site	Christ Church
Midway Church	St. Simons Lighthouse
Fort King George State Historic Site	Cumberland Island National Seashore
	Woodbine Crawfish Festival

When you're ready to head off on your own, *River Street,* a wide brick pedestrian esplanade also known as Riverfront Plaza, is the best place to start. An elevator at Bay and Bull Streets next to the Hyatt Regency Savannah Hotel will take you down to a Savannah Convention & Visitors Bureau Welcome Center, with restrooms, water fountains, and attendants ready to load you up with information, 101 East Bay Street, Savannah 31401, (912) 644–6400, (877) SAVANNAH. As a major plank in the restoration movement, the antebellum brick cotton warehouses were refashioned as seafood restaurants, taverns, touristy shops, and art galleries. Recessed benches are great places to sit and watch the cargo ships cruising to the Georgia Ports Authority docks and heavy industries upriver and the open Atlantic 20 miles downriver.

Browse the shops, have a drink and a bite, then take the elevator or climb up the cobblestoned steps to Bay Street and you're ready for your walk on Savannah's most beautiful street. Few cities are fortunate to be blessed by a thoroughfare as charming as the 10 blocks of *Bull Street* from Savannah's gold-domed City Hall to the green bower of Forsyth Park. Five of Oglethorpe's most picturesque squares are set like gems on this glorious avenue named for a British colonial officer. It divides the historic district into east and west halves. Before you leave, you'll be drawn back time and again to this wonderful, old-worldly street. Revolutionary hero General Nathanael Greene is buried under the granite shaft in Johnson Square. Wright Square honors the founder of the Central of Georgia Railroad, William Washington Gordon.

At Bull Street and Oglethorpe Avenue, Girl Scouts and students of American history should pause at the *Juliette Gordon Low Girl Scout National Center,* (912) 233–4501, www.girlscouts.org/birthplace. Designed by noted early nineteenth-century English architect William Jay, the dignified English Regency mansion was the 1860 birthplace of "Daisy" Low, grandaughter of William Washington Gordon and founder of the Girl Scouts of America. Her paintings and sculpture, personal effects, and GSA mementos are in the high-ceiling rooms. The museum is at 142 Bull Street, Savannah. It's open Monday through Saturday from 10:00 A.M. to 4:00 P.M., Sunday from 12:30 to 4:30 P.M.; closed Wednesday. Admission is $8.00 for adults, $6.00 for senior citizens and students ages 5 to 20.

A bronze statue of General Oglethorpe, by Daniel Chester French (who sculpted the seated statue at Washington's Lincoln Memorial), looks south from its pedestal in *Chippewa Square,* daring the Spanish in Florida to move against his city. Sergeant William Jasper, killed in the 1779 British siege of the city, brandishes the flag atop the monument in the center of Madison Square.

TOP ANNUAL EVENTS

St. Patrick's Celebration,
downtown Savannah, for several days
leading up to March 17,
(800) 444–2427

Jekyll Island Arts Festival,
Goodyear Cottage, mid-March,
(912) 635–3920

Savannah Tour of Homes & Gardens,
late March,
(912) 234–8054

Night in Old Savannah,
mid-April,
(912) 650–7846

N.O.G.S. Tour of Hidden Gardens,
walled gardens north of Gaston Street,
downtown Savannah, mid-April,
(912) 238–0248

Great Golden Easter Egg Hunt,
Jekyll Island Historic District,
Easter Sunday,
(912) 635–3636

Civil War Relic Show & Sale,
Savannah Civic Center, mid-June,
(912) 897–1099

Christmas in Savannah,
throughout December,
(800) 444–2427

Historic St. Marys Christmas Tour,
mid-December,
(912) 927–4976

The tree-shaded benches are usually filled with earnest-looking young people who've drifted over from the Savannah College of Art and Design. Chartered in 1979, with seventy-one students and four faculty, SCAD has grown from the redbrick, late-1800s Guards Armory on the square's east side into an internationally known institution with 5,000 students and 500 faculty and staff. SCAD has restored more than three dozen buildings in the historic district, and all those students infuse the area with electrifying energy.

When Savannah peacefully surrendered to the Union Army in December 1864, General William T. Sherman lodged in the Gothic Revival **Green Meldrim House** (now St. John's parish house) on Madison Square's west side, (912) 233–3845. From the house, he sent a telegram to his commander-in-chief: "Dear Sir, President Lincoln: I beg to present you as a Christmas gift, the city of Savannah with 150 heavy guns and also about 25,000 bales of cotton." You're welcome to walk in and admire magnificent Gothic wood carvings, plasterwork, and spacious rooms. Open Tuesday through Saturday from 10:00 A.M. to 4:00 P.M. Adults, $4.00; students, $2.00.

If you're starting to flag a bit, pep up with a cappuccino or latte at **Gallery Espresso's** indoor or sidewalk tables at 6 East Liberty Street, (912) 233–5348, across from the DeSoto Hilton Hotel. You can also tuck into shepherd's pie and a pint of something from the bar at *Six Pence Pub,* a bit of Olde England at 245 Bull Street, (912) 233–3156.

Patriotic Savannahians named *Monterey Square* for an American victory in the 1840s Mexican War. The monument that's usually in the center of the square salutes Count Casimir Pulaski, a Polish nobleman who gave his all for the American cause during the 1779 British siege. The crumbling, century-old marble shaft was taken down for restoration in 1996 and may or may not be back in place when you visit. *Temple Mickve Israel,* on the east side, is Georgia's oldest Jewish congregation. Spanish and German Jews, who landed five months after Oglethorpe, brought Torahs and other sacred objects and documents that are now part of a collection you're welcome to see. Just knock on the side door Monday through Friday from 10:00 A.M. to noon. No charge.

Savannah's most famous house is directly across the square. Some tour guides used to tell visitors that the *Mercer Williams House Museum* was songwriter Johnny Mercer's boyhood home. Mercer's grandfather built it after the Civil War, but the family never lived in the stately redbrick Italianate mansion at 429 Bull Street. Antiques dealer, social arbiter, and arts patron Jim Williams lived there until he shot his companion to death in 1984 and became fodder for John Berendt's international best-selling nonfiction book *Midnight in*

Savannah's First Scandal

The founder of Methodism had Savannah tongues wagging some 250 years before Jim Williams shot Danny Hansford in the scandal immortalized in *Midnight in the Garden of Good and Evil.* According to John Duncan, book dealer and raconteur extraordinaire, the parson's tale went something like this:

"John Wesley came to Savannah in the 1730s to minister to the Indians, but he became pastor of Christ Anglican Church. His undoing was falling in love with the original Hard-Hearted Hannah, Vamp of Savannah. It was one of those May-December romances, he was 36, Sophia Hopkey was 18. They'd walk hand-in-hand in the moonlight, and read poetry together, but when he asked her to marry him, she dropped him like a hot potato and married another man. After the marriage, when Sophia and her new husband came to services at Christ Church, Wesley refused to give his ex–lady friend communion. Sophia's in-laws sued Wesley for defamation of character. He was indicted, but never came to trial. It was Savannah's first big public scandal, of which we've had many ever since."

For more interesting Savannah tales, you can visit John Duncan at V&J Duncan Antique Maps and Prints, 12 East Taylor Street.

the Garden of Good and Evil, loosely made into a 1997 movie. The house is open for tours of about 30 to 35 minutes Monday through Saturday 10:30 A.M. to 4:00 P.M., Sunday 12:30 to 4:00 P.M. Purchase tickets, $13.25 for adults, $8.48 for students, at Mercer House Gift Shop, behind the main house. Phone (912) 236–6352, (877) 430–6352, www.mercerhouse.com. Jim Williams' sister, Dorothy Kingery, lives full-time in the house.

Another 2 blocks and you're in Forsyth Park. The centerpiece of the twenty-acre sanctuary is an ornate, wrought-iron fountain that looks a bit like a three-tiered wedding cake decorated with swans and water-spouting tritons.

Squares east and west of Bull Street are blessed with landmarks in a variety of styles. *Isaiah Davenport House,* 324 East State Street, Savannah, (912) 236–8097, www.davenport housemuseum.org, on Columbia Square, played a pivotal role in the restoration crusade. Built between 1815 and 1820 and considered one of America's most perfect Georgian mansions, the redbrick house was threatened with demolition in the 1950s to make space for a funeral home parking lot. The Historic Savannah Foundation came to the rescue and went on to help save hundreds of other imperiled structures. The restored Davenport House gleams with Chippendale and Sheraton furnishings, woodwork, and plaster crown moldings. It's open Monday through Saturday from 10:00 A.M. to 4:30 P.M., Sunday from 1:30 to 4:30 P.M. Admission is $8.00 for adults, $5.00 ages 6 to 18. As for the funeral home, it's now Kehoe House, one of the city's grandest historic inns.

blameitonthe general

It's ironic that the city's founder, General James Edward Oglethorpe, may have inbred Savannah's love of hard drink. Although he tried unsuccessfully to prohibit rum (and lawyers) from his colony, Oglethorpe was the first person in the colony to brew beer. He did it, he wrote, "to keep the soliders satisfied." Like the Puritans and Pilgrims in New England, Oglethorpe also believed that drinking beer was a far healthier and more godly endeavor than partaking of polluted water whose very sip was an invitation to disease.

The *Owens-Thomas House, Telfair Academy of Arts & Sciences,* and the new *Jepson Center for the Arts* are part of the same cultural family, with the same hours, fees, and Web site, www.telfair.org. Each is open Monday from noon to 5:00 P.M.; Tuesday through Saturday 10:00 A.M. to 5:00 P.M.; Sunday 1:00 to 5:00 P.M. Adults $9.00, seniors and AAA $8.00, college students $6.00, ages 5 to 12 $4.00. Two-site combination $14, three-site $18.

The Jepson Center for the Arts, dedicated in spring 2006, is a dramatically contemporary expansion of the Telfair Museum in downtown Savannah. With

64,000 square feet in two buildings that are connected by a glass bridge over a historic lane, the glistening white Portuguese stone-clad Jepson, with floor-to-ceiling windows and abundant natural light, includes two galleries for traveling exhibits; dedicated galleries for African-American art, Southern art, and photography and works on paper; a two-level hands-on "experience" gallery for young people; two outdoor sculpture terraces; and an auditorium and cafe.

The $24.5-million Jepson is the first major expansion of the 120-year-old Telfair, designed in 1819 by renowned architect William Jay, whose other Savannah landmarks include the Owens-Thomas House. The Regency-style building was originally the home of the Telfairs, a distinguished Savannah family, and became the South's oldest public art museum in 1875. The stately rooms and a ballroom where the Marquis de Lafayette danced minuets during

A Prophecy Fulfilled

Savannah is full of ghosts and tales of ghosts. Jack Richards, an artist fascinated by the subject, leads true believers and the openly skeptical on "Ghost Talk, Ghost Walk" tours of the historic district. He relates tales of apparitions at the Pirates House and Olde Pink House restaurants, cemeteries, and private homes. One of his favorites is a romantic story about the mother of Girl Scouts founder Juliette Gordon Low. In the 1890s, when workers were digging the foundation in Wright Square for the monument to William Washington Gordon, founder of the Georgia Railroad and grandfather to Juliette Gordon Low, they inadvertently dug up the remains of Tomochichi, the Indian chief who had befriended General James Edward Oglethorpe. They reported the discovery to Eleanor Kinsey Gordon, Gordon's daughter-in-law and Juliette Gordon Low's mother.

Embarrassed by the incident, she ordered the big granite stone now on Tomochichi's grave in Wright Square. Although she asked for a bill several times, the Stone Mountain Granite Company never sent one.

After a decade of repeated requests, she finally got a bill for a dollar, "Due on Judgment Day." She sent a check for a dollar, with a curt note: "I'll be much too busy on Judgment Day to pay my debts."

On the day she died, her prophecy apparently came true. She called her deceased husband's name, as if she were seeing an apparition. He was known as "The Old Captain," his rank in the Confederate Army. Minutes later, as her daughter-in-law, Margaret, rested in the downstairs parlor, a man in a Confederate officer's uniform walked down the stairs and out the front door. He was followed by Margaret's husband, who announced Mrs. Gordon's death. He hadn't seen the mysterious officer. When they walked outside, the family servant was crying. He said, "I just saw the Old Captain and he said, 'I'm taking Miss Eleanor for her afternoon ride.'" Just as she predicted, Mrs. Gordon was too busy on Judgment Day to worry about her debts.

Dashing Through the Spanish Moss

Born in Boston, James Lord Pierpont wrote the popular Christmas song "Jingle Bells" in Savannah in 1857. A distant kin of financial baron J. P. Morgan, Pierpont arrived in Savannah in 1852 and played the organ at the Unitarian church, where his brother was pastor. He married the daughter of Savannah's Civil War mayor and, with visions of New England's snowy landscapes dancing in his head, gave the world the tune that's been played ad infinitum ever since. A historical marker in downtown Savannah's Troup Square commemorates his contribution to the holiday repertoire.

his 1825 visit to Savannah house collections of American and European paintings, sculpture, and decorative arts. You can also view the original "Bird Girl" statue, featured on the book cover of *Midnight in the Garden of Good and Evil.* The Telfair and Jepson are at 121 Barnard Street, Savannah, (912) 232–1177.

The Marquis de Lafayette slept at the Owens-Thomas House on Oglethorpe Square, 124 Abercorn Street, Savannah, (912) 233–9743, during his 1825 farewell-to-America tour. He addressed the populace from the wrought-iron side balcony. William Jay's elegant Regency-style urban villa is filled with art, antiques and intriguing architectural details.

King-Tisdell Cottage/Black History Museum, an 1890s Victorian cottage at 514 East Huntington Street, Savannah, (912) 234–8000, www.kingtisdell.org, displays documents, furniture, and artifacts of Low Country Black heritage. It's the headquarters for Negro Heritage Tours, which includes landmarks of Black history going back to the first slaves. Open Tuesday through Saturday noon to 5:00 P.M. Admission for all ages is $2.50.

Ships of the Sea Maritime Museum, 41 Martin Luther King Jr. Boulevard, Savannah, (912) 232–1511, www.shipsofthesea.org, has moved its extensive collections of sailing ship models, ships in bottles, scrimshaw art, maritime paintings, ornamental figureheads, and other nautical artifacts into spacious galleries in the 1819 Scarbrough House. Open Tuesday through Sunday from 10:00 A.M to 5:00 P.M. Adults, $7.00; students and senior citizens, $5.00.

The role Savannahians played in the 1960s Civil Rights movement is portrayed with memorabilia, photos, documents, and displays at the *Ralph Mark Gilbert Civil Rights Museum,* 460 Martin Luther King Jr. Boulevard, Savannah, (912) 231–8900, www.savannahcivilrightsmuseum.com. It's open Monday through Saturday from 9:00 A.M. to 5:00 P.M. Admission is $4.00 for adults, $3.00 for senior citizens, $2.00 for students. Adult groups of ten or more are $3.00 each.

City Market, once-neglected blocks of brick warehouses on West Congress, West St. Julian, and Barnard Streets, 2 blocks from River Street, has been given reviving doses of adrenaline. You can browse about two dozen artists' studios and enjoy casual dining and nighttime entertainment in a growing number of venues. Several have outdoor tables. Horse-drawn carriage tours begin and end at the Market.

Some of the city's most intriguing sights are outside the historic district. The *Mighty Eighth Air Force Museum,* 175 Bourne Avenue, Pooler, I–95 exit 102 at Highway 80, fifteen minutes west of downtown, (912) 748–8888, www .mightyeighth.org, pays tribute to the juggernaut that was born in Savannah in January 1942. Although its headquarters soon moved to England for the duration of the war, Savannah has always had an affectionate place in its heart for "The Mighty Eighth," which won the WWII air war over Europe. Hundreds of high-tech exhibits, artifacts, films, and dioramas take you on a time trip through harrowing years. *The Darkest Hour,* a documentary film, recounts the Battle of Britain, the Japanese attack on Pearl Harbor, the Holocaust, and other atrocities. Through a doorway, displays trace the U.S. entry into the conflict; the buildup of men, women, and war machines; and the Eighth Air Force's birth. Through another door, you're on a 1943 English airfield. In a small hut, you sit in on a briefing session for crews about to take off on a bombing raid over Germany. Leaving the hut, you're in front of a two-story control tower, similar to hundreds that dotted the English countryside during the war. Original 16 mm color combat film and the sounds of flak, antiaircraft guns, and German fighter planes re-create the terrors Allied crews experienced.

A following exhibit shows the tide of war turning in favor of the Allies, the coming of D-Day, V-E Day, and the atomic bombs on Japan that brought the Pacific war to a close. Open daily from 9:00 A.M. to 5:00 P.M. Admission is $10.00 for adults, $9.00 for seniors and AAA or AARP members, $6.00 ages 6 to 12; free for children under 6.

Old Fort Jackson, on Highway 80/Islands Expressway, Savannah, 3 miles east of downtown, (912) 232–3945, www.chsgeorgia.org, was constructed on the Savannah River between 1808 and 1879. All shipping bound for Savannah's port had to pass by the fort's heavy guns. A tidal moat still guards the stout brick walls. Artifacts include cannon, small arms, machinery, and tools demonstrated at annual events. In summer, uniformed soldiers conduct cannon firings and military drills. Open daily from 9:00 A.M. to 5:00 P.M. Adults, $3.50; students and senior citizens, $2.50.

Oatland Island Education Center, 711 Sandtown Road, Savannah, off the Islands Expressway east of the Wilmington River, (912) 898–3980, www.oat landisland.org, is a fascinating nature experience for all ages. Operated by the

Chatham County Board of Education, the center is a focus of nature education programs and special events. You can walk a nature trail and see an astonishing variety of wildlife secured in natural habitats, including gators, wolves, bobcats, bears, panthers, deer, bald eagles, egrets, and heron. Open Monday through Friday from 8:30 A.M. to 5:00 P.M. Admission is $3.00 per person over age 4.

Fort Pulaski National Monument (912–786–5787), off Highway 80, a half hour east of downtown Savannah, guards the Savannah River's entrance from the Atlantic. The star-shaped fortress took eighteen years to construct. A young West Point engineering grad named Robert E. Lee lent his talents—but it surrendered to Union forces on April 11, 1862, following a devastating attack by new cannon rifles. Historical exhibits, weapons, and uniforms are displayed. Open daily from 9:00 A.M. to 6:00 P.M. Extended summer hours. Admission for adults is $3.00; free for children under 16.

There's not one iota of chic or glamour anywhere on *Tybee Island.* In truth, it's the antithesis of rich and trendy Hilton Head Island, just across the water in South Carolina. Therein lies the charm of this comfortable old shoe of a beach and summer home retreat 20 miles east of downtown Savannah. Many Savannah families spend the torrid summers in cottages near the beach, where the mild Atlantic surf laps 3 miles of hard-packed sand. Stop first at the Tybee Visitor Center, Highway 80, as you enter the island, (912) 786–5444, (800) 868–2322, www.tybeevisit.com.

In warm weather, you'll probably want to make a beeline for the Tybee beaches. The most popular stretch for swimming and sunbathing is the commercial area around Butler Avenue and Sixteenth Street—a quirky time warp straight out of Coney Island, circa 1940. Here's where you'll find ice cream and

BILL'S FAVORITES

Savannah National Historic District	Christ Church
Telfair Art Museum	Little St. Simons Island
Tybee Island	St. Marys Submarine Museum
Midway Church	Cumberland Island National Seashore
Sapelo Island	Dinner at Bistro Savannah
Jekyll Island	Lunch at Mrs. Wilkes Dining Room
St. Simons Island	Little St. Simons Island

fudge shops, hot dog stands, beer joints, old department stores, convenience stores, chair and beach umbrella vendors, motels, condos, and public restrooms. The handsome new Tybee Island Pier & Pavilion, jutting far out into the water, is a fine place to cast your fishing line. It was modeled after the old Tybrisa Pier, where young swains and their belles used to dance to the Dorseys and Benny Goodman.

Don't be disappointed that the Atlantic on the Georgia coast isn't Caribbean blue-green. The grayish-green surf isn't polluted—rivers like the Altamaha flowing down from Georgia's interior leave a silt bottom, rather than a sand bottom that would reflect the sunlight and create more translucent colors.

Tybee Lighthouse and Museum, 30 Meddin Drive, Tybee Island, (912) 786–5801, www.tybeelighthouse.org, are must-see landmarks. You can climb 178 spiraling steps to the 154-foot top of Tybee Light, which first guided ships in between the river and ocean in 1773. Partially destroyed by Confederate raiders during the Union occupation, it was rebuilt after the war. An extensive restoration was completed in 1998. Tybee Island Museum is across from the lighthouse, inside Fort Screven, a Spanish-American War coastal artillery battery. Inside the fort's old bunkers are uniforms, weapons, and displays that reflect the fort's active service through World War II. The museum and lighthouse are open daily except Tuesday from 9:00 A.M. to 5:30 P.M. Adults $6.00, ages 62 and over and ages 6 to 17 $5.00.

Skidaway Island, south of downtown, also has a trove of off-the-beaten-path adventures. *Skidaway Island State Park,* 52 Diamond Causeway, Savannah, (912) 598–2300; www.gastateparks.org, is a 490-acre preserve that's relaxed and quiet even in busy seasons. The one hundred tent and trailer camping sites have electrical and water connections, showers, and restrooms. Amenities include a swimming pool, picnic shelters, nature trails, and a playground. No fishing areas or beaches are inside the park, but they are plentiful nearby. There's a $2.00 per visit parking fee. For camping reservations, call (800) 864–PARK or log on to www.gastateparks.org.

The *UGA Marine Education Center and Aquarium,* 30 Ocean Science Circle, located on Skidaway Island, Savannah, (912) 598–2496, www.uga .edu/aquarium, operated by the University of Georgia, has a twelve-tank aquarium with an array of coastal marine life, including moray eels, barracuda, catfish, pigfish, monkfish, and fifty or so others. Open daily from 10:00 A.M. to 5:00 P.M. Adults $2.00, ages 3 to 12 $1.00.

At *Wormsloe State Historic Site,* 7601 Skidaway Road, Savannah, (912) 353–3023, (800) 864–PARK, www.gastateparks.org, a 1½-mile avenue of live oaks leads to the ruins of the colonial estate built by Noble Jones, one of the contingent of settlers who arrived with General Oglethorpe in 1733. A physician and carpenter in Surrey, Jones was one of the first Georgians to fully realize the American dream. He became a constable, soldier, surveyor, rum agent, and member of the Royal Council. Between 1739 and 1745, he built his fortified tabby home on the Isle of Hope. Tabby was a popular building material made by pouring equal parts of water, lime, sand, and oyster shells into wooden molds. When the substance hardened, the wooden molds were removed and the next layer was poured. It was designed to last forever, but alas it didn't. You can see a model of it in the visitor center, along with artifacts found on the estate and an audiovisual show about the Georgia colony's early years.

Walk a nature trail to the Jones family grave site and the ruins of Noble Jones's great house. During Christmas season, Memorial Day, Labor Day, and Georgia Week in February, staff in period dress demonstrate colonial crafts and skills. Open Tuesday through Saturday from 9:00 A.M. to 5:00 P.M., Sunday from 2:00 to 5:30 P.M. Adults $4.00; children $2.50.

The **Isle of Hope** is a photogenic place for a drive or walk. Go to the end of LaRoche Avenue (off Skidaway Road, southeast of downtown Savannah) and follow Bluff Drive along the Wilmington River. Many lovely homes and a Roman Catholic church are set off by towering live oaks and banks of azaleas.

Fort McAllister State Historic Park (I–95 exit 90), in Bryan County, 25 miles south of Savannah, has some of the South's best preserved earthwork fortifications. Built on bluffs above the south bank of the Great Ogeechee River, the earthworks withstood seven Union land and sea assaults before finally surrendering in December 1864. It was the last major obstacle on General William T. Sherman's "March to the Sea" and led to Savannah's peaceful surrender a few days later. The earthworks and heavy guns have been restored to their wartime appearance. The museum and visitor center has Civil War weapons and other artifacts.

Fort McAllister's recreation area has seventy-five tent and trailer camping

howvalonagot itsname

Communities get their names in many curious ways. A few years ago, I met Mrs. Lewis Graham, then in her 90s, who ran the one-room post office in the tiny McIntosh County shrimping port of Valona. Mrs. Graham's father and uncle founded the town in the 1890s and wanted to named it Shell Bluff, for all the oyster shells piled up on the river bluffs. "When they applied to Washington for a post office," she said, "they were informed that there already was a Shell Bluff, Georgia. They had to have another name. They looked around and saw an Albanian fishing boat called Valona. I believe it was named for a town over there. They reckoned there couldn't be another place in Georgia named Valona, and that's how we got our name."

sites with electricity, water, restrooms, showers, picnic tables, and grills; 5 miles of hiking trails; and boat ramps and docks. There's a $2.00 per visit parking fee. It's at 3984 Fort McAllister Boulevard, Richmond Hill. Drive Highway 144 for 10 miles east of I–95. Phone (912) 727–2339, (800) 864–PARK for reservations or log on to www.gastateparks.org.

As you drive Highway 17 between Savannah and Brunswick, *Midway Church* looms out of the gnarled arms of a live oak grove, like a New England meeting house that's lost its way. The white clapboard church, with its gabled roof and square belfry, traces its heritage to Massachusetts Puritans, who established the Midway Society in 1754. The church dates from 1792. Illustrious parishioners have included two signers of the Declaration of Independence and Theodore Roosevelt's great-grandfather. The fathers of Oliver Wendell Holmes and Samuel F. B. Morse have served as pastor.

Pick up the big iron church key at the neighboring *Midway Museum,* Midway, (912) 884–5837, www.libertytrail.com. The sanctuary's unadorned interior has straightback pews and a slave galley. The churchyard across the highway is the resting place of the church's founders and Revolutionary heroes. Midway Museum has colonial furnishings, documents, and exhibits. Open Tuesday through Saturday from 10:00 A.M to 4:00 P.M., Sunday from 2:00 to 4:00 P.M. Adults, $3.00; children 12 and under, $1.00.

Melon Bluff, 2999 Islands Highway/Georgia Highway 84, 3 miles east of I–95 exit 76, Midway, (912) 884–5779, (888) 246–8188, www.melonbluff.com, is a 10,000-acre nature sanctuary and bed-and-breakfast in the coastal salt marshes and woodlands 35 miles south of Savannah. The Devendorf family, formerly from San Francisco, have regeared a 1930s barn and horse stables as rustically elegant guest rooms with private baths and AC. A two-bedroom 1850s cottage is also available. Rates include full gourmet breakfast. Guests take guided and self-guided hikes through forests inhabited by more than 350 types of birds, deer, raccoons, and armadillos. Kayaking in a tidal creek is the house specialty. Guided trips of an hour or all day are always tied in with a dining experience. Hiking and kayaking are also available to nonguests. Expensive.

The Midway area has two other historic sites. A biracial community effort is restoring *Seabrook Village,* 660 Trade Hill Road, Midway, (912) 884–7008, www.seabrookvillage.org, a post–Civil War African-American community that thrived until the 1930s. Descendants of original former slave settlers lead tours of the one-room schoolhouse, homes, and outbuildings. Open Tuesday through Saturday 10:00 A.M. to 4:00 P.M. Group rates are available.

At *Fort Morris State Historic Site,* 2559 Fort Morris Road, Midway, 7 miles east of I–95 exit 76/Midway, (912) 884–5999, (800) 864–PARK, www.gastate parks.org, a film and museum tell the story of Sunbury, a pre-Revolutionary port that rivaled Savannah and died after the British captured it in 1778. A cemetery is the only physical remains of the town. A marked trail goes around the earthworks of Fort Morris, which failed to protect the town from invasion. A nature trail with excellent bird-watching goes through the woodlands and along the marshes. Open Tuesday through Saturday 9:00 A.M. to 5:00 P.M., Sunday 9:30 A.M. to 5:30 P.M. $2.00 parking fee.

McIntosh County, between Savannah and Brunswick, was the site of a British fort that predated Georgia's founding as a colony in 1733. Marshy bays and coastal islands are home to national marine and wildlife refuges and fleets of fishing boats and shrimping trawlers.

Stop first at the Darien Welcome Center, (912) 437–6684, www.mcintosh county.com, on Highway 17 at the Darien River bridge for general information. The *Fort King George State Historic Site,* a mile off Highway 17, Darien, (912) 437–4770, (800) 864–PARK, www.gastateparks.org, marks an earthwork and pallisaded log fortress South Carolinians built in 1721 to fend off hostile advances by the Spanish in Florida. Most of the fort was destroyed by fire in 1726. A state visitor center and museum has displays, artifacts, and a film about the fort and early Georgia life. Open Tuesday through Saturday from 9:00 A.M. to 5:00 P.M., Sunday from 2:00 to 5:30 P.M. Admission is $3.00 for adults, $2.00 for children 6 to 12. On the way to the fort, you can stop and photograph Darien's shrimp fleet and St. Cyprian's Episcopal Church (1870), McIntosh County's first Black house of worship.

Christ's Memory Chapel, purportedly "America's Smallest Church," was built in 1949 by McIntosh County grocery store owner Agnes Harper, who apparently thought travelers on U.S. Highway 17 needed divine guidance as they traveled the coastal highway between the northeastern United States and Florida. The 10-by-15-foot wooden chapel, with a steeple and imported stained

Fort King George State Historic Site

glass windows, seats thirteen, just large enough, it's said, to accommodate Christ and his twelve Apostles. It's open to the public daily. Donations appreciated. Just switch off the lights when you leave. Take I–95 to the U.S. 17/South Newport exit. The chapel is right beside the highway.

For insights into McIntosh County's modern history—featuring a corrupt sheriff and the Black population's assertion of its civil rights in the 1960s and 1970s—read *Praying for Sheetrock*, Melissa Faye Greene's tell-all nonfiction book.

Unlike its neighboring states, most of Georgia's barrier islands have remained undeveloped. ***Sapelo Island Tours***, conducted by the Georgia State Park system, take you through the fascinating ecology of the state's fourth largest barrier island. The boat leaves from the visitor center/museum at the little fishing community of Meridian. On the thirty-minute voyage, you'll skirt wavering stands of cord grass and scores of small islets and hammocks.

Touring the 10-mile-long, 16,000-acre island on a bus or tram, you'll see marine, bird, and animal life in the Sapelo Island National Estuarine Research Reserve, the University of Georgia Marine Institute, and the R. J. Reynolds State Wildlife Refuge. You'll also pause at the exterior of the mansion North Carolina tobacco baron Reynolds got when he purchased the island from Hudson Motors executive Howard Coffin during the Great Depression. Naturalists will show you how to seine a flounder, explain some of the mysteries of the marshes, and point out deer, wild turkey, and many species of waterfowl that call the island home. You'll have time to walk the beaches and collect shells. Sapelo Island's historic lighthouse has been restored. About 1 percent of the island is owned by Hog Hammock, a black community of slave descendants who operate a small store with sandwiches, cold drinks, and insect repellent.

Tours are conducted year-round on Wednesday from 8:30 A.M. to 12:30 P.M., Saturday from 9:00 A.M. to 1:00 P.M. Friday tours June through Labor Day are from 8:30 A.M. to 12:30 P.M. From March through October, a special tour is available the last Tuesday of each month from 8:30 A.M. to 12:30 P.M. Tickets are $10.00 for adults, $6.00 for those 6 to 18; free for children under 6. Phone (912) 437–3224, www.sapelonerr.org.

Hofwyl-Broadfield Plantation State Historic Site, 5556 Highway 17, Brunswick, 6 miles south of Darien, (912) 264–7333, (800) 864–PARK, www.ga stateparks.org, is the last vestige of the rice culture that once flourished along the Altamaha River. Developed by South Carolinian William Brailsford in 1806–1807, the plantation grew to 7,300 acres, largely on the backs of 350 Black slaves who labored in hellish conditions of heat and disease. A path takes you by the tabby ruins of the rice mill and along the top of the rice field dikes to the antebellum plantation house, furnished as it was in the early 1970s, when it was willed to the state by the last owner. Open Tuesday through Saturday from 9:00 A.M. to 5:00 P.M., Sunday from 2:00 to 5:00 P.M. Adults, $2.00; children, $1.00.

Brunswick and the Golden Isles

"The Golden Isles" are a necklace of lush, subtropical barrier islands snaking languidly along Georgia's 120-mile Atlantic coast. Several of the principal islands are part of Glynn County. Even the most developed islands—St. Simons and Jekyll—are low-key, laid-back, and lightly commercialized compared to other resort islands on the Eastern Seaboard.

Try Your Hand at Brunswick Stew

Brunswick Stew was created in Brunswick. The piquant concoction goes with Georgia barbecue and seafood like ice cream goes with peach cobbler. No two cooks make it quite the same, so there's plenty of room for your own adjustments. A rustic version includes venison, squirrel, and other wild game. This popular recipe makes one gallon.

1 3-pound chicken

1 pound lean beef

1 pound lean pork

3 medium onions, chopped

Place meat in a large, heavy pot.

Season with salt and pepper. Add onions and cover with water. Cook until the meat falls from the bones (several hours). Remove from heat and allow to cool. Tear meat in shreds and return to stock. Add:

4 16-ounce cans tomatoes

5 tablespoons Worcestershire sauce

14 ounces catsup

1 tablespoon Tabasco sauce

2 bay leaves

12 ounces chili sauce

½ teaspoon dry mustard

½ stick butter

Cook 1 hour, occasionally stirring to prevent sticking. Add:

3 tablespoons vinegar

2 16-ounce cans small limas or butter beans

2 16-ounce cans cream-style corn

1 15-ounce can small English peas

Optional: 3 small diced Russet potatoes and a box of frozen, sliced okra

Cook slowly until thick. Serve with barbecue, seafood, and corn bread.

Blessed with long stretches of hard-packed beaches, marshes, inlets, rivers, and Spanish moss–veiled live oak trees, the islands are inviting places to get off the beaten path and commune in solitude with unsullied nature.

Brunswick, the Glynn County seat and a center of Georgia's shrimping and fishing industry (population 18,000), is the gateway to St. Simons, Jekyll, Sea Island, and Little St. Simons Island. Chartered in 1771, Brunswick was named for King George II's German ancestral home. Like Savannah, it was laid out on a precise grid of broad straight streets and public squares named for English places and nobility. Albany, Amherst, Dartmouth, Egmont, George, Gloucester, London, and Newcastle Streets, and Halifax, Hanover, and Hillsborough Squares kept their names after the Revolution. They're in the Old Town National Historic District. Queen Anne, Neo-Gothic, Italianate, Mansard, and Jacobean homes are enhanced by towering live oaks and banks of azaleas, camellias, and dogwoods. Several are charming bed-and-breakfast inns. See "Places to Stay in Coastal Georgia."

Get advance information from the Brunswick–Golden Isles Convention & Visitors Bureau, 4 Glynn Avenue, Brunswick 31520, (912) 265–0620, (800) 933–2627, fax (912) 265–0629, www.bgivb.com. When you get here, pick up maps and information at the Brunswick–Golden Isles Visitors Center at Highway 17 and the F.J. Torras/ St. Simons Island Causeway. Open daily except holidays from 9:00 A.M. to 5:00 P.M. Also visit the Brunswick I–95 Visitors Center, north of the city on I–95.

In downtown Brunswick, the turreted Queen Anne–style City Hall was built in 1883. Around the corner, the Glynn County Courthouse, at Reynolds and G Streets, is a good place to rest a spell. The classical, cupoitaed building sits in a botanical garden of moss-draped oaks, Chinese pistachio, magnolia, and swamp trees and flowering shrubbery.

Get off the beaten path and walk the **Earth Day Nature Trail,** a self-guided tour that takes you on wooden boardwalks over a wading-bird habitat. You'll also see an osprey/eagle nesting platform and wildlife observation decks. The wavering salt marshes, where your favorite seafood begins its life cycle, was immortalized in Sidney Lanier's 1878 poem "The Marshes of Glynn," which goes in part: " . . . Sinuous southward and sinuous northward the shimmering band of the sand beach fastens the fringe of the marsh to the folds of the land." Lanier was inspired by the same view you'll see from **Marshes of Glynn Overlook Park.**

If you'd like to go deep-sea fishing or just get out on the open water for a spell, many charter boats are at the Brunswick docks at the end of Gloucester Street. Get information at the Brunswick–Golden Isles Convention & Visitors Bureau.

Jekyll Island

Jekyll Island is connected to Brunswick by a 6-mile causeway and a high-span bridge ($3.00 per car) that allows boats to go under while you head unimpeded for your holiday. You can fish from the mothballed, forty-five-year-old bridge. Stop first at the Jekyll Island Welcome Center at the island end of the bridge, 901 Jekyll Causeway, Jekyll Island 31527, (912) 635–3636 or (877) 4–JEKYLL, www.jekyllisland.com. Open daily from 9:00 A.M. to 5:00 P.M. On the island, the Jekyll Island Museum Visitors Center, 100 Stable Drive, (912) 635–4036, (877) 4-JEKYLL; www.jekyllisland.com, has exhibits on the island's "Millionaires' Era" and carriage tours and Sea Turtle Walks.

Between 1886 and 1942, Jekyll was the winter home of many of America's richest and most famous families. From the Gilded Age until early in World War II, Astors, Pulitzers, Vanderbilts, Morgans, Rockefellers, Cranes, Goodyears, and other aristocrats lived in secluded luxury on their remote Georgia island. Shortly after Pearl Harbor, they boarded up their elegant "cottages" and left the island for the last time. After the war, the state of Georgia paid $675,000 for the island and turned it into a state park. Although the purchase price now seems a pittance, Governor M. E. Thompson, who championed it, was widely lambasted for what political enemies labeled "Thompson's Folly."

According to the legislation creating the state park, only 35 percent of the island can be developed. That's a blessing for vacationers, who can hike and bike and bird-watch in a wilderness as pristine as when it was created, and enjoy amenities the old plutocrats could never have imagined. One side of the island is skirted by nearly 10 miles of hard-packed Atlantic beaches, washed by a usually mild surf perfect for young children and waders. Several beachfront hotels welcome pets, which have a ball chasing seagulls and each other and splashing in the waves. A rock wall intended to stop erosion prevents your Fidos from racing off the beach into woods where they're hard to find. Free showers, restrooms, and

Jekyll Island Hotel

changing rooms are at regular intervals along the beachfront. Even on the busiest holiday weekends, there's plenty of room to get away from everybody else. The island's mainland side is washed by the Intracoastal Waterway and scenic salt marshes. Deer, raccoon, armadillo, wild turkey, and many species of waterfowl roam the marshes, live oak, and pine forests.

Tours of the *Jekyll Island Historic District* start at the Visitors Center. You can see a video presentation about Jekyll's colorful history, and guided tram tours take you inside several of the millionaires' restored cottages. Indian Mound Cottage, Standard Oil director William Rockefeller's shingled Cape Cod–style cottage, has been furnished as it was when the family began wintering here in 1917. You'll probably wonder why there's no kitchen in most of the houses. The Club House, now the Jekyll Island Hotel, was the social center, where members gathered for meals, cards, and other activities. Other stops on the tour include Mistletoe Cottage, a Dutch Colonial Revival with a collection of sculpture by noted artist Russell Fiore, a longtime Jekyll resident. Cypress-shingled Faith Chapel is illuminated by Louis Comfort Tiffany and D. Maitland Armstrong stained-glass windows. Jekyll's recreational riches include sixty-three holes of golf that wind through marshes and woodlands, indoor and outdoor tennis, a fishing pier, marinas, a water slide park and wave pool, rental bikes, picnic grounds, and hiking trails.

Former shop buildings and servants quarters now house an array of unique shops. Nature's Cottage, built in 1916 for the island's engineer, has handcarved wooden ducks, bears, birds, and other wildlife. The Servants Dining Hall, from 1900, now sells beautiful sterling silver jewelry and Native American crafts. The Island Design Store, in the 1905 butlers' and valets' dormitory, specializes in casual clothes and decorative arts. For a rainy day at the beach, check out the new, used, and rare books at Jekyll Books and Antiques in the 1890s Furness cottage.

Jekyll hosts 114 monitored sea turtle nests, so it's only natural that the *Georgia Turtle Center* is the island's newest amenity. Located in the former 1903 power plant, the $2 million facility has a museum-style learning center, a state-of-the-art rehabilitation center, and a veterinary clinic. Guided turtle walks are conducted nightly from May through August.

St. Simons and Sea Islands

The toll-free F. J. Torras Causeway takes you to *St. Simons Island.* The most developed of the four Glynn County "Golden Isles" has seen a big increase in hotels, condos, restaurants, and shopping areas in recent years, but that hasn't dimmed the natural glories of the Manhattan-size island's salt marshes, beaches, and live oak forests wrapped in Spanish moss. You can swim and sunbathe on long strands of beach—all Georgia beaches are public domain—fish, ride horseback, play golf and tennis, and visit historic sites dating back to the early eighteenth century.

Fort Frederica National Monument, Frederica Road, St. Simons Island, at the island's northern end, includes remnants of a tabby fortress the British built in the 1730s as a bulwark against Spanish invaders from Florida. Leading up to the fort are foundations of homes and shops once occupied by 1,500 troops and civilians. The fort was never tested. The Spanish attacked in 1742, and their defeat at the nearby Battle of Bloody Marsh kept England firmly in control of Georgia's coast. Stop first at the National Park Service Visitors Center (912–638–3639, www.nps.gov/fofr) for a film and historical displays. Bring insect repellent, and don't step on the fire ant mounds! Open daily from 9:00 A.M. to 5:00 P.M. Admission is $1.00; free for children 16 and under.

Christ Church, a Gothic wooden sanctuary on the road to Fort Frederica, is the island's most beloved (and most photographed) landmark. The site of services John and Charles Wesley conducted for Frederica's garrison, the original church was built in 1820. Desecrated by Union soldiers, it was rebuilt in 1884 by the Reverend Anson Phelps Dodge, whose life was chronicled by late St. Simons novelist Eugenia Price in *Beloved Invader.* The church is framed by an arbor of live oaks, dogwoods, and azaleas. The interior is illuminated by stained-glass windows. The church is at 6329 Frederica Road, St. Simons Island, (912) 638–8683, www.christchurchfrederica.org. Open daily, donations appreciated. Episcopal services are conducted every Sunday.

St. Simons Lighthouse, St. Simons Island, (912) 638–4666, www.saint simonslighthouse.org, at the island's southern end, has been a landmark since 1872. The present 104-foot brick sentinel—still maintained as an operational beacon by the U.S. Coast Guard—stands on the site of an 1810 lighthouse that was destroyed by retreating Confederate troops in 1861. The old lightkeeper's cottage houses the **Museum of Coastal History,** with collections of colonial furniture, shipbuilding tools, and changing exhibits of coastal art. Open Monday through Saturday from 10:00 A.M. to 5:00 P.M., Sunday from 1:30 to 5:00 P.M. Admission for adults is $5.00; ages 6 to 11 $2.50; under 6 free.

Neptune Park, around the lighthouse, has seaside picnic tables, a playground, and steps down to the

ghostlylight

If you stand outside the walls of Christ Church burying ground late at night, you might see a light flickering through the darkness. Legend says a young woman with a terrible fear of the dark was buried there. To ease her spirit, her husband brought a lighted candle to the grave site every night, and long after his own death, the candle still burns.

beach. You can fish from the beach or take a cooler and lawn chair onto the Municipal Pier and angle for flounder and whiting, even pull up a startled hammerhead shark or barracuda. No license is required for saltwater fishing. The pier, lighthouse, and Neptune Park are in The Village, around Mallory Street, St. Simons's original commercial area, where you'll find restaurants, shops, and lodgings.

Massengale Park, on Ocean Boulevard, between the King & Prince Hotel and the Coast Guard Station, has several miles of public beach, picnic areas, and restrooms.

Whatta you do on a rainy day at the beach? The *Maritime Center at the Historic 1935 Coast Guard Station* on St. Simons' East Beach, opened in April 2006, invites visitors to learn about life as a "Coastie" in the early 1940s. "Ollie," a fictional Coast Guardsman from the '40s, is the "tour leader." Through his "letters home" and his field journal entries, we learn the ropes of being a Coastie and explore the beaches and marshes that surround his base. The

Little St. Simons Low Country Boil

Occasionally, the LSSI kitchen staff hauls a big iron kettle out to the beach and invites everyone to join.

Water as needed for thick stew-like consistency

3 new potatoes per person

1 box commercial shrimp boil per 2 pounds shrimp

1 teaspoon vinegar per pound shrimp

½ teaspooon Tabasco sauce per pound shrimp

1 teaspoon black pepper per 4 pounds shrimp

½ pound kielbasa, or other smoked sausage, per person

1 ear shucked corn per person

2 onions per person

1 carrot per person, cut in fourths

1–2 crabs per person

½ pound raw shrimp in shell per person

Boil water in a large kettle on stove or outdoor cooker. Add potatoes and all spices, bring to boil, and cook 5 minutes. Add sausage and bring back to boil for 5 minutes. Add corn, onions, and carrots and boil 5 minutes.

Check ingredients, especially potatoes, for doneness. Add crabs, boil 5 minutes. Add shrimp and boil until just done—they will be bright pink. Drain and pour onto platters. Have cole slaw, corn bread, cocktail sauce, and Dijon mustard on hand. A real crowd pleaser!

museum's seven galleries are filled with hands-on exhibits that include "Coasties in Training," lifesaving techniques, "Digging for Fossils," a radar training school, the area's marine life, shrimping and fishing, weather and hurricanes, and the perils of German U-boats off the Georgia coast in the early days of WWII. The Maritime Center is open Monday through Saturday from 10:00 A.M. to 5:00 P.M. Adults $6.00, $3.00 ages 6 to 11.

The world is truly not much with us on *Little St. Simons Island.* By the time we've made the twenty-minute launch crossing from "big" St. Simons, the world's problems have vanished in the sunlight of another glorious Low Country morning. A fortunate set of circumstances has left the island—6 miles long by 2 to 3 miles wide—very nearly as nature created it.

Through the 1800s, the 10,000 acres were the domain of one rice planter family. In 1903 a pencil company bought the island, but when the red cedars proved too wind-gnarled for writing instruments, it became an off-the-beaten-path retreat, now open to the public.

Congenial hosts at *The Lodge* on Little St. Simons Island will put you up in rustic but comfortable, air-conditioned guest rooms and cottages that accommodate up to thirty. At mealtime, sit at a communal table and relive your day's adventures. Things to do are bountiful: horseback riding, sunbathing, and swimming in a pool or in 7 miles of wild beaches, boating, canoeing, crabbing, bird-watching, fishing, and walking through forests inhabited by deer, raccoon, armadillos, pelicans, red-tailed hawks, great blue heron, egret, and more than 200 other species of birds. Gators cruise like ironclad vessels in marshes and rivers. All meals and activities are included in double occupancy daily rates. You can even rent the whole island for $3,400 to $5,400. Phone (912) 638–7472 or (888) 733–5774, fax (912) 634–1811, www.littlestsimonsisland.com. Write P.O. Box 21708, St. Simons Island 31522. Expensive.

Only *Sea Island* homeowners and guests at the exclusive Cloister Resort are allowed on the island.

Cumberland and Crawfish

Cumberland Island National Seashore is an intricate web of nature's rarest, most wondrous gifts. Maintained by the National Park Service, the island—18 miles long and 1 to 2 miles wide—preserves astonishing treasures of marshes and dunes, pristine beaches, live oak forests, lakes, ponds, estuaries, and inlets. "Natives" include great blue heron, wood storks, egrets, and dozens of other bird species, many rarely seen beyond these shores; giant sea turtles, which plod over the beaches to regenerate their endangered kind; fiddler, hermit, and ghost crabs; shrimp, oysters, and flounder; deer, armadillo,

Aaron Burr Slept Here

After being indicted for murder for killing popular founding father Alexander Hamilton in an 1804 pistol duel, U.S. Vice President Aaron Burr fled south, first to Cumberland Island, where he was unwelcome, then to the home of his Princeton law school classmate, Major Archibald Clark, in St. Marys. Mistress Clark reportedly didn't cotton to an accused murderer under her roof, so Burr, who was never tried for Hamilton's death, returned to Washington. A bronze plaque on the front of the *Clark-Bessant House* on Osborne Street (St. Marys' oldest house, 1801) notes Burr's visit and that of Gen. Winfield Scott, who R&R-ed on returning from Indian wars in Florida. The house's current occupants, and owners of A. Clark Antiques, are descendants of Archibald Clark.

mink, wild horses, and wild boar; playful otters; and gators that cruise the waterways like men o' war.

Mankind's 4,000-year habitation began with ancient Guale Indians, followed by sixteenth-century Spanish missionaries, eighteenth-century British troops, and pre–Civil War indigo and cotton planters. Thomas Carnegie, of the Pittsburgh Carnegies, bought the entire island in the 1880s. His family's splendid estates were mostly abandoned when the Gilded Age gave way to the Roaring Twenties, and high society discovered more fashionable wintering places. With only a few intrusions, the island has passed into public trust largely as it was created.

Unless you own your own boat, the only way to enjoy Cumberland's glories is via a forty-five-minute ride on the **Cumberland Queen** from St. Marys. With a capacity of 150, the *Queen* departs St. Marys daily from March 1 to November 30 at 9:00 A.M. and 11:45 A.M., arriving at Cumberland at 9:45 A.M. and 12:30 P.M., respectively. The rest of the year, it operates at the same times daily except Tuesday and Wednesday. Including taxes, fares are $15.00 for adults, $12.00 for those 65 and older, $10.00 for children 12 and under. When you arrive on the island, the National Park Service will collect a $4.00 per person user fee. For information and reservations, phone (912) 882–4336, (877) 860–6787, www.nps .gov/cuis. The NPS visitor center on the St. Marys waterfront is open Monday through Thursday from 8:00 A.M. to 4:30 P.M.; Friday, Saturday, and Sunday 8:00 A.M. to 6:00 P.M.

Bear in mind that sailing times are as precise as Swiss trains. If you miss the last ferry from the island, you'll have to hire a boat from St. Marys or Florida's Fernandina Beach. Campers have a choice of developed and primitive campgrounds available for a small cost, which varies according to the site you choose. Sea Camp, five minutes' walk from the ferry dock, has bathrooms and showers ($4.00 per person per day, plus $4.00 one-time day-use fee); primitive campsites, a 3½- to 10-mile hike from the dock, have trench latrines and cold water spigots ($2.00 per person per day, plus $4.00 one-time day-use fee). If you're a day-tripper, you can walk several nature trails, or swim and sun and view the remains of Dungeness, the Carnegies' fabulous estate destroyed by fire in the 1950s. Park Service rangers lead history and nature walks. There's nothing at all for sale on the island, so remember to bring food, cold drinks, insect repellent, and sunscreen.

The *Greyfield Inn* is Cumberland's only hotel-type accommodation. The late John F. Kennedy, Jr., and his wife, Carolyn, had their wedding reception in the Carnegie family's old Georgian-style mansion after taking their vows at the island's African American chapel. Staying overnight is a one-of-a-kind experience. Guests sleep in seventeen air-conditioned rooms with four-poster beds, bathe in claw-footed tubs, and relax amid family portraits and mementos. All meals, boat transportation from Fernandina Beach, Florida, and walks with naturalists are included in the rates. Contact Greyfield Inn, P.O. Box 900, Fernandina Beach, FL 32035-0900, (904) 261–6408, (866) 410–8051, www.greyfieldinn.com. Expensive.

St. Marys Submarine Museum, 102 St. Marys Street, St. Marys, on the St. Marys waterfront, (912) 882–2782, www.stmaryssubmuseum.com, will tell you everything you ever wanted to know about submarines, with special emphasis on the nuke fish at nearby Kings Bay Submarine Base. You can also see diving equipment, research documents, uniforms, and a re-created sub interior. Looks pretty cozy, eh? Imagine spending several months in these quarters without seeing the surface of the seas you're cruising under. Open Tuesday through

Spanish Moss

Spanish moss, which isn't a moss at all, but an air plant loosely related to pineapple, hangs in wispy picturesque veils from live oak trees in the southern and coastal parts of the state. It's lovely to look at, but the very devil to touch. Chiggers (aka redbugs) are voracious little pests that make their home in Spanish moss. They enjoy nothing better than feasting on a fresh, tasty smorgasbord of anybody unwary enough to think the moss would be picturesque in a home garden or stuffed in a pillow. Chiggers attack en masse and make you itch and scratch until you think you'll lose your sanity. Modern medications like Benadryl can relieve the torture, but many Southerners prefer old-fashioned remedies like Epsom salt baths, nail polish, and Chapstick. A couple of years ago on Little St. Simons Island, I saw a little boy come out of the forest with his arms loaded with the stuff and strands of it draped around his neck. I bet the poor kid is still itching.

Saturday from 10:00 A.M. to 4:00 P.M., Sunday from 1:00 to 5:00 P.M. Admission is $3.00 adults, $2.00 retired military, $1.00 children 6 to 18. Contact the St. Marys Tourism Council, P.O. Box 1291, St. Marys 31558, (912) 882–4000, (800) 868–8687, www.stmaryswelcome.com.

The Cumberland Island National Seashore Museum in downtown St. Marys tells the story of the War of 1812's "forgotten invasion." In the early morning hours of January 13, 1815, five days after Andy Jackson's back-woodsmen and Jean Lafitte's French pirates bested the British at New Orleans, effectively ending the war, 600 British sailors landed at Point Peter, a fort guarding St. Marys. They overwhelmed the 130 American defenders in what was the war's belated last battle. Nearly two centuries later, musket balls, uniform buttons, pottery shards, cooking utensils, and other artifacts recovered at Point Peter are on display at the National Seashore Museum. The museum also exhibits artifacts and photos of Cumberland Island's human history, from ancient Guale Indians, through the Gilded Era of the Carnegies and the island's acquisition as a national seashore in 1972. The museum is on Osborne Street, a few steps from St. Marys' waterfront. Open daily 1:00 to 4:00 P.M. Free admission. Phone (912) 882–4336.

The *Woodbine Crawfish Festival* takes over the tiny Camden County seat the last weekend of April. The chance to see beauty queens, marching bands, parades, and arts and crafts and put away mountains of delicious crustaceans—fried, gumbo'd, étouff!éed, jambalaya'd, and boiled in savory Cajun herbs—lures crowds from all over the Georgia coast, even down into Florida. Phone (912) 576–3211 for information.

Places to Stay in Coastal Georgia

SAVANNAH (HISTORIC DISTRICT)

Bed & Breakfast Inn,
117 West Gordon Street,
(912) 238–0518,
(888) 238–0518,
www.savannahbnb.com
History and charm at moderate prices. A pair of 1835 Federal-style townhouses have fifteen guest rooms. A garden suite and two cottages have kitchens and sitting areas. Full Southern breakfast included. Moderate.

Foley House,
14 West Hull Street,
(912) 232–6622,
(800) 647–3708,
www.foleyinn.com
Danish-born Inge Svensson presides over this elegant 1896 Victorian townhouse with nineteen guest rooms, several with oversize whirlpool tubs and working fireplaces. Continental breakfast, afternoon tea, and cordials included. Expensive.

The Gastonian,
220 East Gaston Street,
(912) 232–2869,
(800) 322–6603,
www.gastonian.com
Sumptuous seventeen-room inn in a matched pair of 1868 townhouses. Georgian and Regency antiques and all the modern comforts. Honeymooners prefer the Caracalla Suite, with an antique four-poster bed and a draped whirlpool bath as big as Cleopatra's barge. The rate includes gourmet breakfast. Expensive.

Mansion on Forsyth Park,
700 Drayton Street,
(912) 238–5198,
www.mansiononforsyth
park.com
The Savannah Historic
District's newest luxury hotel
blends a restored 1890s
redbrick mansion with a
seamless new addition.
Overlooking beautiful Forsyth
Park, the hotel's Victorian
exterior is contrasted with
more than 400 pieces of
original contemporary art,
Brazilian mahogany, Italian
marble, antique mirrors, and
other materials. The 126
guest rooms have many
deluxe amenities. Guests
and visitors may enjoy the
eclectic 700 Drayton
Restaurant, cooking school,
lounges, and spa. Expensive.

The Marshall House,
123 East Broughton Street,
(800) 589–6304,
fax (912) 644–7896,
www.marshallhouse.com
Beautifully restored mid-
nineteenth-century hotel,
with sixty-eight guest rooms
and suites, private baths, full-
service restaurant, bar, and
jazz room. In the heart of the
downtown historic district,
near the riverfront, restaurants, shops, and museums.
Rates for doubles and suites:
expensive.

Mulberry Inn,
601 East Bay Street,
(912) 238–1200
and (877) 468–1200.
The 121-room historic district
hotel, in a onetime Coca-
Cola bottling plant, is a
Holiday Inn franchise, but
you'd never guess it from the
antiques and other Old
Savannah decor and furnishings. Full restaurant and bar.
Expensive.

More than three dozen historic bed-and-breakfast inns
surround you with the aura of
Old Savannah. For information and reservations, phone
Bed & Breakfast
Reservations of Savannah,
(800) 729–7787 and
(912) 232–7787 (RSVP),
and Savannah Historic Inns
and Guest Houses,
(800) 262–4667. Chain
hotels and motels are also
abundant.

TYBEE ISLAND

Hunter House,
1701 Butler Boulevard,
(912) 786–7515,
www.hunterhouseinn.com
Fits Tybee like a hand in a
glove. Simply furnished guest
rooms range from singles to
four-room suites. Some have
kitchens and fireplaces for
brisk winter days by the sea.
The upstairs restaurant and
bar, with an outside deck,
specializes in coastal
seafood, steaks, pastas, and
potent drinks. Lend an ear
during afternoon happy hour,
and you'll find out what's
happening on the island.
Moderate seasonal rates.

If you'd like to rent a condo
or a beach house, contact
Tybee Island Rentals, P.O.
Box 1440, Tybee Island
31328, (800) 755–8562.

Tybee's chain motels include
Days Inn, (800) 325–2525
and (912) 786–4576;
Econo Lodge Beachside,
(912) 786–4535; and
Best Western Dunes Inn,
(912) 786–4591.

For general information,
contact Tybee Island Visitor
Center, (800) 868–2322.

**Lighthouse Inn Bed
& Breakfast,**
61 Meddin Drive,
(912) 786–0901,
(866) 786–0901,
www.tybeebb.com
Innkeeper Susie Morris's
three guests rooms in a tree-
shaded 1910 beach house
have private entrances,
phone, minifridge, claw-foot
tubs, and coffeemakers. The
inn is close to beaches,
Tybee Lighthouse, and
restaurants. Moderate rates
include full breakfast.

BRUNSWICK

Brunswick Manor,
825 Egmont Street,
(912) 265–6889,
www.brunswickmanor.com
Built in 1886 as the home of
a former Union Army officer,
the redbrick Romanesque
mansion is decorated with
antiques and period furnishings. Four suites have
queen-size beds and private
baths. Two have kitchens
and breakfast nooks. A separate cottage sleeps eight.
Inexpensive to moderate
rates include full breakfast
and high tea.

McKinnon House,
1001 Egmont Street,
(912) 261–9100 and
(866) 261–9100.
Victorian splendor in a handsomely restored Queen Anne
mansion with elaborate
woodwork and fine New
Orleans and Charleston furniture. Full breakfast and afternoon refreshments. Three
guest rooms with private
baths. Inexpensive to
moderate.

JEKYLL ISLAND

Buccaneer Beach Resort,
85 South Beachview Drive,
(912) 635–2261,
(877) 84BEACH,
www.buccaneerbeach
resort.com
There are 208 rooms and
efficiencies. Inexpensive to
moderate.

Jekyll Island Campground,
North Beachview Drive,
(912) 635–3021
and (866) 658–3201,
www.jekyllisland.com
Eighteen wooded acres with
full hookups, restrooms,
showers, laundry, and camp
store. Pets allowed on leash.
Near beaches, fishing, and
golf courses. Nightly rates
are $17. Weekly and monthly
rates available.

Jekyll Island Hotel,
371 Riverview Drive,
(912) 635–2600,
(800) 535–9547,
fax (912) 635–2600,
www.jekyllclub.com
The millionaires' turreted,
four-story former clubhouse
has been transformed into a
deluxe hotel graced by
stained glass, plaster mold-
ing, and other rich architectural details. Swim in the
outdoor pool, take carriage
rides, and play croquet on
the emerald lawns. The 134
guest rooms and suites have
all the first-class comforts.
Expensive.

Villas by the Sea Resort,
1175 North Beachview Drive,
(912) 635–2521,
(800) 841–6262,
fax (912) 635–2569.
There are 168 one- to
three-bedroom villas with
fully equipped kitchens for
expensive rates.

ST. SIMONS ISLAND

Days Inn,
1701 Frederica Road,
(912) 634–0660
and (800) 870–3736,
www.daysinnstsimonsisland
.com
Complimentary continental
breakfast and microwave
and refrigerator in all 101
rooms. Bike rentals on site.
Inexpensive.

Epworth-by-the-Sea,
100 Arthur Moore Drive,
(912) 638–8688;
www.epworthbythesea.com
Methodist conference center,
spiritual retreat, and vacation
center has 218 modern
motel rooms, an inexpensive
cafeteria, a swimming pool,
tennis courts, and fishing
piers. No alcohol or unmar-
ried couples allowed.
Inexpensive.

**King & Prince Beach &
Golf Resort,**
201 Arnold Road,
(800) 342–0212,
www.kingandprince.com
On its own Atlantic beach,
the K&P has been catering
to St. Simons vacationers
since its original building
opened in 1935. Now a
deluxe, full-service resort, its
187 accommodations
include guest rooms and
suites, oceanfront cabanas
and two- and three-bedroom
villas. Amenities include an
indoor pool, spa, restaurants
and bars, tennis courts and
golf privileges at nearby
courses. Expensive.

Queen's Court,
437 Kings Way,
(912) 638–8459,
www.queenscourtmotel.com
Old-fashioned but clean and
comfortable motel with some
kitchenettes. In The Village,
near shops, dining, the lighthouse, and Neptune Park.
Inexpensive.

**St. Simons Inn by the
Lighthouse,**
609 Beachview Drive,
(912) 638–1101,
www.stsimonsinn.com
Thirty-four modern, attractive
guest rooms and pool
around the corner from The
Village shops, restaurants,
pier, and lighthouse. Micro-
waves and refrigerators in
every room. Moderate, including continental breakfast.

ST. MARYS

During the past fifteen years,
the Kings Bay Nuclear
Submarine Base—home port
for eight Trident missile
nuclear subs—has mush-
roomed St. Marys' popula-
tion from 2,000 to nearly
9,000. A flood of fast-food
outlets, video rental stores,
and chain stores has grown
up on the outskirts, but the
historic old town on the St.
Marys River is as quaint and
unchanged as ever.

Crooked River State Park,
Highway Spur 40,
7 miles north of St. Marys,
(912) 882–5256.
Has campsites and cottages,
swimming pool, fishing
areas, and playgrounds.
There's a $2.00 per visit
parking fee. For camping and
cottage reservations, call
(800) 864–PARK,
www.gastateparks.org.

Emma's Bed & Breakfast,
300 West Conyers Street,
(912) 882–4199,
www.emmasbedandbreak
fast.com
Beautifully decorated inn,
with southern pine floors and
working fireplaces, has four
main house guest rooms and
five others in an adjacent
cottage, each with private
bath. The Honeymoon Suite
has a red heart-shaped
Jacuzzi and a private deck.
Full breakfast with inexpensive to moderate rates.
Picnic lunches can be
packed for Cumberland
Island trips. The house is on
four wooded acres, with
deer, birds and other wildlife.

**Goodbread House Bed and
Breakfast,**
209 Osborne Street,
(912) 882–7490,
www.eagnet.com/
goodbread
Has four guest rooms with
private baths in an 1870s
Victorian house. Children are
welcome, and pets can stay
in the fenced yard.
Inexpensive to moderate
rates include full breakfast.

Spencer House Inn,
200 Osborne Street,
(912) 882–1872 and
(888) 840–1872,
www.spencerhouseinn.com
The 1872 National Register
House is a short walk from
the Cumberland Island ferry.
Fourteen rooms have private
baths, claw-foot tubs, TV,
and phone. Guests relax in
the library and on verandas
with cypress rockers. Full
breakfast. Inexpensive.

Places to Eat in Coastal Georgia

SAVANNAH (HISTORIC DISTRICT)

Bistro Savannah,
309 West Congress Street,
City Market,
(912) 233–6266.
The Bistro's fresh market cuisine is a contemporary spin
on healthy, vibrant foods
enjoyed in the Low Country
before the Civil War.
Specialties include coastal
seafood bouillabaisse, crisp
pecan chicken with bourbon
sauce, and veal and wild
mushroom meat loaf. Dinner
served Monday through
Saturday. Expensive.

Express Cafe,
39 Barnard Street,
(912) 233–4683.
Popular City Market drop-in
serves sandwiches, soups,
salads, pastries, and crois-
sants in a cheerful black-
and-white-tiled former
drugstore. Inexpensive.

Gryphon Tea Room,
337 Bull Street, at
Madison Square,
(912) 238–2481.
A century-old pharmacy has
been transformed into a
romantic European tearoom.
Sit back and enjoy your tea,
coffee, soups, sandwiches,
and desserts amid the
beauty of Honduran
mahogany, fourteen original
stained-glass windows,
Tiffany-style globes, and lace
curtains. Open daily morning
to night. Inexpensive.

Il Pasticcio,
Bull and Broughton Streets,
downtown,
(912) 231–8888.
Fresh pastas, grilled vegetables, shrimp, risotto, oak
fired pizza, rotisserie chicken,
real Italian gelato, and fresh-
baked goods in a stylishly
converted Art Deco women's
dress shop with floor-to-ceiling windows overlooking the
busy corner. Owner/artist
Floriana Venetico's second-
floor art gallery is a before-or-
after dinner treat. Lunch and
dinner daily. Moderate to
expensive.

Mrs. Wilkes Dining Room,
107 West Jones Street,
(912) 232–5997.
Mrs. Wilkes Dining Room is a
treasure hidden away in a
historic district townhouse.
You know you're there by the
long lines waiting outside.
Family-style lunch fills the
tables with bottomless platters of fried chicken, fried
fish, Southern-style vegetables, corn bread, biscuits,
and dessert. Come for
breakfast and you'll be
treated with feather-light biscuits, eggs, sausage, and
buttery grits. Monday
through Friday, breakfast and
lunch only. No credit cards.
Inexpensive.

The Old Pink House,
Reynolds Square,
23 Abercorn Street,
(912) 232–4286.
This is the ticket for a romantic, candlelight dinner. The
stunning eighteenth-century
mansion's dining rooms are
graced by colonial paintings
and decor, a perfect dress-
up place for Low Country
she-crab soup, crispy flounder, sautéed shrimp, country

ham served over grits, and Vidalia onion stuffed with sausage. Before or after dinner, sit by the fireplace and enjoy the pianist in the cozy downstairs tavern. Dinner daily. Expensive.

Six Pence Pub,
245 Bull Street,
(912) 233–3156.
General Oglethorpe might feel at home in this cozy British pub in downtown Savannah's historic district. Locals and tourists meet for shepherd's pie, fish and chips, soups, salads, sandwiches, and a raft of imported and domestic brews and a full bar. Lunch and dinner daily. Inexpensive.

TYBEE ISLAND

Cafe Loco Waterfront Bar & Grill,
Lazzaretto Creek Marina,
(912) 786–7810.
The quintessential seafood shack, with wooden booths, a long bar, and an outside deck overlooking the marina, is a laid-back place for sand-

wiches, burgers, shrimp, crab, and steak. Way into the wee hours, the place boogies to the beat of local blues and rock bands. Open from 11:00 A.M. to 2:00 A.M. daily. Off Highway 80, the marina is also headquarters for dolphin-watching tours, deep-sea fishing excursions, and gambling cruises on the *Atlantic Star*. Phone (800) 242–0166. Inexpensive.

The Crab Shack,
40A Estill Hammock Road,
(912) 786–9857.
As the sign of the happy crab says, THE PLACE WHERE THE ELITE EAT IN THEIR BARE FEET, The Crab Shack epitomizes Tybee's laid-back ambience. Sit on a big open deck by the water or in the screened-in dining room, and tuck into monster platters of fried and broiled shrimp, oysters, crabs, and fish at very moderate prices. Open continuously for lunch and dinner daily. Inexpensive.

North Beach Grill,
41A Meddin Drive,

(912) 786–9003.
Behind the Tybee Museum, across from the lighthouse, this longtime Tybee favorite delivers a flavorful blend of Southern and Caribbean cooking. Genial owner/chef George Spriggs wows his patrons with Jamaican-style jerk (marinated) chicken, pan-seared snapper, eggplant parmigiana, crab cake sandwiches, Cuban-style pot roast, and many other wonderful creations. Open daily for lunch and dinner. Inexpensive to moderate.

Snappers,
107 Bryan Wood Road,
off Highway 80 near Wilmington River bridge,
(912) 897–6101.
A great place for family dinner, especially after a big day at the beach. Big plates of Low Country shrimp, oysters, deviled crabs, and pecan and key lime pies. Lunch Monday through Saturday. Inexpensive.

Spanky's Beachside,
165 Strand, across from

HELPFUL WEB SITES

Savannah Convention & Visitors Bureau,
www.savannahvisit.com

Jekyll Island Visitors Bureau,
www.jekyllisland.com

Brunswick-Golden Isles Visitors Bureau,
www.bgivb.com

St. Marys Visitors Bureau,
www.stmaryswelcome.com

Little St. Simons Island,
www.littlestsimonsisland.com

Tybee Island,
www.tybeevisit.com

the Tybee Pier,
(912) 786–5520.
A popular drop-in for cold beer, seafood, and sandwiches and casual meeting and mingling. Open daily. Inexpensive.

BRUNSWICK

Cargo Portside Grill,
1423 Newcastle Street,
(912) 267–7330.
Former Atlanta restaurant owner Alix Kenagy has turned a former marine warehouse in downtown Brunswick into a cozy, sophisticated dining room, with fresh local seafood and innovative beef, pork, pasta, chicken, and veal dishes, complemented by a large wine selection and a full bar. Dinner Monday through Saturday. Moderate to expensive.

The Georgia Pig,
2712 Highway 17 South,
(912) 264–6664.
The place for Brunswick stew at the source, plus delectable barbecue pork plates with all the trimmings. Lunch and dinner daily. Inexpensive.

SUNBURY

Sunbury Crab Company,
Fort Morris Road,
(912) 884–8640.
A well-off-the-beaten path gem that's worth the detour, this seafood shack overlooking the coastal rivers and marshes serves shrimp, oysters, fish, and blue crab just

out of the water. Crab cakes, fresh steamed crabs, and fried shrimp are house specialties. Full bar. Open Wednesday through Friday 5:00 to 10:00 P.M., Saturday and Sunday from noon to 10:00 P.M. Inexpensive. From I–95 take exit 76, go east on GA 38/Islands Highway about 3 miles, then left on Fort Morris Road and 3 miles to a left fork in the road and half-mile to the Sunbury Crab Company, just past the historic Sunbury Cemetery and a condo development. You can rent kayaks for self-guided adventures in rivers, creeks and marshes. You can also explore the Revolutionary-era Fort Morris State Historic Site and learn about the "lost town" of Sunbury, which died after being sacked by the British in 1778.

JEKYLL ISLAND

Blackbeard's,
200 North Beachview Drive,
(912) 635–3522.
Fresh Low Country seafood dishes are the specialties at this popular beachfront eatery. Moderate.

Cafe Solterra,
Jekyll Island Club Hotel,
371 Riverview Drive,
(912) 635–2600.
Pick up sandwiches, salads, pizza, and desserts, and enjoy them inside or at outdoor tables. Inexpensive.

The Grand Dining Room,
Jekyll Island Hotel.
(See "Places to Stay.")
Dine in the splendor of the Gilded Age, amid candlelight, fine crystal, china, and silver. The extensive menu includes innovative continental cuisine, steaks, fresh seafood, and pasta. The yards-long Sunday brunch shouldn't be missed. Expensive.

SeJay's Waterfront Cafe & Pub,
Jekyll Harbor Marina,
1 Harbor Road,
(912) 635–3200.
Low Country seafood, steaks, and Brunswick stew in a casual dining room overlooking the shrimp and pleasure boats and sunset on the marshes. Moderate.

ST. SIMONS

Bennie's Red Barn,
5514 Frederica Road,
(912) 638–2844.
Fresh coastal seafood and steaks grilled over a wood fire have made this rustic off-the-beaten-path old barn a dining landmark since 1954. Moderate to expensive.

Fourth of May Cafe & Deli,
321 Mallory Street,
at the main Village corner,
(912) 638–5444.
Has daily potluck specials—meat or seafood with two fresh vegetables, for about $6.00. Also has huge deli sandwiches and desserts. Lunch and dinner daily. Inexpensive.

J. Mac's Island Restaurant & Bistro,
407 Mallory Street,
(912) 634–0403.
A cool, classy place for rack of lamb, soft-shell crabs, lobster, steaks, pasta, cocktails, wine, and live musical entertainment. Dinner Monday through Saturday. Moderate.

ST. MARYS

Pauly's Cafe,
Osborne and St. Marys Streets,
(912) 882–3944.
On the St. Marys waterfront, a few steps from the Cumberland Island Visitors Center, the snug little cafe serves local seafood, Italian dishes, subs, steaks, and beer and wine at lunch and dinner daily. A cold beer or a glass of wine with almond-crusted fresh grouper or lobster scampi (baby lobster tails sauteed in garlic butter) is a perfect way to celebrate a Cumberland Island adventure. Inexpensive.

Northeast Georgia

Depending on which direction you've pointed your hiking boots, the 2,015-mile *Appalachian Trail* either begins or ends with 79 miles of northeastern Georgia mountainland. Many AT veterans acclaim the Georgia section as the most beautiful in all the fourteen states between here and Mount Katahdin, Maine.

The AT's southern terminus is atop 3,782-foot *Springer Mountain,* in Dawson County, 75 miles northeast of Atlanta. An 8-mile approach trail begins at Amicalola Falls State Park. There hikers can camp out, get their gear together, and have their packs weighed by park rangers.

From Springer Mountain the AT's Section I is a 22.3-mile easy-to-strenuous hike to Highway 60 at Woody Gap. Section II, 10.7 miles from Woody Gap to Neels Gap, has just one long uphill stretch and is popular with one-day and weekend hikers. At Neels Gap, the trail crosses Highway 19/129 and goes "indoors" as it passes through a covered breezeway of the *Mountain Crossing/Walasi-Yi Center.* At this stone-and-log legacy of the 1930s Civilian Conservation Corps, hikers can get trail information and replenish supplies of dehydrated foods and camping gear, do their laundry, and enjoy a hot shower.

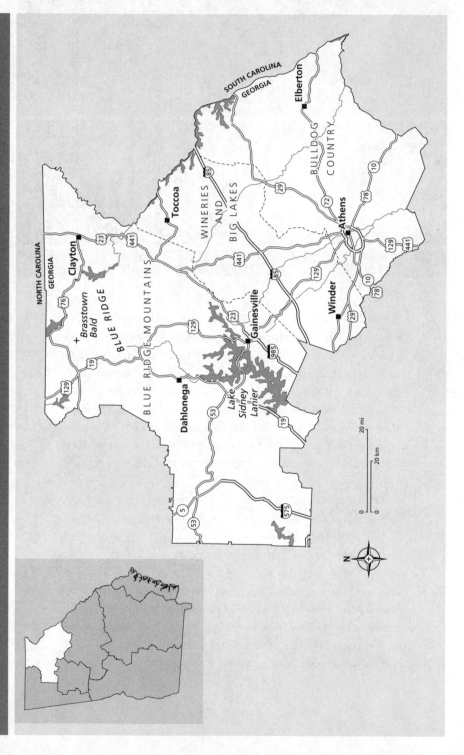

NORTHEAST GEORGIA

Motorists stop by for mountain handicrafts and short hikes on the trail. Phone (706) 745–6095, www.mountaincrossings.com. From Walasi-Yi, Section III is a moderately difficult 5.7 miles to Tesnatee Gap on the Richard Russell Scenic Highway (Highway 348). Sections IV–VI carry the trail upward and onward. At Bly Gap, near the Rabun County/Towns County border, you bid adieu to Georgia and cross into the North Carolina Great Smokies. Mount Katahdin, here we come!

NORTHEAST GEORGIA'S TOP HITS

Appalachian Trail

Chattooga River Rafting

Lake Rabun Hotel/Rabun Beach Recreation Area

Tallulah Gorge Park and Terrora Park and Campground

Foxfire Museum

Black Rock Mountain State Park

Moccasin Creek State Park

Georgia Mountain Fair

The Reach of Song

Lake Chatuge

Chattahoochee National Forest

Brasstown Valley Resort

Russell-Brasstown Scenic Highway

Vogel State Park

Lake Winfield Scott Recreation Area

Mark of the Potter

Babyland General Hospital

Old Sautee Store/Stovall Covered Bridge

Alpine Helen

Unicoi State Park

Anna Ruby Falls

Smithgall Woods Conservation Area

Dahlonega Courthouse Gold Museum

Amicalola Falls State Park

Lake Lanier Islands

Georgia Mountains Museum

Elachee Nature Science Center

Hart State Park

Tugaloo State Park

Victoria Bryant State Park

Travelers Rest

Chateau Elan Winery & Resort

Fort Yargo State Park

Crawford W. Long Museum

Elberton Granite Museum/Georgia Guidestones

Bobby Brown State Park

Richard B. Russell State Park

University of Georgia

Oconee Cultural Arts Foundation

Blue Ridge Mountains

In Georgia's far northeast corner, up against the North Carolina and South Carolina borders, Rabun County is the heart of the state's dramatically rugged Blue Ridge Mountain country. About 80 percent of the county is included in national forests and state parks. Outdoor adventures range from tranquil trout fishing in mountain streams, canoeing, swimming, off-the-beaten-path hiking, and browsing for handmade crafts at country stores to the ultimate heart-pounding adventure: ***Chattooga River rafting.***

Until the early 1970s, when Jon Voight, Burt Reynolds, and the rest of the *Deliverance* movie crew let the world in on the secret, the Chattooga River was the remote domain of mountain folk along the Georgia–South Carolina border. Nowadays daredevils come from early spring through late fall to test their courage against the river's steep sluices, whirlpools, and roller-coaster rapids. To see that they accomplish their missions safely, the U.S. Forest Service licenses professional outfitters to conduct the trips, which are made in sturdy six-person rubber rafts and are led by guides who know every rock and rill along this tempestuous waterway.

Outfitters offer a variety of Chattooga experiences. Beginners usually test their wings on Section III, a seven-hour, 6-mile ride that sweeps them through many of the *Deliverance* landmarks. At lunchtime guides pull a small deli out of their waterproof packs and spread the feast at the foot of a waterfall.

Section III is a mere warm-up for "The Ultimate Challenge," the Chattooga's wild and woolly Section IV. Suggested only for well-seasoned white-water hands in top physical condition, this rip-snorting seven-hour cruise carries you through swiftly moving currents; steep, wooded gorges; up and over, down and around such potential perils as Seven Foot Falls, Corkscrew, and Jawbone. At day's end, the Chattooga finally turns you loose, into the peaceful waters of Tugaloo Lake.

For those who really want to get to the heart of the river, outfitters offer two-day trips, which include overnight camping, a steak dinner, and a bountiful breakfast. Some packages offer the option of lodgings at rustic inns and cabins.

Day trips on Section III are about $60 on weekdays, $10 higher on weekends. For Section IV, figure on paying around $70 on weekdays, $90 on weekends. You'll be supplied with all the necessary equipment and transportation to and from river access points. You'll also get a briefing on paddling techniques and safety rules, expert guide service, lunch, and a place to shower and change clothes at the end of your ride. Half-day trips are also offered. Contact Nantahala Outdoor Center, (800) 232–7238, www.noc.com; Wildwater Limited, (800) 451–9972, www.wildwaterrafting.com; and Southeastern Expeditions, (800) 868–7238, www.southeasternexpeditions.com.

If the Chattooga sparks memories of *Deliverance*, **Lake Rabun,** near the little town of Tallulah Falls, may remind you of the film *On Golden Pond*. Ringed by the soft green humps of the Blue Ridge Mountains and unpretentious summer cottages, some dating back to the 1920s and 1930s, this small, off-the-beaten-path lake is the embodiment of peace and quiet.

Built in 1922, the **Lake Rabun Hotel** is the perfect complement to the lake. New owners have spruced up the sixteen-room wood-and-stone lodge, polished the mountain laurel and rhododendron furniture, added baths to some rooms, and put in heat for spring and fall guests. You'll still have to go somewhere else for a television, telephone, or air-conditioning. What the Lake Rabun does offer is rare tranquility and hospitality that draws guests back year after year. In the evenings you can sit by the flagstone hearth, play parlor games, swap tips on local eateries and "secret" waterfalls, and store up energy for the next day's boating, fishing, and hiking. The hotel's Boar's Head Saloon serves beef, seafood, and desserts with a full bar. Doubles, with breakfast, are inexpensive. Major credit cards are accepted. Closed December to April. Contact Lake Rabun Hotel, Lake Rabun Road, Lakemont, (706) 782–4946, www .lakerabunhotel.com.

Fishing boats and canoes may be rented at **Hall's Boat House,** next to the hotel. **Lake Rabun Road,** which twists and turns about 15 miles between Highway 441 near Tallulah Falls, to Georgia Highway 197, is a very scenic drive. It curves around Lake Rabun and Seed Lake, with many lovely vistas of the water and woodlands. Ask the proprietors of the Lake Rabun Hotel for directions to **High Branch Falls,** also known as Minnehaha Falls. It's a little tricky to find but well worth the search. During the summer **Rabun Beach Recreation Area,** (706) 782–3320, www.fs.fed.us/conf, is a relaxing place to swim, have a picnic, and enjoy boating, hiking, and fishing. Campsites have electrical and water hookups.

The Rabun County Visitors Bureau and Welcome Center, 232 Highway 441 North, Clayton 30525, (706) 782–4812, www.gamountains.com, can give you further tips on off-the-beaten-path outdoor adventures.

It may be difficult to imagine now, but early in the twentieth century, **Tallulah Falls** was one of the South's most popular summer resorts. Honeymooners, families, and other nature-loving city folk came to admire the cataracts of the Tallulah River, which stormed through a gorge 820 feet across and more than 1,200 feet deep. All that ended in the early 1920s, when a series of hydroelectric dams diverted water from the falls but at the same time created Lake Rabun, Lake Burton, and other recreational areas.

Tallulah Gorge State Park invites hikers to explore the depths of the gorge. The parks department and Georgia Power Company periodically open the floodgates and allow kayakers to experience the falls' glorious power. The park area has a fishing pier and picnic tables on the Tallulah River. Exhibits explain Georgia Power's conservation efforts. Fifty campsites have water and electrical hookups. Phone (800) 864–PARK for reservations. If you'd like to hike the gorge, you'll need to register, free of charge, at the Jane Hurt Yarn Interpretive Center, which has exhibits on the gorge's plant and animal life and a film on the gorge's fascinating ecology. For general information, contact Park Superintendent, P.O. Box 248, Tallulah Falls 30573, (706) 754–7970 or (800) 864–7275, www.gastateparks.org. The most strenuous hike takes you down 400 steep metal stairs to a suspension bridge swaying 80 feet above the river and rocky floor. Another 200 steps go the rest of the way down to the bottom of the gorge. Bring plenty of water and stop for breathers and views of the gorge, the river, and waterfalls. Depending on your physical fitness, going back up can seem two or three times as far. A bit of trivia: 1930s actress Tallulah Bankhead was named for the gorge by her grandparents, who vacationed at the resort in its heyday.

Tallulah Gallery (706–754–6020) has a beautiful selection of paintings, pottery, weaving, and other mountain handicrafts in the parlors of a Victorian mansion built by the president of the now-extinct local railroad. The two-story home is on Highway 441 in the center of the small community. Open daily. Closed in winter.

If you're fond of kitschy local folk arts, stop by the *Co-Op Craft Store,* on Highway 441, in the old Tallulah Falls train depot (706) 754–6810. They've got a great selection of scenes hand-painted on saw blades and shovel, axe, and hoe heads. They depict hunting dogs, deer, farmhouses, pigs, pastures, tractors, and other rural motifs. While you're there, browse the made-in-Georgia jams and jellies, pottery, wooden toys, patchwork pillows, pot holders, place mats, and other crafts. It's open daily year-round.

Traveling on Highway 441 between Tallulah Falls and Clayton, Dillard, and Mountain City, you'll be sorely tempted by a raft of mountain-craft shops and art galleries. *Lofty Branch Art and Craft Village,* 6 miles south of Clayton, (706) 782–3863, is a scattered complex of studios offering mostly high-quality weaving, woodwork, leather, pottery, and glass.

If you've read the Foxfire books and magazines or would like to learn more about the vanishing Appalachian Mountain culture, plan a visit to the new *Foxfire Museum* complex, up a mountain road from the old museum on Highway 441. (If you're not familiar with the Foxfire books, they chronicle research by students who scour the mountains to preserve elements of the old, isolated mountain lifestyle.) The complex's more than twenty log structures include an authentic 1820s one-room home that raised three generations; "dog trot" cabins; a chapel; animal barns; a folk art museum; and complete gristmill,

TOP ANNUAL EVENTS

Tallulah Falls Whitewater Festival,
early April,
(706) 754–8590

Bear on the Square Mountain Festival,
mid-April, Dahlonega,
(706) 864–7817

Athens Home & Garden Tour,
late April,
(706) 353–1801

Southworks Arts Festival,
late May, Watkinsville,
(706) 769–4565

Mountain Laurel Festival,
mid-May, Clarkesville,
(706) 754–2296

Helen-to-Atlantic Hot Air Balloon Race and Festival,
early June,
(706) 878–2271

Oktoberfest,
September and October, Festhalle, Helen,
(706) 878–2271

Sorghum Festival,
mid-October, Blairsville,
(706) 896–5789

Mule Camp Market,
mid-October, Gainesville,
(770) 532–7714

Georgia Mountain Fall Festival,
early to mid-October, Hiawassee,
(706) 896–4191

Toccoa Harvest Festival,
early November,
(706) 886–2132

Alpine Helen Winter Festival,
November–January,
(706) 865–5356

Lighting of the Chateau,
Thanksgiving weekend, Chateau Elan Winery, Braselton,
(770) 932–0900

blacksmith shop, and working craft shops, where classes are held. The Zurow Wagon is the only existing wagon known to have taken Cherokees to Oklahoma on the 1830s "Trail of Tears." The visitor center/gift store sells Foxfire books and handmade Appalachian crafts. You can take a self-guided tour or a guided tour with groups of six or more. Motor homes and other large vehicles can't negotiate the steep, winding mountain road. Call ahead and someone will come and pick you up on the highway. The museum is at 220 Foxfire Lane, off Highway 441, Mountain City, (706) 746–5828, www.foxfire.org. Open Monday through Friday 8:30 A.M. to 4:30 P.M. Self-guided tour, $5.00, age 10 and under, free.

Beechwood Inn Bed & Breakfast, P.O. Box 120, Clayton 30525, (706) 782–5485, (866) 782–2485, fax (706) 782–5485, www.beechwoodinn.ws, is one of the mountain country's nicest small lodgings. Innkeeper Marty Lott fastidiously restored this old Rabun County summer vacation house, originally built in

1922. On a rise, among terraced gardens, the house has dramatic views of the neighboring mountains. Five guest rooms have queen-size or twin beds. All have their own baths, and some have working fireplaces. Marty sends you off in the morning with an excellent full breakfast. The location on Georgia Highway 76, east of Clayton, is especially convenient to launching points for Chattooga River rafting adventures. Moderate rates include a big mountain breakfast.

Two scenic state parks in Rabun County offer a wealth of outdoor activities and overnight lodgings. *Black Rock Mountain State Park,* 1,500 acres of brawny beauty atop a 3,600-foot elevation of the Blue Ridge Mountains, has an eighteen-acre lake, many miles of wooded nature trails, waterfalls, and campsites with electrical and water hookups and kitchens. Contact Park Superintendent, Black Rock Mountain, P.O. Drawer A, Mountain City 30562, (706) 746–2141, (800) 864–PARK, www.gastateparks.org.

Moccasin Creek State Park, on Lake Burton, has a boat ramp and docks, a trout hatchery, hiking trails, and campsites. For reservations, phone (800) 864–PARK. Contact Park Superintendent, Moccasin Creek State Park, Route 1, Box 1634, Clarkesville 30523, (706) 947–3194, www.gastateparks.org.

For twelve days every August, the normally unhurried Towns County seat of *Hiawassee* (population 1,985) throbs with the energy of the *Georgia Mountain Fair*. Against a backdrop of Blue Ridge Mountains, forests, and blue-green lakes, the fair takes Hiawassee and the rest of Georgia's "Little Switzerland" literally by storm.

The fairgrounds resound with the music of bluegrass fiddlers, gospel singers, clog dancers, and some of the very big names of the country music entertainment world. Scores of craftspeople show off their skills at woodworking, pottery, cornshuck and applehead dolls, painting, leatherwork, furniture and toy making, jewelry, basket weaving, needlework, quilting, and macramé.

Pioneer Village is like a walk through a mountain town of yesteryear. You can peruse the canned goods and bolt cloth in the mercantile store, see the hickory switch in the one-room schoolhouse, visit the smokehouse, and stop in at the hand-hewn log cabin. Elsewhere on the forty-two-acre grounds, you can enjoy midway rides, taste just-squeezed apple cider, and see a "moonshine" whiskey still up close. "Revenooers" keep a close guard against any free samples. For information contact Georgia Mountain Fair, P.O. Box 444, Hiawassee 30546, (706) 896–4191, www.georgia-mountain-fair.com.

From early June to early August you can enjoy **The Reach of Song.** Georgia's official state historic drama tells the story of the mountain folk with fiddling, gospel singing, dancing, tale swapping, and problem sharing. It's performed from late June to late August in the auditorium on the Young Harris College Campus, (800) 241–3754, (706) 379–4312, www.mountaintopga.com.

Also at the college, the Rollins Planetarium has seasonal shows on Friday night and free telescope viewings.

Most of the year *Lake Chatuge* is a great place to play. The 7,500-acre Tennessee Valley Authority reservoir on the western edge of the Hiawassee is a tranquil retreat for trout and bass anglers, waterskiers, swimmers, and boaters. Several marinas and public boat docks offer easy access to the lake. You'll also find picnic grounds, tennis courts, a sand beach, playgrounds, and camping sites at the 160-acre *Towns County Park* on the lakeside. Contact Lake Chatuge Recreation Area, (706) 745-6928, www.fs.fed.us/conf.

The *Chattahoochee National Forest* blankets much of Towns County with Georgia pines and hardwoods. Sections of four national wilderness areas in the county afford you the opportunity to get well off the beaten track. During certain times of the year, the Appalachian Trail, crossing Towns County near Brasstown Bald Mountain, gets downright busy as hikers test their stamina on the 2,000-mile Maine-to-Georgia route described at the beginning of this chapter.

Brasstown Bald Mountain, 4,784 feet, is Georgia's highest point. A steep, winding road off Highway 180 takes you to a parking area a half mile from the top, where you'll find restrooms and a gift shop. You can hike the paved, moderately strenuous trail to the visitor center and observation platform, or take a shuttle van, $1.50 per person. There's a $2.00 parking fee in the lot. Be sure your car is up to the task before heading up the mountain. Many a vehicle has been left overheated and steaming by the roadside.

You can follow the 5½-mile Arkaquah Trail from the crest of Trackrock Gap and the less strenuous 2½-mile Jack's Trail Knob to the foot of Brasstown. Wagon Train Road meanders 6 miles to a pastoral valley that cradles the pretty town of Young Harris and the campus of Young Harris College.

A short drive from Brasstown Bald Mountain, *7 Creeks Housekeeping Cabins,* 5109 Horseshoe Cove Road, Blairsville, (706) 745–4753, (888) 241–0425, fax (706) 745–2904, www.7creeks.com, is an answered prayer for anyone who's ever dreamed of "getting away from it all." In the midst of gorgeous mountain scenery, the seven cabins have baths, full kitchens, grills, and picnic tables. You can swim and fish in a private lake, pet farm animals, and play badminton and horseshoes. Furnished cabins (guests bring towels and bedsheets) sleeping four, six, and eight are inexpensively priced. There is a two-night minimum.

Brasstown Valley Resort, opened in 1995 on a scenic 503-acre Blue Ridge mountainscape, has all the upscale resort bells and whistles: 134 attractively appointed guest rooms in the four-story main lodge and adjacent cottages; 18-hole, 7,000-yard Scottish links–style golf course; and tennis, horseshoes, trout fishing, horseback riding, indoor/outdoor pool, fitness center, and full-service restaurant and lounge. It's a great place to roost for a while and an excellent base while sightseeing in the surrounding mountainlands. Lodge rooms and cottages are moderately to expensively priced. Brasstown Resort, 6321 U.S. Highway 76 East, Young Harris, (706) 379–9900 and (800) 201–3205, www.brasstownvalley.com.

Deer Lodge, a hideaway near the junction of Highways 66 and 75, is another heaven-sent place to park a while and savor the glories of the mountains. Hospitable proprietors Richard and Willene Haigler serve some of the biggest, best, and lowest-priced steaks and trout anywhere in these parts. Cabins secluded in the nearby woods are inexpensive. Contact Deer Lodge, 7900 South Highway 17/75, Hiawassee, (706) 896–2726.

The *Russell-Brasstown Scenic Highway,* in White and Union Counties, takes you through the heart of some of northeastern Georgia's most spectacular mountain country. Designated as Highway 348, the 14-mile paved highway takes you from the outskirts of Georgia's "Alpine Village" of Helen, across the Appalachian Trail, to the state's highest mountain and a picture-perfect state park. Several parking areas and overlooks give you the chance to stop and admire the rugged beauty of the Blue Ridge Mountains. The drive is especially striking in mid-October to early November, when the hardwoods turn a brilliant orange, yellow, and scarlet.

One of the Scenic Highway's "high points" is 3,137-foot Tesnatee Gap, where the Appalachian Trail crosses on its way between Maine and Springer Mountain, Georgia. You can get out of your car here and mingle a while with the earnest hikers. At its northwestern end the Scenic Highway intersects with Highway 180. If you turn right, you can explore 4,784-foot Brasstown Bald. A steep, paved road ends at a parking area 930 feet below the summit. From here either hike to the crest of Georgia's highest peak or take a commercial van up to the view of four states.

A left turn at Highway 180 will lead you to Highway 19 and *Vogel State Park.* Cradled in mountains, beside a pretty lake, Vogel is a delightful place for fishing, boating, warm weather swimming, and year-round hiking on woodland trails. The park's seventy-two campsites have electricity, water, hot showers, and restrooms; thirty-six rustic but very snug cottages, by the lake and in the adjacent woodlands, are equipped down to sheets, towels, pots, and pans. For reservations, phone (800) 864–PARK. The park also has a $2.00 one-time parking fee. The park office is open from 8:00 A.M. to 5:00 P.M. Contact Vogel State Park, 7845 Vogel Park Road, Blairsville, (706) 745–2628, (800) 864–PARK, www.gastateparks.org.

Georgia Highway 180, which joins U.S. Highway 19 north of Vogel Park, is a 22-mile scenic mountain route to the little community of Suches. Along the way stop at *Sosebee Cove Scenic Area,* (706) 745–6928, www.fs.fed.us/conf, where a half-mile loop trail takes you through a second-growth forest with wildflowers and rhododendron. Farther along, **Lake Winfield Scott Recreation Area,** (770) 297–3000, www.fs.fed.us/conf, has a thirty-two-acre, thirty-six campsite campground with showers ($6.00 a night) and an eighteen-acre fishing and swimming lake. There is a $2.00 parking fee for noncampers. A large furnished cabin rents for $75 a night, two-night minimum.

Habersham County claims some of northeast Georgia's most photogenic Blue Ridge Mountain country. These mountains and valleys, thousands of acres of Chattahoochee National Forest, and scores of lakes and streams offer limitless opportunities to take a hike, ride a bike, camp out, and fish, swim, and otherwise unwind.

Habersham is one of Georgia's major apple producers. Rich soil and a cool climate encouraged English and Canadian families to initiate the apple-growing arts here in the 1920s. In October, roadside stands overflow with Red Delicious, Stayman Winesaps, dark red Yates, and bright yellow-green Granny Smiths. You can buy 'em by the sackful or the carload and also purchase homemade apple jelly, apple butter, and ice-cold, freshly squeezed sweet apple cider by the glass and gallon jugful. As a rule Habersham owners don't allow visitors to come in and pick their own fruit.

The Big Red Apple, in front of the old train depot in downtown Cornelia, is a tribute to Habersham County's apple industry. Weighing in at about 5,200 pounds, the 7-foot-tall Grande Pomme, with a 22-foot "waist," has defied winds, rains, worms, and schoolboy vandals since its dedication in 1926.

Elvis fans who've been to Graceland and think they've seen it all may think again after seeing Joni Mabe's Panoramic Encyclopedia of Everything Elvis at

Where Wallenda Walked on Air

On July 18, 1970, 65-year-old Karl Wallenda walked across Tallulah Gorge. While 35,000 spectators held their breath, the patriarch of the Flying Wallendas trapeze family stepped onto a thin steel cable strung 700 feet across the 1,200-foot-deep gorge. Balancing a 36-foot pole, he did a pair of handstands before reaching the other side. He earned $10,000 for his eighteen minutes of fame, which set a new record for cable height. His luck and pluck ran out on March 22, 1978, when he fell to his death from a cable between two hotels in San Juan, Puerto Rico. You can read about his feat at Tallulah Point Overlook, a privately owned snack bar and souvenir shop, with a covered porch overlooking the gorge. It's on Historic Highway 441 in the town of Tallulah Falls, (706) 754–4318, www.tallulahpoint.com. Just up the highway, the Jane Hurt Yarn Interpretive Center at Tallulah Gorge State Park has a display on Wallenda's walk, with his gold-fringed powder blue costume.

the **Loudermilk Boardinghouse Museum** in Cornelia. An Athens artist, Mabe's 30,000-piece collection includes hundreds of photos, show posters, newspaper and magazine articles, and souvenirs in varying degrees of taste and two rarities: Mabe found the "Maybe Elvis Toenail" in the shag carpeting at Graceland and acquired the "Elvis Wart" from Presley's dermatologist, who removed it before the King was inducted into the army. "The Big E Celebration," honoring his August death anniversary, is the Loudermilk Museum's big day. Impersonators croon his big hits and toast his memory with his favorite food, fried peanut butter and banana sandwiches. The Loudermilk Boardinghouse Museum is at 271 Foreacre Street, Cornelia, (706) 778–2001, www.joni mabe.com. Self-guided tours Friday and Saturday, 10:00 A.M. to 5:00 P.M., other times by appointment. Admission is $5.00.

Clarkesville, Habersham's snug little county seat, is a happy hunting ground for antiques and mountain handicrafts. Several shops around the courthouse square on Highway 441 are loaded with handcrafted furniture, pottery, paintings, weaving, leatherwork, handmade baskets and quilts, toys, dolls, jellies, jams, and preserves.

The **Glen-Ella Springs Hotel** sits on seventeen pastoral acres, off Highway 441/23 between Clarkesville and Tallulah Falls. Owners Barrie and Bobby Aycock have converted the hundred-year-old hotel building into a sixteen-room country inn, full of rustic touches and modern conveniences. In warm weather, enjoy the outdoor swimming pool. All the rooms have porches with rocking chairs, antiques, and heart-pine paneling. Some have fireplaces and whirlpools. The dining room features fresh mountain trout but varies from traditional mountain fare with veal dishes, pasta, scallops, fresh fish, and other American/continental entrees. Doubles are moderately to expensively priced, including full breakfast. Contact the Aycocks, Route 3, Bear Gap Road, Clarkesville 30523, (706) 754–7295, (877) 456–7527, www.glenella.com.

"myoldwarhorse"

General James Longstreet, the Confederate hero who Robert E. Lee called "My Old War Horse," survived his numerous Civil War battles and retired to Gainesville, where he lived from 1875 until his peaceful death in 1904. After he hung up his uniform and sidearms, Longstreet ran a hotel, a farm, and a vineyard and became a leader of the Republican Party. He and his family are buried in Gainesville's Alta Vista Cemetery.

Burns-Sutton House, 855 Washington Street, Clarkesville, (706) 754–5565, www.bbonline.com/ga/burns-sutton, an imposing early 1900s Queen Anne house, has been tastefully restored by innkeeper Jaime Huffman. Seven guest rooms have period furnishings, heart-pine floors, and woodwork. Some have shared bath. Enjoy the mountain breezes on the wrap-around front porch. Moderate rates include full breakfast.

Highway 197, twisting and turning north between Clarkesville and Clayton, is considered one of north Georgia's prettiest drives. The **Mark of the Potter,** 9982 Highway 197, Clarkesville, 9 miles north of Clarkesville, (706) 947–3440, www.markofthepotter.com, is a favorite stop for mountain visitors. The weathered old white frame corn-grinding mill, by the rapids of the Soque River, sells some of the finest work of Georgia's most accomplished craftspeople. Shelves are laden with superb pottery, colorful fabrics, metal, and leatherwork.

Browsing inevitably will take you onto the porch overhanging the Soque to throw treats to the fat, pampered trout swimming in the river's pools. Mark of the Potter is open daily. Habersham also shares Tallulah Falls and Tallulah Gorge with Rabun County.

South of Clarkesville, the little town of **Demorest,** on Highway 441, is worth a visit. A couple of antiques shops are on the short main street, and you can stroll through the peaceful campus of Piedmont College.

When your children pose that age-old question—"Where do babies come from?"—take them to **Cleveland** and show them. At Cleveland's **Babyland General Hospital,** 73 West Underwood Street, Cleveland 30528, (706) 865–2171, www.cabbagepatchkids.com, some very special "babies" come from a cabbage patch. Originally a doctor's turn-of-the-century clinic, the white frame "hospital" is where the soft-sculpted Cabbage Patch Kids, created by White County's own Xavier Roberts, first see day's light. Uniformed "nurses" lead you through the nursery, day-care center, and delivery room. At the magic moment, a "doctor" in surgical garb plucks a newborn Kid from a patch of sculpted cabbage leaves to "oohs" and "aahs" all around. You can take home a cuddly Cabbage Patch Kid of your very own. Just remember, they're "babies," not "dolls"; not "bought," but "adopted." The hospital is open Monday through Saturday from 9:00 A.M. to 5:00 P.M., Sunday from 10:00 A.M. to 5:00 P.M. Free admission.

If the sheer granite escarpments of **Mount Yonah,** off Highway 75 north of Cleveland, set your rock-climbing juices flowing, make plans to scale the heights with commercial outfitters in Atlanta. **High Country Outfitters,** 3906 Roswell Road, (404) 814–0999, will put you in the proper climbing gear and send you up Yonah's 150- to 300-foot cliffs with experienced guides. Mount Yonah is also one of Georgia's best and most popular hang-gliding points.

Driving up to the **Old Sautee Store** (706–878–2281, (888) 463–9853, www.sauteestone.com) at the junction of Highways 17 and 255, you might imagine an old-time mercantile stocked with bolts of cloth, seeds, farm implements, and sacks of cornmeal. Walk inside and what do your wondering eyes behold, but an array of tempting goods from Scandinavia: Norwegian and Icelandic sweaters, jackets, and coats; crystal, dinnerware, needlework, gourmet foods, jewelry, and unique gifts from Sweden, Denmark, and Finland. Open daily.

The *Northeast Georgia Folk Pottery Museum* illuminates two centuries of pottery making by Georgia's mountain artists. The 3,200-square foot exhibition hall is a centerpiece of the Sautee-Nacoochee Center, a former mountain school that houses a local history museum, art studio, gallery, and theater. Constructed of heavy timbers with soaring windows overlooking the Sautee-Nacoochee Valley's rolling countryside, the Folk Pottery Museum features farm churns, kitchenwares, and other utilitarian pottery, as well as face jugs and other decorative pieces by such acclaimed pottery makers as the Meader, Hewell, and Ferguson families and newer generations of pottery artists. The museum is located at 283 Highway 255, Sautee-Nacoochee, (706) 878–3300, www.folkpotterymuseum.com. Open Monday through Friday from 10:00 A.M. to 5:00 P.M., Saturday and Sunday noon to 5:00 P.M. Admission $2.00.

You can spread a picnic by the *Stovall Covered Bridge,* in a small park by Chickamauga Creek on Highway 255, between Helen and Batesville. Only 36.8 feet long, it's the shortest covered bridge anywhere in Georgia.

The *Stovall House,* nearby on Highway 255, is one of the nicest country inns anywhere in the state. Built in 1837, the handsome two-story frame house is in the heart of the scenic Sautee Nacoochee Valley. Five guest rooms are decorated with country antiques and all the modern comforts. The dining room features Southern and continental cooking and is one of the best anywhere in the mountains. For pure, sweet relaxation, settle yourself into a porch swing and listen to the absolute peace of this lovely countryside. Moderate rates; all rooms with private bath and breakfast. Contact the Stovall House, Route 1, Box 103-A, Sautee 30571, (706) 878–3355, www.stovallhouse.com.

Highway 17 cuts a most picturesque path through the Sautee-Nacoochee Valley as it meanders westerly toward Helen. You may want to stop for a picture—or attend Sunday services—at *Crescent Hill Baptist Church,* on a wooded hillock near the intersection of Highways 17 and 75. The pretty Carpenter Gothic church was built in the 1870s by the same well-off gentleman who built the grand Victorian house and gazebo atop the Indian mound at Highways 17 and 75.

Going north on combined Highway 17/75, stop off at *Nora Mill Granary & Store* (706–878–1280, 800–927–2375, www.noramill.com). Founded in 1876 on the banks of the Chattahoochee River, the mill's current owners still grind corn into meal and grits in the tried-and-true old-fashioned way. It's open daily. Free.

BILL'S FAVORITES

Chattooga River rafting	Lodge at Smithgall Woods
Lake Rabun	Dahlonega's town square
Lake Burton	Amicalola Falls State Park
Brasstown Valley Resort	Downtown Athens dining, entertainment
Vogel State Park	
Unicoi State Park	State Botanical Garden
Anna Ruby Falls	Oconee County's arts community

Don't try to pinch yourself awake as you drive by the WILKOMMEN signs of *Alpine Helen.* You haven't wandered onto a Disney film set. About twenty-five years ago this then-humble mountain hamlet underwent a wholesale transformation into a make-believe Alpine village. Nowadays, the red-tile roofs, flower boxes, biergartens, and stucco-fronted shops selling cuckoo clocks, Christmas ornaments, Tyrolean hats, and loden coats put the once-quiet village very much on the well-beaten path. Outlet stores, with all the usual suspects, are amassed on the south end of town.

Like it or disdain it, Helen's worth at least a short stroll and a browse. The many inns and "hofs" around town are good bases for more off-the-beaten-path adventures, such as the Appalachian Trail, Russell-Brasstown Scenic Highway, and Chattahoochee National Forest. In trout season, you can don your waders and cast in the Chattahoochee River, which rises near here and wends its bonny way through the middle of town.

More Blue Ridge than Bavarian, *Betty's Country Store* (Main Street, Helen, 706–878–2943), on the north end of town, has grown into a full-blown supermarket. The modern store with some rustic ambience is loaded with jams and jellies, fresh vegetables, gourds, cookbooks, canned goods, cheeses, fresh meat and fish, gourmet coffee, apple cider, and other goods.

Hofer's of Helen, across from Betty's, 8758 North Main Street, (706) 878–8200, fits tongue-in-groove with Helen's Bavarian motif. Walk in the door and you'll be intoxicated by the aromas of fresh-baked breads, cakes, cookies, and strudels. In the cozy dining room, treat yourselves to Belgian waffles with maple syrup and whipped cream, Alpine French toast, and a variety of bountiful omelets; the lunch menu includes bratwurst and sauerkraut, German-style meat loaf, smoked pork chops, and grilled and deli sandwiches. Breakfast and lunch daily.

At *Troll Tavern,* Castle Inn, Main Street, Helen, (706) 754–5566, sit on an outdoor terrace by the Chattahoochee and watch the tubers float gently through Helen. The menu includes bratwurst, smoked pork chops, chicken, fish, deli sandwiches, German beer, and wine. Lunch and dinner are served Monday through Saturday.

If you've never made it to Munich for Oktoberfest, *Helen* has a scaled-down replica. In late September and early October, the town's pavilion resounds to oompah bands and thousands of folk-dancing feet. In late October and early November, the mountain hardwoods change their colors as brilliantly as those in New England, making this an especially worthwhile time to visit. It's also prime season for freshly squeezed apple cider and boiled peanuts. Simmered in brine in huge iron kettles, the goobers are warm, salty, sticky, and a special mountain delicacy that not everyone goes for, but that should at least be experienced. Contact Helen-White County Visitors Bureau, 726 Brucken Strasse, Helen 30545, (706) 878–2181, (800) 858–8027, www.helenga.org.

Unicoi State Park, just north of Helen, is a treat that everyone can enjoy. With 1,081 acres of highlands and woodlands, threaded by streams, lakes, and waterfalls, there's plenty of off-the-beaten-path solitude.

Swimming, canoeing, and fishing focus on a picture-postcard fifty-three-acre lake. You can take solitary walks on 12 miles of trails and take part in nature walks led by park naturalists. Craftspeople share the secrets of pottery, quilting, dulcimer and furniture making, and other mountain arts. The handicraft shop in the Unicoi Lodge sells an array of beautiful items.

Also in the lodge the cafeteria-style dining room serves excellent breakfast, lunch, and dinner at extremely low prices. The park's accommodations include ninety-six camping sites, with water, electricity, nearby showers, and restrooms; and two- and three-bedroom, completely furnished cottages. For reservations, call (800) 864–7275. Contact Park Superintendent, P.O. Box 849, Helen 30545, (706) 878–2201, (800) 864–PARK, www.gastateparks.org.

Anna Ruby Falls is the awesome showpiece of a 1,600-acre Chattahoochee National Forest recreation area that neighbors Unicoi. From the parking area follow a moderately strenuous half-mile trail through the woodlands bordering a swift-flowing stream. An observation platform sits at the base of Anna Ruby's two cascades, which drop dramatically 153 and 50 feet over the edge of Tray Mountain. Back at the parking area, restore your energy with a picnic by the water's edge. A handsome visitor center has an excellent gift shop and a porch from which you can toss treats to some of creation's fattest trout. A Trail for the Blind identifies trees and plants in Braille. There is a $2.00 per car parking fee.

The ***Lodge at Smithgall Woods,*** west of town, is a peaceful counterpoint to the hyper Alpine village. In 1994 north Georgia publisher Charles Smithgall made his pristine 5,600 acres of woodlands and streams a gift-purchase to the state. Although it's administered by the state park system, the similarities to other parks are few. Virtually no car traffic is allowed. Visitors who wish to hike the preserve's three wilderness trails and catch-and-release trout in 4-mile Dukes Creek sign in at the visitor center and take a free shuttle bus to their destinations. Mountain bikers can use 12 miles of improved roads. On the Martin's Mine Historic Trail, hikers can stop at the site of an 1893 gold mine, with a 125-foot-deep shaft and a 900-foot-long tunnel. Guests have full access to Dukes Creek trout fishing, rated in the top 100 by Trout Unlimited. In order to give everybody casting room, only fifteen are allowed on the creek at the same time. A $2.00 parking pass is the only charge. Overnight guests stay in five deluxe cottages, including Charles Smithgall's former Montana lodgepole pine retreat. Nudged alongside Dukes Creek's rushing waters, the cottages are furnished with plush sofas and chairs, fieldstone fireplaces, twin and queen-size beds, stocked kitchens, open porches, TVs, phones, computers, and Internet access. The staff prepares three full meals daily, with wine. Rainbow and brown trout, fresh from the creek, are the kitchen's tour de force. Naturalists lead waterfall and wildflower hikes. Double occupancy rates include all meals and activities. Open daily, it's located at Highway 75-Alt, 3 miles west of Helen, and just south of the Richard B. Russell Scenic Highway (Highway 348). Phone (706) 878–3087 and (800) 318–5248, www.smithgallwoods.com, 61 Tsalaki Trail, Helen. Expensive.

The Nacoochee Valley gets its name from a Native American version of *Romeo and Juliet.* According to legend, Cherokee Princess Nacoochee fell in love with a warrior from an enemy tribe. Her father captured the suitor and had him executed. In her grief, Nacoochee leaped to her death from Mount Yonah on the western end of the valley. Some say her tearful laments can still be heard on moonlit nights.

In 1828 a trapper named Benjamin Parks allegedly stubbed his toe on a rock in ***Dahlonega*** and shouted the Georgia version of "Eureka!" as he gazed at a vein of gold that soon sent prospectors streaming into these hills. *Dahlonega* is a Cherokee Indian word meaning "precious yellow," and until the War Between the States, the substance flowed into a major U.S. Mint right here. Although it's no longer a major industry, enough gold is still mined here to periodically releaf the dome of Georgia's state capitol building and intrigue visitors who pan for it at reconstructed camps. The Dahlonega Visitors Center on the square has restrooms and information on anything you could possibly be interested in. Phone (706) 864–3711, (800) 231–5543, or access www.dahlonega.org.

True to its heritage, the *Dahlonega Courthouse Gold Museum State Historic Site,* Public Square, Dahlonega, (706) 864–2257, (800) 864–PARK, www.gastateparks.org, in the center of the little town of 2,800, chronicles the gold rush and the numerous mines that flourished in these parts. A twenty-eight-minute film upstairs in the old courtroom is especially worthwhile. Operated by the Georgia Department of Natural Resources, the Gold Museum is open Tuesday through Saturday from 9:00 A.M. to 5:00 P.M., Sunday from 2:00 to 5:30 P.M. Admission is $3.00 for adults, $2.50 for seniors, $1.50 for children 6 to 18; free for children 5 and under.

Buildings around the square have a rustic frontier look. Shops purvey gold-panning equipment, ice cream, fudge, mountain handicrafts, gold jewelry, and antiques. Many people make the 70-mile drive north from Atlanta just to feast at the famous *Smith House.* It's off the square at 202 South Chestatee Street, Dahlonega, (706) 867–7000 and (800) 852–9577, fax (706) 867–7000, www.smithhouse.com. The Smith House puts out huge family-style spreads with fried chicken, chicken and dumplings, beef stew, shrimp, numerous vegetables, biscuits, relishes, and dessert for a moderate price. They also serve breakfast and have a cafeteria line for those not up to the full board. It's open daily except Monday.

You can stay close to the chow line in the Smith House's sixteen guest rooms, all with private baths. Inexpensive to moderate. Many other restaurants, inns, and motels are close to the square.

The *Worley Homestead Inn,* at 410 West Main Street, Dahlonega, (706) 864–7002, (800) 348–8094, www.bbonline.com/ga/worley, is a short stroll from the Gold Museum, restaurants, and shops on Dahlonega's square. Seven guest rooms in the mid-nineteenth-century Victorian house are full of antiques and pictures of Worley family ancestors. Each has a private bath, some with claw-foot tubs. There are even rumors of a friendly resident ghost. The moderate tariff qualifies you for a huge country breakfast.

Gold Rush Days, the third weekend of October, celebrates the gilded heritage with arts and crafts, clog dancing, and lots of bluegrass fiddling and singing. You can pan for gold year-round at *Crisson's Gold Mine,* 2736 Morrison Moore Parkway, Dahlonega, (706) 864–6363, www.crissongoldmine.com. You'll feel some of old Benjamin Parks's excitement and might even whoop out "Eureka!" when you spot a few grains gleaming amid the mud in your pan.

You can also take a guided walk through the tunnels of the old *Consolidated Mine.* In the early 1900s it was the largest and richest gold mine in the eastern United States. It went mysteriously bankrupt in 1906, and much of the old equipment is still in place. Phone (706) 864–8473, www.consolidated goldmine.com. Open daily 10:00 A.M. to 5:00 P.M. Adults $11.00, ages 4 to 14

$7.00. Located off Georgia Highway 60, 3.7 miles south of Dahlonega. Dahlonega is a popular gateway to the northeastern Georgia mountain vacation areas. From here Highway 19 snakes north toward Vogel State Park, while other roads aim toward Helen, Cleveland, and Amicalola State Park.

One of northern Georgia's most interesting and unusual dining and lodging places is off the beaten path among the green hills and marble quarries of Pickens County. The **Woodbridge Restaurant and Inn** at Jasper departs joyously and deliciously from the culinary path most often trod in rural Georgia.

German-born Joe Rueffert and his Georgia-born wife, Brenda, have been the hospitable proprietors of the Woodbridge Restaurant and Inn for more than fifteen years. On the surface, the rustic pre–Civil War inn, with the checkered tablecloths and big windows with panoramic views of the mountains, gives few hints of surprises. It's only when Joe dons his chef's hat and parades from the kitchen with grilled swordfish steaks, fresh grouper, and mahi-mahi with rich creamy sauces; chateaubriand forestière and steak au poivre; veal dishes with silken béarnaise and hollandaise sauces; roast duckling with orange sauce; bananas Foster and other luscious desserts, that the wealth of this "find" finally sinks in.

You may select American or European wines and beers—there is also a full bar—from the Woodbridge list. After your feast, you're only a few steps from your lodgings in the inn's moderately priced guest rooms and cabins. Comfortably furnished and air-conditioned, the eighteen large rooms come with complimentary mountain views. The dining room serves lunch on Wednesday and Sunday and dinner Monday through Saturday. Prices are moderate to expensive, and major credit cards are accepted. Contact Woodbridge Inn, 411 Chambers Street, Jasper, (706) 253–6293, www.woodbridgeinn.net. Inexpensive to moderate.

The inn is, true to its name, across a wooden bridge, at the northern edge of the bucolic town of Jasper. If you've forgotten how sweet and peaceful a town of 5,000 can be, take a leisurely constitutional on Jasper's main street, and chat with the folks in the stores and around the Pickens County Courthouse. The Rueffens don't serve breakfast, so you may wish to indulge in the grits and eggs at one of Jasper's hometown cafes.

Amicalola Falls State Park and the **Appalachian Trail approach trail** are a scenic half-hour drive from Jasper, in neighboring Dawson County. The 400-acre park, centered on a majestic 729-foot waterfall, has hiking trails above and below the falls, picnic areas, fishing, campsites—with electricity, water, hot showers, and restrooms—and furnished cottages with fireplaces. The handsome **Amicalola Falls Lodge** has fifty-seven guest rooms with spectacular views and all the modern comforts. For reservations phone (800) 864–PARK, www.gastateparks.org. Contact the park at Star Route, Box 215, Dawsonville

30534, (706) 265–8888. The Appalachian Trail is described at the beginning of this chapter.

As its name suggests, the secluded *Len Foote Hike Inn,* operated by Georgia State Parks, is accessible only by a moderately strenuous 5-mile hike through woodlands and hilly terrain that begins at Amicalola Falls State Park. Twenty rooms with bunk beds open onto a wraparound porch. A common room looks east into a spectacular sunrise. The inn furnishes bed linens and towels, rib-sticking family-style meals, trail lunches, and snacks. Rooms have no electrical outlets, TV, or heat. Reservations must be made eleven months in advance. Phone (706) 265–4703, (800) 581–8032, www.hike-inn.com. Inexpensive.

The mountain may not have come to Muhammad, as the old saying goes, but in 1957, an inland sea came to northeastern Georgia's Hall County. The U.S. Army Corps of Engineers closed the Buford Dam on the Chattahoochee River and created Lake Sidney Lanier. Nowadays about 25,000 of the lake's 38,000 acres and some 380 miles of its green and hilly 550-mile shoreline cover former Hall County farmlands and forests.

Lake Lanier Islands is the huge waterway's biggest recreational package. Developed by the state on wooded hilltops that bobbed above the water after the dam was closed, the islands have a lifeguarded, Florida-sand swimming beach; an 850,000-gallon wave pool; mild and hair-raising water slides; miniature golf and championship golf; all kinds of rental boats, such as houseboats, pontoon boats, sport boats, ski boats, sailboats, fishing boats, and paddleboats; horseback riding; picnic grounds; campgrounds; and a deluxe resort hotel. *Emerald Pointe Resort,* (770) 945–8787, (800) 840–5253, www.lake lanierislands.com, with 224 guest rooms and full amenities, invites guests and nonguests to challenge its par-72 championship-style Emerald Pointe golf course. While you're admiring the scenery, beware of thirteen water holes! Both resorts are moderate to expensive.

The Islands' 300 lakeside campsites are equipped with water, electricity, and some sewer hookups. Campers also have their own fishing pier, outdoor pavilion, and boat launch ramp. For reservations, phone (770) 932–7200 or (800) 840–5253, www.lakelanierislands.com. Admission to the Islands' wave pool and water slides, including the swimming beach, is $25.99 for adults and $16.99 for children 42 inches and under; children 2 and under are free. For information, contact Lake Lanier Islands, 6950 Holiday Road, Lake Lanier Islands 30518, (770) 932–7200 or (800) 840–5253; and Gainesville-Hall County Convention and Visitors Bureau, 117 Jesse Jewell Parkway, Gainesville 30501, (770) 536–5209, (888) 536–0005, www.gainesvillehallcvb.org.

Gainesville, the Hall County seat (population about 30,000; Hall County, 140,000), is a popular gateway to northeastern Georgia vacationlands. Before heading for the hills, enjoy a leisurely stroll through the **Green Street Historical District.** The wide, tree-lined thoroughfare, also designated as Highway 129, holds a wealth of late-nineteenth- and early twentieth-century Victorian and Neoclassical Revival residences.

Also in the Green Street Historical District, the **Quinlan Art Center,** 514 Green Street Northeast, Gainesville, (770) 536–2575, www.quinlanartscenter .org, shows the works of state, regional, and national artists Monday through Saturday from 10:00 A.M. to 4:00 P.M., Sunday from 2:00 to 5:00 P.M. at no charge.

The **Northeast Georgia History Center,** 322 Academy Street, Gainesville, (770) 297–5900, features a permanent exhibit that details the history and culture of Northeast Georgia. One of the most popular exhibits is the "Ed Dodd Room," dedicated to the Gainesville native son who created the "Mark Trail" comic strip adventurer. You'll also see excellent displays on Native Americans, Black history, textiles, Gainesville's vital poultry industry, spinning, weaving, and pioneer life. Two blocks from the main museum, the affiliated **Railroad Museum** houses memorabilia in a renovated baggage car. Open Tuesday through Saturday. Free admission.

Elachee Nature Science Center, at 2125 Elachee Drive, Gainesville, (770) 535–1976, www.elachee.org, is a great place to get lost in the woods for a while and learn something about the world around us. The heavily wooded, 1,200-acre preserve's many fascinating experiences include please-touch fish, amphibians, reptiles, and a 300-gallon trout tank. The interactive, computer and contemporary music–enhanced "If Everyone Lived Like Me" exhibit looks at the effects of our lifestyles on our environment. Enjoy the tranquil beauty of the Chicopee Woods Nature Preserve on 2½ miles of nature trails, where you can take a close look at animal and plant habitats. Open Monday through Saturday from 10:00 A.M. to 5:00 P.M. Donations appreciated.

If you enjoy unusual monuments, bring your camera to **Poultry Park,** where a rooster atop a granite obelisk hails Gainesville's distinction as "Poultry Capital of the World." Some 2.6 million broilers leave here every week for kitchens around the world.

The Big Rabbit commemorates a time when the small community of Rabbittown on the northside of Gainesville owed its livelihood to the commercial farming of bunnies. In 1993 residents of the "Hoppin' Little Place" chipped in for the 20-foot stone rabbit that waves a hospitable "Howdy" in front of the **Rabbittown Cafe,** 2415 Old Cornelia Highway, I–985 exit 24, (770) 287–3695, www.rabbittowncafe.com, which serves first-rate Southern breakfast, lunch, and dinner daily. The Rabbittown Celebration, Saturday the week before Easter, starts with breakfast at the cafe, followed by an Easter parade, Easter egg hunt, gospel singing, and clog dancing.

As Scarlett O'Hara's Aunt Pittypat might exclaim: "Kangaroos in Georgia! However did they get here?" The answer's simple: Debbie and Roger Nelson brought their 'roos and other Down Under and African critters to **Kangaroo Conservation Center,** an 87-acre Dawson County "Outback," in the 1990s. The Nelsons breed the largest collection of the hip-hopping marsupials outside of Australia—200 and counting—and exotic birds and animals for zoos and sanctuaries as far away as China. Visitors on a two-hour tour can blink their eyes and imagine they're in the middle of Aussie nowhere. "Mobs" of kangaroos—as groups of them are called—hop up close to the open-air army truck and gaze at you with big, soulful eyes. Newborn "joeys" peek from mama's pouch. The tour also includes a visit to a barn, where you get a closer look at the kangaroos, which weigh up to 150 pounds, and the lovable little dik-dik, a miniature East African antelope no bigger than a house cat. Kangaroo Conservation Center is at 222 Bailey–Waters Road, Dawsonville, (706) 265–6100, www.kangaroocenter.com. Visits are by reservation Saturday, Sunday, Tuesday, and Friday, April to October. Adults, $27.50; ages second grade to 18, $22.50; age 56 and over, $26.13.

Wineries and Big Lakes

Created by U.S. Army Corps of Engineers impoundments of the Savannah River, **Lake Hartwell** is a vast inland sea whose 55,000 acres offer limitless off-the-beaten-path opportunities for fishing, boating, swimming, and nature hikes. You can headquarter at two state parks on the lake and play another park's 9-hole golf course. While meandering the green, hilly backroads of Hart, Stephens, and Franklin Counties, you can rest a while at an eighteenth-century stagecoach inn and reminisce with old-timers, who still remember baseball's "Georgia Peach," Ty Cobb.

Hart State Park, 330 Hart Park Road, Hartwell, (706) 376–8756, reservations (800) 864–PARK, www.gastateparks.org, spreads 417 acres along the lakeshore. Set up housekeeping in eighty-three camping sites, with utility hookups, adajcent restrooms, and showers, and in furnished cottages. Enjoy swimming, boating, waterskiing, hiking, and fishing for largemouth bass, bream, black crappie, walleye, pike, and rainbow trout.

Tugaloo State Park, on a wooded peninsula jutting into Lake Hartwell, 1763 Tugaloo State Park Road, Lavonia, (706) 356–4362, (800) 864–PARK, www.gastatepark.org, is another mother lode of bass and other fish fry favorites. Nonfisherfolk can play tennis and miniature golf, swim and waterski from a sand beach, and hike and bike on trails threading through the woodlands. Lodgings include twenty furnished cottages and 122 tent and camper sites.

After driving all day, are you tantalized by thoughts of a round of golf, a swim, maybe some late-afternoon fishing? *Victoria Bryant State Park,* off I–85 near Royston, 1105 Bryant Park Road, Royston, (706) 245–6270 or (800) 864–PARK, (706) 245–6770, www.gastateparks.org, may be the answer to your search. The park's 5,421-yard, 18-hole course is hardly a monster, but clusters of Georgia pines, hills, and plenty of water hazards will keep you on your toes. Rental clubs and pull carts are available at the clubhouse, which also has showers, changing rooms, and a snack bar.

Nongolfers can enjoy the swimming pool and angle for bass, bream, and catfish in stocked ponds. The park's twenty-five camping sites have utility hookups, with access to restrooms and showers.

The *Ty Cobb Museum,* in his hometown of Royston (population 2,700), honors baseball legend Tyrus Raymond "Ty" Cobb. From the early 1900s to the 1920s, "The Georgia Peach" was one of major league baseball's most exceptional players. While leading the Detroit Tigers to American League and World Series championships, his fierce competitiveness earned him a lifetime batting average of .367, the highest in baseball history. He won a record twelve batting titles, hit safely 4,191 times, scored a major-league-record 2,245 runs, and stole 894 bases.

He may have been ruthless on the field, but Cobb was a humanitarian. He helped fund the Cobb Memorial Hospital in Royston, dedicated to his parents, and the Cobb Health Care System, with facilities in three northeast Georgia counties. The museum, in the Joe A. Adams Professional Building, exhibits vintage photos, artwork, uniforms and equipment, and a film with rare action footage and interviews. It's at 461 Cook Street, Royston, (706) 245–1825, www.tycobbmuseum.org. Open Monday through Friday from 9:00 A.M. to 4:00 P.M., Saturday 10:00 A.M. to 4:00 P.M. Adults $5.00, seniors $4.00, students $3.00, ages 5 and under and military free.

In the 1830s and 1840s—more than a century before Ty Cobb headed to the majors—travelers enduring the bone-jarring stagecoach trip through the northern Georgia wilderness took solace in the thought that by and by they'd reach *Travelers Rest,* 8162 Riverdale Road, Toccoa, off Highway 123, 6 miles northeast of Toccoa, (706) 886–2256, (800) 864–PARK, www.gastateparks.org.

The sturdy, fourteen-room plank structure was built in 1833 as the plantation home of wealthy planter Devereaux Jarrett. As more and more travelers streamed through the region, the enterprising Jarrett turned his home into an eighteenth-century B&B. South Carolina statesman John C. Calhoun was a guest, and Joseph E. Brown, Georgia's Civil War governor, spent his honeymoon here.

Now a state historic site maintained by the Georgia Department of Natural Resources, the fourteen rooms are furnished with four-poster beds, rocking chairs, vanities, marble-topped tables, goose feather mattresses, spinning wheels, china, cutlery, glassware, and memorabilia of Travelers Rest's days as a post office. The grounds are shaded by a huge white oak tree, believed to be well into its third century, and several century-old crape myrtle trees. Open Tuesday through Saturday from 9:00 A.M. to 5:00 P.M. Admission is $4.00 for adults, $2.50 for children 6 to 18; free for children under 6.

Approaching the Winder/Chestnut Mountain exit (126) on I–85, 30 miles north of Metro Atlanta's I–285 Perimeter Highway, what appears to be a sixteenth-century French castle, surrounded by vineyards, rises from the piney landscape. It's no mirage. ***Château Élan Winery & Resort,*** 100 Rue Charlemagne, Braselton, (678) 425–0900, www.chateauelan.com, was established in 1982 as Georgia's first major winery since the end of Prohibition. Inside the Château's "castle," you're welcome to stroll around a movie-set French marketplace and purchase jams, mustards, wine guides, cookbooks, picnic hampers, and other gourmet foods and gifts. Before purchasing the Château's grape, take the winery tour, followed by a free tasting. In a short time, cabernet sauvignon, chardonnay, Riesling, pinot noir, zinfandel, and other varieties bearing the Château Élan label have won more than fifty-five awards in national competitions. Southerners are partial to the sweet, fruity Summerwine, a blend of peaches and muscadine grapes. Wines are about $6.00 to $12.00 a bottle.

Six restaurants include the Marketplace Cafe with quiche, pâté, chicken breast, salads, cheeses, and other light luncheon fare. Candlelit Cafe Closs serves a five-course dinner with appropriate wines (and appropriate prices). For a taste of another old country, stop in the Château's Paddy's Irish Pub. Constructed in Ireland, dismantled, and shipped to Georgia, it was reassembled by Irish craftsmen and staffed with smiling young lasses and laddies. The rough-hewn timber ceiling, beer barrel tables, slate floors, and stacked stone fireplace—and a menu that includes Irish lamb stew, Irish whiskey mousse,

Château Élan Winery & Resort

North Georgia's Wineries

Before Prohibition turned the state bone-dry, Georgia ranked sixth among the nation's wine-producing states. With Château Élan leading the way, a dozen North Georgia wineries now produce a variety of vintages. Most of them welcome visitors for tours and tastings.

Blackstock Vineyards,
5452 Town Creek Road,
Dahlonega 30533,
(770) 983–1371.

Crane Creek Vineyards,
916 Crane Creek Road,
Young Harris 30582,
(706) 379–1236,
www.cranecreekvineyards.com

Dahlonega Tasting Room,
16 North Park Street,
Dahlonega 30533,
(706) 864–8275.

Fox Vineyards and Winery,
225 Highway 11,
Social Circle 30279,
(770) 787–5402.

Frogtown Cellars,
330 Damascus Church Road,
Dahlonega 30533,
(706) 865–0687,
www.frogtownwines.com

Georgia Winery Taste Center,
I-75 exit 350/Battlefield Parkway,
Ringgold 30736,
(706) 937–2177,
www.georgiawines.com

Habersham Winery,
7025 South Main Street,
Helen 30545,
(706) 878–9463,
www.habershamwinery.com

Persimmon Creek Vineyards,
81 Vineyard Lane,
Clayton 30525,
(706) 212–7380,
www.persimmoncreekwine.com

Three Sisters Vineyards and Winery,
439 Vineyard Way,
Dahlonega 30533,
(706) 865–9463,
www.threesistersvineyards.com

Tiger Mountain Vineyard and Winery,
2592 Old Highway 441,
Tiger 30576,
(706) 782–9256.

Wolf Mountain Vineyards,
180 Wolf Mountain Trail,
Dahlonega 30533,
(770) 992–4120,
www.wolfmountainvineyards.com

and Irish ales, stouts, and whiskeys—make the pub seem like a cozy corner of Eire transplanted to the Georgia hills.

The 3,100-acre resort also has three championship golf courses with 63 stem-winding holes, tennis, and an indoor heated pool. You can overnight in the deluxe 245-room Château Inn, in furnished *Golf Villas,* and at the moderately priced Days Inn–Château Élan. The ***Château Élan Spa*** has diet and nutrition services, smoking cessation programs, massages, mineral baths, herbal wraps, saunas, and fourteen guest rooms.

Fort Yargo State Park, on Georgia Highway 81 at nearby Winder, takes its name from a still-standing log blockhouse that white settlers built in 1792 as protection against hostile Creeks and Cherokees. The park's big green lake is an inviting place to swim and fish and to rent paddleboats, rowboats, and canoes. You can also enjoy tennis and miniature golf, hike nature trails, and set the youngsters loose on the playground. ***Will-A-Way Recreation Area,*** inside the park, has facilities for handicapped persons, including specially equipped, furnished cottages. There are also furnished cottages and campsites not so equipped. For reservations, phone (800) 864–PARK. Contact Park Superintendent, P.O. Box 764, Winder 30680, (770) 867–3489, www.gastateparks.org.

At Christmas, many people bring their holiday mail to the post office in the nearby little community of Bethlehem for that special postmark.

The ***Crawford W. Long Museum,*** 28 College Street, Jefferson, (706) 367–5307, www.crawfordlong.org, in Jefferson honors the physician who first used ether for surgical anesthesia. Dr. Long, then a young Jackson County practitioner, performed the first painless surgery on March 30, 1842. The museum displays his personal papers and a diorama depicting the first operation. An 1840s doctor's office and apothecary and a general store are also part of the museum. The outdoor herb garden grows many plants commonly used in nineteenth-century medicine. Open Tuesday through Saturday 10:00 A.M. to 4:00 P.M. Donations appreciated.

Bulldog Country

Ever wonder where all the tombstones come from? The answer is ***Elbert County.*** "The Granite Capital of the World" is home to more than forty quarries and 150 finishing plants, which produce hundreds of tons of blue-gray stone shipped to all fifty states and several foreign countries. The multimillion-dollar Elberton granite industry had a simple, bizarre birth in 1898, when the first finishing plant was built expressly to create a Confederate soldier for Elberton's Public Square. But when the seven-foot "Johnny Reb," on a fifteen-foot-tall pedestal, was unveiled, townfolks' Rebel Yells turned to jeers and tears.

With his round face, squat legs and a uniform that looked suspiciously Union, wiseacres said he was "a cross between a Pennsylvania Dutchman and a hippopotamus" and dubbed him "Dutchy." Resentment grew and in 1900 Dutchy was pulled from his perch, "lynched," and buried face down, a military sign of disgrace.

Fearing for his own life, the sculptor, who apparently didn't know a Reb from a Yank, fled town and never returned. But from "Dutchy's" seed, Elberton granite grew dramatically.

"Just in Case"

If you fancy Civil War oddities, don't miss the "Double-Barreled Cannon," a whimsical piece of memorabilia that was a spectacular failure. Cast in Athens in 1862, each barrel was to be loaded with cannonballs connected to each other by an 8-foot chain. When fired, the missiles were supposed to exit together, pull the chain tight, and sweep the cannon across the battlefield like a scythe. In reality, the barrels weren't synchronized, and instead of devastating Yankees, the errant shots went in different directions, plowing up a cornfield, knocking down a tree and a log cabin chimney, and killing a cow. It was permanently retired and rests today on the City Hall grounds, pointing north, "just in case."

Forgotten for eight decades, Dutchy was exhumed from the public square in 1982, pressure washed and, in recognition of his pioneering status, given a place of honor in the *Elberton Granite Museum & Exhibit.*

Georgia Guidestones, a sort of Elbert County Stonehenge, is granite country's most curious landmark. In 1979 a mysterious stranger calling himself "R. C. Christian," commissioned the monument on a hilltop 7 miles north of Elberton. He told the president of an Elberton granite finishing company that what he called the "Georgia Guidestones" would be "for the conservation of the world and to herald a new Age of Reason." He also said his name wasn't really Christian, but he was a patriotic Christian who represented a group outside of Georgia that shared his beliefs. Only the Elberton banker who handled "Mr. Christian's" substantial deposit ever knew his true identity. The banker reportedly took the secret to his grave, and no group has ever taken responsibility.

Quarrying, cutting, and etching the stones and putting them in place took nearly a year. Fewer than 100 people came for the March 1980 dedication. A minister denounced it as a potential shrine for devil-worshippers. Perhaps to calm his fears, a self-proclaimed witch twice drew pentagrams around each stone, once to drive away negative forces, the second to invoke positive forces.

Like the 4,000-year-old original on England's Salisbury Plain, the Guidestones are arranged in a circle. The central stone, which weighs 20,957 pounds, is 16 feet, 4 inches high, 3 feet by 3 feet wide, and about a foot and a half thick. It's surrounded by four upright slabs radiating from it like spokes on a wagon wheel. Each slab weighs 42,437 pounds and measures 16 feet, 4 inches high and 6 and a half feet wide. A 9-foot, 8-inch capstone is across the top. Slots drilled in the center stone allow visitors to track summer and winter solstices and other celestial events.

On the four upright slabs, "Guides to the Age of Reason," etched in 4,000 four-inch letters, in English, Spanish, Russian, Hebrew, Hindi, Chinese, and

Swahili, read like New Age Ten Commandments:

- Maintain humanity under 500 million in perpetual balance with nature.
- Guide reproduction wisely, improving fitness and diversity.
- Unite humanity with a new living language.
- Rule passion, faith, tradition, and all things with tempered reason.
- Protect people and nations with fair laws and just courts.
- Let all nations rule internally, resolving external disputes in a world court.
- Avoid petty laws and useless officials.
- Balance personal rights and social duties.
- Prize truth, beauty, love, seeking harmony with the infinite.
- Be not a cancer on the earth, leave room for nature.

While some who speak the living languages may find their way to this isolated monument adjoining a northeast Georgia cow pasture, only a scholar of dead languages will be able to read the admonition, "Let these be Guidestones to an Age of Reason," etched on the capstone. It's written in Egyptian hieroglyphics, Sanskrit, Babylonian cuneiform and classical Greek.

Elberton is on Highway 17, 36 miles south of I–85 Lavonia exit 173. The Elberton Granite Museum and Exhibit, on College Avenue, a half-mile west of downtown, is open from 2:00 to 5:00 P.M. Monday through Saturday, (706) 283–2551, www.egaonline.com. You can see Dutchy, a model of the Guidestones, and a film and exhibits about the granite industry. Free admission. Georgia Guidestones is on Highway 77, 7.2 miles north of town. Free admission. You can walk right up to it.

Two state parks on the Savannah River's big reservoirs are happy hunting grounds for bass and trout fishing. *Bobby Brown State Park,* Georgia Highway 72, 21 miles southeast of Elberton, Box 232, Elberton 30635, (706) 213–2046, (800) 864–PARK, www.gastateparks.org, has boat ramps, picnic areas, a swimming pool, and campsites on 70,000-acre Clarks Hill Lake. Just upriver, *Richard B. Russell State Park,* Georgia Highway 77, 8 miles northeast of Elberton, Box 118, Elberton 30635, (706) 213–2045, (800) 864–PARK, www.ga stateparks.org, also has campsites, cottages, a swimming beach, boat ramps, an 18-hole golf course, and fish that aim to please. Both parks have a $2.00 per visit parking fee.

Athens throbs with the vitality of 30,000 *University of Georgia (UGA)* students, who almost balance "The Classic City's" 45,000 townies. Founded in 1785, America's oldest chartered state university existed only on paper for sixteen years before the legislature provided funds for land and academic buildings in 1800. The first classes met in 1801. That same year Athens was founded on hills above the Oconee River—hopeful of Olympian inspiration, the rude little settlement was named for Greece's hub of classical learning. Planters and literati embellished the campus and Athens's elm- and oak-lined thoroughfares with Greek Revival, Georgian, and Federal architecture. Over the ensuing decades, "town and gown" have coexisted in peace and harmony only seriously disrupted when 85,000 Bulldog football fanatics shake the skies over Sanford Stadium with exhortations of "Go-oooo Dawgs!"

Stop first at the Athens Welcome Center in the ***Church-Waddel-Brumby House,*** 280 East Dougherty Street, Athens, (706) 353–1820, (800) 653–0603, www.visitathensga.com. The fine Federalist house was built in 1820 for Alonzo Church, who became one of UGA's early presidents. Dr. Moses Waddel, who succeeded him in the president's chair, also lived in the house, believed to be the city's oldest surviving residence. You may view the lovely rooms and pick up walking and driving tours of the Athens Historic District and information about other attractions.

As Athens and the university have grown, much of the city's antebellum heritage has been lost. Many antebellum homes have been torn down, others turned into UGA sorority and frat houses, funeral homes, commercial offices, and academic buildings. Only the ***Taylor-Grady House,*** 634 Prince Avenue, Athens, (706) 549–8688, is open as a museum. It was built in 1845 by General Robert Taylor. In 1863 Major William S. Grady purchased the house and his son, Henry W. Grady, lived in it while studying journalism at UGA. Grady went on to become the nationally renowned editor of *The Atlanta Constitution* and spokesman for the post–Civil War "New South." UGA's journalism school is named for him. Open Monday through Friday 9:00 A.M. to 5:00 P.M. Donations appreciated.

The ***State Botanical Garden,*** 2450 South Milledge Avenue, Athens, (706) 542–1244, www.uga.edu/botgarden, is a serene oasis 3 miles from UGA's high-energy campus. The three-story glass and steel Visitors Center and Conservatory is the gateway to the 313-acre sanctuary, which UGA created in 1968 as a "living laboratory" for the study and enjoyment of plants and nature.

After a ten-minute audiovisual introduction, stroll among orchids, ferns, bamboo, bougainvillea, birds of paradise, and other lush tropical and semi-tropical plants that flourish along man-made streams and ponds. You can have lunch in the sunny indoor/outdoor ***Garden Room Cafe*** and browse among plants, books, and gardening paraphernalia in the gift shop. Revolving exhibits highlight botanical and horticultural paintings by regional and national artists.

Five miles of color-coded trails wind through hardwood forests and along ravines of the Middle Oconee River. As you admire azaleas, wildflowers, rhododendron, 125-year-old beech trees, and other plants and trees native to the

Georgia piedmont, you might spot white-tailed deer, rabbits, foxes, opossum, and a remarkable variety of birds.

Theme gardens display roses, dahlias, mums, camellias, hollies, ornamentals, and other seasonal plants. There are plenty of spots for quiet musings. Eleven collections in the three-acre International Garden follow the history and culture of botany back to the beginnings of civilization. Grounds are open daily from 8:00 A.M. to sunset. Visitors Center hours are 9:00 A.M. to 4:30 P.M. Monday through Saturday and 11:30 A.M. to 4:30 P.M. Sunday. Free admission.

UGA's contemporary vitality is a dichotomy with antebellum Athens. Stop at the **UGA Visitors Center,** Four Towers Building, College Station Road, Athens, (706) 542–0842, www.uga.edu/visctr, in a refurbished dairy barn on the edge of UGA's new East Campus, for information about campus landmarks and activities. Open Monday through Friday from 9:00 A.M. to 5:00 P.M., Saturday from 9:00 A.M. to 5:00 P.M., Sunday from 1:00 to 5:00 P.M. The campus is a crazy quilt of classical and modern architecture. According to tradition, freshmen may not walk under the three-columned **University Arch,** which was forged in cast iron in 1857 and is the centerpiece of Georgia's Great Seal, representing WISDOM, JUSTICE AND MODERATION. Walk under it and you're on the historic **North Campus.** Listed on the National Register of Historic Places, "Old North's" landmarks include Phi Kappa Hall, an 1836 Greek Revival; Federal-style Waddel Hall, 1820; Palladian-style Demosthenian Hall, 1824; Greek Revival University Chapel, whose bells clamor joyously when the Bulldogs win one on the gridiron; and Old College, where Crawford W. Long, a Georgian who pioneered the use of anesthesia for surgery, was the 1832 roommate of Alexander Hamilton Stephens, who became vice president of the Confederacy.

The **Georgia Museum of Art,** 90 Carlton Street, Athens, (706) 542–4662, www.uga.edu/gamuseum, exhibits more than 7,000 paintings, sculptures, and other works by regional, national, and international artists. It hosts more than twenty annual special exhibits and educational programs and film series. Open Tuesday through Saturday from 10:00 A.M. to 5:00 P.M., Sunday from 1:00 to 5:00 P.M. Free admission.

With its thousands of perpetually ravenous students, finding a place to eat is no problem. Restaurants, casual cafes, coffeehouses, and snack bars line Broad Street across from the University Arch and spill over onto adjacent streets.

When it comes to music, Athens is a spawning ground for modern rock groups. The **40 Watt Club,** 285 West Washington Street, Athens, (706) 549–7879, still lives on its reputation as the launching pad for REM and the B-52s back in the 1970s. Widespread Panic is the latest Athens group to make the big time. Local bands and touring groups play at the early 1900s **Morton**

Theater, 199 West Washington Street, (706) 613–3770, www.mortontheater .com. Once the state's most famous Black vaudeville theater, the Morton has recently been restored to its former glory.

Oconee County

Knock on a farmhouse door down a rutted dirt road in the backwoods of Oconee County, or stop by a tidy house on a shady street in *Watkinsville,* the 200-year-old county seat, and don't be surprised when an artist invites you in. The rural, but rapidly suburbanizing county of 25,000, just south of Athens, boasts what people here proudly claim is one of Georgia's most extraordinary congregations of creative talent. From Watkinsville (population 2,100) down pasture roads and in the woods around Farmington, Bishop, and Bogart, a hundred or more virtuosos are painting, throwing pottery, and making jewelry; metal, marble, and papier-mâché sculptures; decorative woodcraft; calligraphy; ceramics; woven rugs; forged iron; folk art; custom furniture; and blown and fused glass and fabric wall hangings that sell in shops from here to Alaska.

The *Oconee Cultural Arts Foundation* (OCAF) fosters many of the county's visual and performing arts programs. With the enthusiastic support of local governments and a wellspring of donated time, labor, and money, a 1902 redbrick school building has been regeared as a setting for exhibitions, plays, and educational workshops.

Works by Oconee's artists span the spectrum from representational to anarchic, folkloric to contemporary. There are Christmas ornaments that would fit in your pocket and steel and marble sculptures that require an army to move—and a philosopher to interpret. Some artists are homegrown, but many move here initially to study in the University of Georgia's nationally respected visual arts programs.

A few artists work in close communities, but most prefer to labor alone in barns, cabins, old industrial buildings, and refitted farmhouses around the county. You can search for them by riding through the rolling piedmont coun-

Georgia's Many Symbols

From its official state bird (brown thrasher) to official state wildflower (azalea), Georgia has more than a dozen official state symbols. Some of the others are butterfly, tiger swallowtail; fish, largemouth bass; fossil, shark's tooth; fruit, peach; game bird, bobwhite quail; gem, quartz; insect, honeybee; marine mammal, right whale; mineral, staurolite; reptile, gopher tortoise; seashell, knobbed whelk; character, "Pogo" Possum; tree, live oak; vegetable, Vidalia onion; and two official state songs, "Our Georgia," a waltz, and "Georgia on My Mind," by Albany native Ray Charles.

tryside, a patchwork of pecan and peach orchards, cornfields, covered bridges, pine forests, and cattle farms, but many artists live and work hidden away on isolated roads, with no clue to the creative endeavors transpiring behind the trees.

The surest way to locate them is to stop first at the *Eagle Tavern Welcome Center,* across from the courthouse on Watkinsville's 1-block, back-in-time Main Street, Watkinsville, (706) 769–5197, www.oconeecounty.com. The tavern has been a landmark since 1820, when it was a frontier stagecoach stop. "The Oconee County Guide to the Arts," a free foldout guide, lists more than fifty artists, and director Bonnie Murphy will point you in the right directions. For an overview of the art scene, walk down to *Art Masters Gallery & Framing,* 8 North Main Street, (706) 769–4450. Owner Peggy Holcomb has revamped a huge old building, where she displays the works of many local artists, conducts classes, sells art supplies, and does framing. Open Monday through Saturday.

Most people trace the arts community's birth to 1970, when Jerry and Kathy Chappelle came down from Minnesota to teach pottery at the University of Georgia. The Chappelle's *Happy Valley Pottery,* a collection of old farm buildings and workshops 9 miles south of Watkinsville, 1210 Carson Graves Road, Watkinsville, (706) 769–5922, is one of the county's largest one-stop arts sources and one of the few that keep regular hours. Their high-fire stoneware is characterized by colorful fruit, flowers, and mountainscapes. *The Chappelle Gallery,* a beautiful two-year-old shop in the historic Haygood House in downtown Watkinsville, 25 South Main Street, (706) 310–0985, carries the work of fifty-seven artists who work in painting, pottery, photography, wood, fabric, copper, pewter, and other media.

Places to Stay in Northeast Georgia

GAINESVILLE

Whitworth Inn Bed & Breakfast,
6593 McEver Road,
Flowery Branch,
(770) 967–2386,
www.whitworthinn.com
Has ten light, airy guest rooms, all with private baths, a few minutes from Lake Lanier. Enjoy the cool mountain air on open porches. Innkeepers Ken and Christine Jonick send you off in the morning with a full country breakfast. Doubles are inexpensive.

HARTWELL

The Skelton House,
97 Benson Street,
(706) 376–7969,
(877) 556–3790,
www.theskeltonhouse.com
An excellent B&B alternative to state park cottages and campgrounds. The Skelton family's 1896 home, fully restored in 1997, has eight guest rooms, all with private baths, TV, balconies, and porches and full breakfast. Inexpensive to moderate.

ATHENS

Foundry Park Inn & Spa,
295 East Dougherty Street,
(706) 549–7020,
(800) 9ATHENS,
www.foundryparkinn.com
Downtown Athens's only

boutique-style hotel has 119 deluxe guest rooms and suites in buildings that replicate 1820s row houses. Full-service restaurant, pub, spa, and conference center are a short walk to restaurants, shops, and the University of Georgia. Expensive.

Grand Oaks Manor Bed and Breakfast,
6295 Jefferson Road,
(706) 353–2200,
www.bbonline.com/ga/grandoaks
On 34 wooded acres on the edge of town, Grand Oaks Manor, an 1820s farm house, has eight guest rooms with Victorian antiques, private baths, TV, and phone. Moderate rates include breakfast.

Magnolia Terrace Guest House,
277 Hill Street,
(706) 548–3860,
www.bbonline.com/ga/magnoliaterrace
The handsome Colonial Revival mansion, built in 1912, is close to downtown and the UGA campus. Innkeeper Dottie Sigmund's eight guest rooms have claw-foot tubs and modern fixtures. There's a spacious front veranda and outdoor seating for breakfast. Moderate.

WATKINSVILLE

Ashford Manor Bed-and-Breakfast,
5 Harden Hill Road,
(706) 769–2633,
www.ambedandbreakfast.com
This B&B was opened in 1997 by two Chicago brothers and a partner. They've beautifully decorated and furnished seven rooms in an 1893 Victorian mansion, which sits on five acres of lawns, gardens, and woods within walking distance of downtown shops. Pets are welcome at an adjacent cottage. Moderate rate includes breakfast.

Watson Mill Bridge
State Park, on Highway 22, 6 miles south of Comer,
(706) 783–5349,
(800) 864–PARK for camping reservations,
www.gastateparks.org
The site of Georgia's longest covered bridge. The century-old bridge's four spans stretch 236 feet over the South Fork of the Broad River. It's an idyllic place for a picnic, canoeing, and an overnight stay in the campgrounds.

Places to Eat in Northeast Georgia

DAHLONEGA

Corkscrew Cafe,
51 Main Street,
(706) 867–8551.
The urbane dining room, with an outdoor terrace, near Dahlonega's Public Square, prepares a varied menu, from

HELPFUL WEB SITES

bistro sandwiches and paninis, soups, and salads, to rack of lamb, duck, beef, and seafood. Large wine list. Lunch and dinner Tuesday through Sunday. Inexpensive to expensive.

The Crimson Moon Cafe & Gallery,

24 North Park Street, Public square, downtown, (706) 864–3982.

A coffeehouse and sandwich, salad, and dessert shop by day, featuring organic and locally grown products, this long, narrow 1858 storefront across from the Dahlonega Gold Museum turns into an energy-buzzing acoustic music venue after the sun goes down, with performances by local and visiting groups playing a variety of styles. The Gallery sells pottery, paintings, and other mountain crafts. Specialty coffees, beer, and wine are served. Open daily. Inexpensive.

Wolf Mountain Vineyards,

180 Wolf Mountain Trail, (706) 867–9862, www.wolfmountainvineyards.com

One of northeast Georgia's new breed of small wineries, Wolf Mountain, 5 miles up a winding mountain highway north of Dahlonega, serves its wines with an elaborate Sunday blues and jazz buffet from March until October. Dine inside or on the outdoor patio with Blue Ridge Mountain vistas. The multicourse buffet, $25.00 a person, is complemented by a tasting of Wolf Mountain wines, for $8.00, and a souvenir tasting glass. Tours and tastings are conducted Thursday through Sunday

from March to December, and food and wine pairings are available on Friday and Saturday from noon to 3:00 P.M.

GAINESVILLE

Poor Richard's,

1702 Parkhill Drive, (770) 532–0499.

Gainesville's choice for steaks, prime rib, chateaubriand, baby back ribs, shrimp, lobster, and chicken since 1977. They'll also serve you a hefty hamburger, salads, sandwiches, and wine. Dinner is served Monday through Saturday. Moderate to expensive.

Rudolph's On Green Street,

700 Green Street, (770) 534–2226.

This is a baronial English Tudor rich with dark, exposed beams, stained-glass windows, Oriental carpets, and Duncan Phyfe furnishings. Lunch and dinner entrees are equally impressive: broiled baby salmon, chicken Florentine, roast duckling, several veal dishes, and Georgia mountain trout complemented by wines from California, Georgia, and Europe. Lunch Tuesday through Thursday. Dinner Monday through Saturday and Sunday brunch. Moderate to expensive.

ATHENS

East West Bistro,

351 East Broad Street, (706) 546–4240.

Serves Athens's most adventurous international cuisines. It's really two restaurants in one. The casual street-level

dining room, with big comfortable booths and a large bar area, serves Spanish tapas, pastas, seafood, and Asian, Southwestern, and Mexican dishes and great desserts. The more formal white-tablecloth upstairs dining room has a classical Italian menu. Continuous lunch and dinner service daily. Moderate.

Five & Ten,

1653 South Lumpkin Street, (706) 546–7300.

Canada native Hugh Acheson, who has cheffed at some of San Francisco's finest restaurants, came to Athens when his wife, Mary, enrolled in UGA's graduate school. At Five & Ten, a white-tablecloth restaurant in the Five Points neighborhood, he combines classical French and traditional Southern cooking. He introduced Athens to red grouper wrapped in peanut beurre blanc, plantation quail on a bed of Red Mule cheese grits, New Orleans–style "dirty rice" with maple-brined pork, and Canada's Jackson-Triggs ice wines for dessert. Dinner nightly. Moderate to expensive.

The Grill,

171 College Avenue, (706) 543–4770.

Fills up those hungry students and townies with great hamburgers, fries, shakes, egg muffins, bagels, and other tasty stuff around the clock daily. Inexpensive.

The Grit,

199 Prince Avenue, (706) 543–6592.

REM's Michael Stipe owns the building, but native Brit Mark Dalling rules the kitchen of this "renegade vegetarian" restaurant that's so good even nonvegans wait in line for tofu chicken salad, lentil and roasted garlic soup, and other specialties. Lunch and dinner daily. Inexpensive.

Harry Bisset's New Orleans Cafe,

279 East Broad Street, (706) 353–7065.
The place for Cajun and New Orleans Creole-style cooking. Favorite dishes include soft-shell crab, jambalaya, oysters, shrimp, crawfish étouffée, and bread pudding. Lunch Tuesday to Friday, dinner Monday through Saturday, Sunday brunch. Moderate.

Weaver D's,

1016 East Broad Street, (706) 353–7797.
Dexter Weaver's white cinder block diner on the edge of downtown Athens serves classic African-American soul food: crisp chicken straight from the fryer basket, nutmeg-spiked sweet potato soufflé, collard greens swimming in fatback potlikker, and squash casserole enriched with cheddar. Weaver admonishes UGA students skipping their veggies: "How about some greens? Come on, make your mama proud!" His motto, "Automatic for the People," inspired REM's hit album. Lunch Monday through Saturday. Inexpensive.

Indexes

Entries for Festivals and Folk Plays, Museums, National Parks and Historic Sites, and State Parks and Historic Sites appear only in the special indexes on pages 221–224.

GENERAL INDEX

FESTIVALS AND FOLK PLAYS

MUSEUMS

NATIONAL PARKS AND HISTORIC SITES

STATE PARKS AND HISTORIC SITES

About the Author

William Schemmel is a full-time freelance writer and photographer who travels from Paris, Texas, to Paris, France, but most enjoys telling others about his native state of Georgia. His work appears regularly in numerous magazines, newspapers, and guidebooks. A member of the Society of American Travel Writers, he has experienced adventures on Georgia's off-the-beaten paths for more than twenty-five years. He invites you to get off the interstate highways and make your own fascinating discoveries.